*To the Memory of Mary Lauchline McNeill and
Charlotte Johnston McNeill, my sisters
and Mary MacNeill of Barra,
my friend*

Florence Marian McNeill (1885-1973), was born and brought up in an Orkney manse, where her father, a university graduate in divinity and medicine, kept up many of the old customs. Her secondary education was undertaken in Glasgow and in private schools in Paris and the Rhineland, before returning to Glasgow University to graduate with an Arts degree. Among her friends and contemporaries at this time were James Bridie and Donald and Catherine Carswell.

In the following years F. Marian McNeill travelled abroad, visiting Greece, Egypt and Palestine among other countries, working in London as part of the suffragette movement, and later as a freelance journalist. Excited by the modern Scottish renaissance in literature and culture, she returned to Edinburgh to stay in 1926, working for a time as a researcher for the Scottish National Dictionary. Her only novel, *The Road Home* (1932), was loosely based on her years in Glagow and London.

A life-long interest in traditional Scottish lore first found expression in *The Scots Kitchen* (1929), and later *The Scots Cellar* (1956). These well-loved books of old recipes and convivial customs amount to a social history of Northern domestic life and its contacts with Europe. Marian McNeill's greatest contribution to the study of Scottish folk life was published in four volumes as *The Silver Bough* (1957-68). The first volume is this classic collection of national folk lore and folk belief; the next two books deal with seasonal festivals from Candlemas to Yule, while the final volume describes local festivals from all parts of the country.

The Silver Bough is a four volume study of Scottish Folklore and National and local festivals. Volume I, Scottish Folklore and Folk Belief: TWO, A Calendar of Scottish National Festivals, Candelmas to Harvest Home; THREE, A Calendar of Scottish National Festivals, Hallowe'en to Yule; FOUR, The Local Festivals of Scotland. The complete four volume set is available only in hardback editions from Stuart Titles Ltd, 268 Bath Street, Glasgow.

F. Marian McNeill
THE SILVER BOUGH

VOLUME ONE

SCOTTISH FOLK-LORE
AND FOLK-BELIEF

Introduced by Stewart Sanderson

CANONGATE
CLASSICS
24

First published in 1956 by William MacLellan, First published as a Canongate Classic in 1989 by Canongate Publishing, 17 Jeffrey Street, Edinburgh EH1 1DR. Copyright © Mrs E. R. McNeill. Introduction copyright © Stewart Sanderson.

The publishers gratefully acknowledge general subsidy from the Scottish Arts Council towards the Canongate classics series and a specific grant towards the publication of this volume.

Set in 10 pt Plantin by Falcon Graphic Art Ltd, Wallington, Surrey. Printed and bound by Cox and Wyman, Reading.

Canongate Classics
Series Editor: Roderick Watson
Editorial Board: Tom Crawford, J. B. Pick

British Library Cataloguing in Publication Data
McNeill, F. Marian (Florence Marian),
1885-1973
The silver bough.
1 Scottish folklore
I. Title
398′.09411

ISBN 0-86241-231-5

Contents

ACKNOWLEDGMENTS

I have to thank the following authors, owners of copyright and publishers for giving permission to include prose passages in this book. John R. Allan and Robert Hale for two passages from *The North-East Lowlands of Scotland*; Blackie and Son for two passages from the late Donald A. Mackenzie's *Scottish Folklore and Folk-life*; the late G. K. Chesterton and Hodder and Stoughton for a passage from *St Francis of Assisi*; Robert Crottet and *Time and Tide* for a passage from an article, *Children of the Wild*; Dr W. Y. Evans Wentz and the Oxford University Press for three passages from *The Fairy Faith in Celtic Countries*; the Folklore Society for two passages from the late Mrs Macleod Banks's *British Calendar Customs: Scotland*, and one from an article, *Scottish Lore of Earth, its Fruits and the Plough*, published in *Folklore;* *The Listener* for a passage from an article, *Christian Values in a World of Conflict*, by W. B. Honey; Aldous Huxley, Chatto and Windus and Harper and Brothers for a passage from *Ends and Means*; Sir Thomas Innes of Learney and W. and A. K. Johnston and G. W. Bacon, Ltd., for a passage from the Introduction to *The Clans, Septs and Regiments of the Scottish Highlands* by the late Frank Adam; Sir Thomas Innes of Learney and Oliver and Boyd for a passage from *Scots Heraldry*; Macmillan and Co. for two passages from Sir James Frazer's *The Golden Bough*; Methuen and Co. for a passage from the late G. Lowe Dickinson's *The Greek View of Life; The Modern Churchman* for a passage from an article, *Retrospect and Prospect*, by W. R. (Dean) Inge, and another from an article, *Reverence for Human Personality*, by E. J. Strover; and the Society of Authors for a passage from George Bernard Shaw's *The Adventures of the Black Girl in her Search for God*. I am also indebted to Mrs Murdina Mackenzie for revising the Gaelic Notes.

FOREWORD

The Silver Bough of the sacred Apple-tree, laden with crystal blossoms or golden fruit, is the equivalent in Celtic mythology of the Golden Bough of classical mythology—the symbolic bond between the world we know and the Otherworld. The analogy of the title with that of Sir James Frazer's stupendous work may well make it seem a pretentious choice—the more so as I have made no attempt to cover the whole corpus of Celtic folk-lore, but only so much as is necessary for the better understanding of our national and local festivals, which are dealt with in the subsequent volumes in this series. It is thus no more than a sturdy spray of the Silver Bough that I offer, paradoxically, to a country in search of its roots.

Two other books have borne the title, *The Silver Bough*. (Actually, I discovered them both only after I had made my own choice.) One is an anthology of Irish poetry, the other a book by that distinguished Highland novelist, Neil Gunn. A volume of verse, a novel, a study in folk-lore—what more diverse kinds of book? Yet in all three, I like to think, one may detect the scent of the apple-blossom.

F. M. MCN.   *Edinburgh, December 1956*

Introduction

In one of his essays Robert Louis Stevenson asks why Scotsmen of all kinds feel themselves to be different from their English neighbours. Highlanders and Lowlanders, with all their diversity of race, history and experience, speak in a babel of Gaelic, several varieties of Scots, and English; yet they all speak with what he calls 'a strong Scotch accent of the mind'.

The reasons for this he attributes mainly to the cultural institutions of our country, and in particular to the distinctive character of the Scottish kirk, of Scots law, and of the Scottish educational system. The argument still holds good, though it was no doubt a better one in Stevenson's day than ours; the extra century since the Union has had its eroding effect. But there is a further influence, likewise eroded with the passing of time, which helps to shape a sense of unified cultural identity. Stevenson hardly hints at it in his essay although it operates powerfully in some of his own best work.

This cohesive force is to be found in the national heritage of folklore and folk traditions. For all its variations of local detail, there is a common unity of pattern in our folk culture. It runs as a continuous motif through the fabric of Scottish life, and not only of Scottish life, one might add, but of Scottish literature. As well as the long rollcall of those who have collected and published folklore material in Scots and Gaelic, many creative writers have turned folk belief and custom to their purposes, or have echoed in verse and prose themes drawn from old songs, ballads and folktales, often invoking a mysterious other world of magic and the supernatural. Indeed not only writers, but in varying degrees painters and musicians also, have found inspiration in the folklore heritage, in the unofficial, as opposed to the formally institutionalised, culture of Scotland; and its potent effect on their imagination and creativity is mirrored in public response to their work—which is of course always the sum of personal responses. Amongst the many individuals who have been fascinated by this aspect of our national culture, the author of *The Silver Bough* stands out conspicuously.

Florence Marian McNeill was born on 26 March 1885, one of three daughters of an Orkney manse. Her father, the Rev Dr Daniel McNeill, was of Highland stock; her mother, Janet Dewar, came of a Lowland line of bonnet lairds, lawyers and divines. With these two strains in her ancestry and the Norse world lying around her childhood, the direction her enthusiasms were to follow is not perhaps surprising. Moreover her father encouraged his children to take an interest in Gaelic songs and folklore, and liked to keep up the old customs and traditions of the past. Though a minister of the United Free Church, he found neither conflict of principle nor theological difficulty in walking sunwise round his manse at midnight on Hogmanay to bring good luck on the house. It was left to his daughter to interpret this in after years as a pagan practice inappropriate to a man of the cloth. At the same time she proclaimed her gratitude to him for imparting to his family a liberal theology. But Daniel McNeill was a man of exceptional parts who qualified in medicine at Glasgow University after his studies in both Arts and Divinity. He became minister of Holm West in Orkney in 1869 and retired in 1914.

In 1904 Florence McNeill in her turn entered the University of Glasgow to read for an arts degree. A spirited and vivacious nineteen-year old, she flung herself into student life in what was at that time a particularly exciting community. Her peers included Osborne Mavor (the playwright James Bridie), Jimmy Maxton, Walter Elliot and W. L. Renwick, all busy in student politics and journalism, while in the Faculty of Arts W. MacNeile Dixon, the Professor of English Literature, actively encouraged his young men and women to write as well as read, kept a friendly eye on *GUM* (the *Glasgow University Magazine*), and eventually edited an anthology of verse from its pages. Florence was soon selected to the Students' Representative Council, wrote under the pen name Orcades, and even had romantic poems pseudonymously addressed to her by *GUM*'s editor. But these triumphs were achieved at the expense of academic success. Floss McNeill left the University in 1908 with many friends but without graduating, and it was not till 1912 that she took enough class certificates to qualify for an ordinary MA degree.

Meanwhile she continued to lead an active and varied life. She spent a year each in France and Germany as English assistant in girls' schools, worked for five years in London as secretary of charitable organisations for the suffragette movement and the protection of homeless women, and after the first war spent some time in Athens where she gave English lessons.

These adventurous years she liked to refer to as 'a sort of gaberlunzie life'. They fed her experience and imagination; no doubt they also, as for so many Odyssean Scots, fostered increasing nostalgia for her native land. Returning to Edinburgh in 1920 she supported herself once more by secretarial work, including a stint with the Scottish National Dictionary; and at the same time she sought by her writing and other activities to make a personal contribution to the current revival in Scotland's cultural past and political future. The success of her best-known book, *The Scots Kitchen: Its Traditions and Lore* (1929), eventually allowed her to turn full-time author and journalist; she also became a Vice-President of the Scottish National Party. In later years, however, although her books continued to be well enough received and her services to Scottish life and letters were recognised by the award of the MBE, her fortunes as an author waned, and when she died in 1973 she was in sadly constrained and lonely circumstances.

The four volumes of *The Silver Bough* (1957–68) were planned as part of her contribution to the better understanding of Scotland's cultural heritage. They are in many ways the product of her emotional identification with the nation's past history and its future aspirations. Deeply conscious of the important role of popular traditions in shaping the way people feel and react and think, she offered this wide-ranging folklore survey, as she herself wrote, to a 'country

in search of its roots'. In the first volume she set out to
illuminate the complex patterns of belief in magic and the
supernatural and to unravel the strands of their history;
the second and third volumes survey seasonal festivals and
customs throughout Scotland; the fourth deals with spe-
cifically local festivals.

It is in this first volume that F. Marian McNeill's en-
thusiasm and delight in her subject is particularly apparent.
Quite apart from the intrinsic interest of the material itself,
her freshness of approach and the width of her reading and
personal knowledge of traditions make this a fascinating
introduction to Scottish folklore. Even her occasional way-
wardness of interpretation has its own interest. Often the
reflection of theories which more recent scholarship has revised or rejected, it constitutes a kind of folklore in itself,
illustrating the commonly held beliefs of educated people
about folklore and its origins. These beliefs, like the body
of traditional folklore, are sometimes self-contradictory, as
alert readers of *The Silver Bough* will note. To take but one
example, the notion that the religion of the Celtic Druids
was some kind of sun cult (see Chapter Three) stems
from the misguided speculations of seventeenth and eighteenth century antiquarians who thought that the neolothic
monuments of Avebury and Stonehenge were Druid temples. But contemporary classical authors, including Caesar
as quoted here, make no mention of sun worship and tell us
that the cardinal doctrine of Druidism is the transmigration
of souls, something which, if one is looking for Celtic origins
for Scottish folklore, accords well with Gaelic belief about
the nature of fairies.

When *The Silver Bough* first appeared, academic scholars
cavilled at Miss McNeill's uncritical attitude to her sources
and at her failure to distinguish between what we really
know, and what we can only guess about the past, especially before the written record. They were also irritated
by the chaotic numbering of her reference notes and the
sketchiness of the bibliography, and these anomalies have
been at last corrected in this edition. What remains is a
book of genuine virtue, for the first volume of *The Silver
Bough* brings together an extraordinary range of material

which is scattered throughout many printed sources; it is enlivened with fresh information and a host of insights from the author's own observations; and it points the reader towards other books on the subject.

Especially it has the virtue of opening portals upon a world that is mysterious, often inexplicable, irrational, yet powerfully charged with instinct and emotion, and deeply rooted in human consciousness. These glimpses of another world of thought and feeling extend our perceptions of Scotland's cultural heritage; they also reveal the landscapes and atmosphere of some of our most compelling literature, from the ballads to Scott, from the Stevenson of Tod Lapraik and Thrawn Janet to John Buchan's *Witchwood* through to writers of our own age. *The Silver Bough* provides an unforgettable entrée to that strange terrain.

Stewart Sanderson

Reason discounts for the most part
All stray overflowing of life's deeper flood,
Instincts, intuitions, religion, art,
   And though a small part of the whole
   Would fain have entire control.

But who reason well know all too well
That that unseen tide now and again
Lifts into consciousness far greater truths
Than reason itself can attain,
   Truths to thought I wis
   As thought to feeling is.
   HUGH MACDIARMID *Thalamus*

ONE

Introductory

Those of us who grew up in homes where our national festivals were celebrated know how much warmth and colour
they brought into our childhood. In some of us, at least, they
seemed to stir a racial memory and link us more closely to
the generations that had gone before us.[1]

In our own time, the development of science has tended
to estrange us from our racial traditions. We are so clever at
making things, we moderns—all sorts of fascinating things
from telephones and microphones to submarines and aero-
planes—that we may be excused a little childish vanity in
our achievements and a measure of preoccupation with
them. But presently we shall take them for granted, shall
perhaps weary of them a little, and shall come to feel with
the poet:

> I care not if you bridge the seas,
>   Or ride secure the cruel sky,
> Or build consummate palaces
>   Of metal and of masonry.
>
> But have you wine and music still,
>   And statues and a bright-eyed love,
> And foolish thoughts of good and ill,
>   And prayers to them that sit above?[2]

These are the vital things, the enduring things, and our
blood asserts it, whatever our reason may say.

Living, as I did mainly while writing this book, in Edinburgh, where the bright young people of one's acquaintance ran to cinemas, dance halls and cocktail parties, and
the more sober ones discussed the merits and demerits
of Epstein and Einstein, Communism, Fascism, Douglas
Credit and the rest, the world I knew as a child in the
'nineties seemed as remote and unreal as a dream. That
was an island in Thule, where the sound of wind and

waves was always in our ears, and in our nostrils the smell of heather and peat-reek and the salt sea spray. On wild winter nights the wind howled in the chimney-pots, the windows rattled in their sockets, and fearful shadows leapt from their ambush as one crept upstairs to bed by the light of a flickering flame. In contrast were the opalescent beauty of the summer nights, when sunset merged into dawn, and the crystalline beauty of the autumn nights, when the stars shone bright in a frosty sky and the northern heavens were lit up by the aurora borealis or 'the merry dancers', as we called them. We lived in an eerie borderland between the seen and the unseen worlds, and, Manse bairns and all as we were, duly trained in the Shorter Catechism and in respect for the eternal verities, we had (like most Scots, I fancy) more than a dash of the pagan beneath our Presbyterian veneer. What a thrill we got from an unchancy encounter with an old wife reputed to have the evil eye, an uncanny tapping on the window-pane, or the appearance of a 'shroud' in the candle-flame; whilst the sight of a cat walking widdershins on Hallowe'en—that was a thing to send a shiver down the spine! Dominated by a great arch of sky, surrounded by wide seas, and looking out to far horizons, we could not if we would escape the sense of mystery and awe that is engendered by long and close contact with the elements; and though in due course we came south and studied logic and mathematics, and read Shaw with avidity and Wells with an effort, we found ourselves always a little out of tune with this brave new world of the twentieth century. It is an age of science, they say. Maybe so, but the province of science is bounded by the five senses, and how much lies beyond![3]

'When the mind of man looketh upon secondary causes scattered,' writes Bacon, 'sometimes it resteth in them, but when it beholdeth them confederate and knit together, it flieth to Providence and Deity.'

Even if the glass is clearing a little, we still see 'in a glass, darkly.' The Mystery remains unsolved.

But what, it may be asked, has all this to do with the subject of Festivals?

The answer is, quite a lot.

'The religious sense,' writes Ronald Campbell Macfie, 'always involves, with a sense of wonder and mystery, the sense of an infinite Intelligence and Power behind all things—and though there always have been, and perhaps always will be, men who are blind to the mystery of things—men who may be said to lack the sense of Final Cause . . . yet to-day science has elevated and confirmed intuitive religion by showing the vastness of the universe, and the disciplined energy and fruitful intelligence at work in all natural processes, and especially in the processes of life.'[4]

It is to this sense of wonder and mystery in our remote forebears, and to the same instinct or intuition on which modern theism is based, that we trace our ancient Scottish festivals—which, of course, like those of every other nation, are not national in origin, but are world festivals that have acquired a national complexion.

In every age and in every land, the spirit of a people finds expression not only in its music, its art, and its literature, but also—and most revealing of all—in its religion. Besides myth and dogma, we find in all the great religious systems a series of symbolic rites and ceremonies associated with a ritual that has developed in accordance with the spiritual needs of the times. The great seasonal festivals have always played an important part in the religious life of mankind. Yet, strange as it may seem, they are less mystical than utilitarian in origin, deriving directly from the concern of primitive man with his food supply. The two strongest human instincts are self-preservation and race-preservation, or, in other words, the two main interests of primitive (and not so primitive) man are food and children.[5] It is not easy for us moderns, living in a world where scientific agriculture and rapid transport have ensured abundance of food at all seasons (though the plight of Europe after two World Wars gave us an inkling), to realise what it meant to our forefathers to be entirely dependent upon local produce and to live in constant dread of the failure of the harvest.

Primitive man could never escape from the menace of famine, and the object of his religious festivals was, first and foremost, to placate the earth-powers, the hidden life-giving forces of nature, and so ensure fertility in the soil he tilled, in his domestic animals, and in his own family.

Primitive man was an intense realist: otherwise he could not have survived. If he worshipped the sun and the moon and the heavenly bodies, it was not primarily for their inherent mystery, as Miss Jane Harrison has noted,[6] but because they mysteriously regulated the seasons and brought him food. He observed that at certain seasons the plants and the animals which formed his food appeared and disappeared, and the dates of his festivals synchronise with the focal points of his interest in the food supply. On these dates, which vary, of course, in different climates, he kindled bonfires, offered up sacrifices, and performed certain symbolic acts in order to encourage the bounty of Nature.

The supreme event in Nature's calendar is the resurrection of vegetation in Spring. The prototype of the great class of resurrection gods, whose worship originates in the intense desire of man that nature, which seems dead, shall live again, is the Egyptian Osiris, whose Greek equivalent is the god Dionysos.

'In the ancient days,' writes Plutarch, 'our fathers used to keep the feast of Dionysos in homely, jovial fashion. There was a procession, a jar of wine, and a branch; then someone dragged in a goat; another followed bringing in a wicker basket of figs, and, to crown all, the phallos.'[7]

'It was just a festival of the fruits of the whole earth,' comments Miss Harrison; 'the wine and the basket of figs and the branch for vegetation, the goat for animal life, the phallos for man. No thought here for the dead; it is all for the living and food.'[8]

It is probable that the mariners who brought the first seeds and agricultural implements to Britain, traversing the route marked by the megalithic monuments of North Africa and Western Europe, introduced at the same time the agricultural calendar and the magical or religious rites associated with it.

THE CALENDAR
The whole life of nature is, as we know, dominated by periodic events. The rotation of the earth produces day and night; the rotation of the earth round the sun produces the

cycle of the seasons; the phases of the moon, which before the introduction of artificial light were of vital importance to man, are also recurrent; and primitive calendars are based upon this periodicity.

Our forefathers were profoundly conscious of the rhythm of life, of the secular wheeling of the seasons. At the approach of winter, they rent their garments and bewailed the death of vegetation, and at the approach of spring they hailed its resurrection with frenzied dancing and orgiastic rites. Our modern urban civilisation has cut us off from the old close contact with nature, and we have come to take such natural phenomena for granted; yet so deep is it in our blood, that we have never entirely lost our awareness of the long, slow pulse of the seasons.

To our remote ancestors the phases of the moon were much more obvious than the solstices and equinoxes, and in the pre-Christian era the calendar in general use was lunar; time-reckoning was lunar; festivals began on the rising of the moon—that is, on their eve; and many agricultural operations were governed by its phases. In the first century BC, there was a reaction against the lunar calendar throughout the Roman Empire, and in 46 BC, under Julius Caesar, there was drawn up what we know as the Julian calendar, in which the motion of the moon was ignored and the civil year regulated entirely by the sun.

In 1582, Pope Gregory XIII had the Julian calendar amended in such a way as to check the slow backward movement of the seasons. The Gregorian calendar was immediately adopted in Catholic countries and slowly in Protestant ones. In Great Britain, the change was not made until 1751, by which time the discrepancy between the Julian and Gregorian calendars amounted to eleven days; but since 1752 was not a leap year, the 'new and old styles of reckoning now differed by twelve days—i.e., 1 January, Old Style, became 13 January, New Style. The change met with strong opposition from the people, who clamoured for their lost days. Well into the latter half of the nineteenth century, Scottish country folk still kept their festivals by the Old Style reckoning, and in some of the remoter parts of Shetland, the Hebrides, and elsewhere, the custom has not yet entirely died out.

The date of the New Year varies in different periods and in different countries. The ancient Celtic year began with the entry of winter on 1 November, or, more correctly, on its eve (our modern Hallowe'en). In 527 AD, New Year's Day was fixed by the learned Dionysius at 25 March —the day already long observed as such in the Jewish calendar—and not until a thousand years later was 1 January substituted. In Scotland, James VI decided that the turn of the century was an appropriate time for the change, and by an Act of the Privy Council passed at Holyroodhouse in December, 1599, it was ordained that the first day of the following month should be reckoned the first day of the new year, in conformity with the new Continental calendar.

As regards the Christian festivals, only so much of the ritualistic ceremonial as derives from pre-Christian sources will be dealt with in this book.

TWO

Ethnic Origins of the Festivals

Our Scottish national festivals, like those of every other nation, are infinitely older than the nation itself. Nationality and race are far from being synonymous terms, and the European nations of to-day, dating, as they do, only from the Middle Ages, when they emerged from the chaos that followed the disruption of the Holy Roman Empire, are all of mixed racial strains. The origins of the festivals are therefore not national, but racial.

In tracing nations to their particular sources, we used to rely mainly upon philology; but a no less valuable method has been discovered in the study of folk-customs, and contemporary anthropologists owe an immense debt to Sir James Frazer, who in *The Golden Bough* has surveyed the customs and folk-lore of primitive peoples the world over and, incidentally, has shown us those of his native Scotland in their true perspective against a European background. Since the middle of the nineteenth century, with the development of the two sciences of comparative grammar and comparative mythology our knowledge of the habits and thoughts of the whole human race has enormously increased. We know, for instance, that the various tribes who left their home in or about Mesopotamia, where the 'Garden of Eden' or cradle of the human race is popularly thought to have been situated (though this is by no means proved), to discover Europe in the north and India in the south, carried with them a common speech and a common mythology; that from this common speech is derived the so-called 'Aryan' family of languages—Greek, Latin, Celtic,[1] Teutonic and Slavonic—together with the Oriental languages of Persia and India; and that from their common mythology are descended the gods of Greece, Gaul, and Northern Europe.

7

Within the British Isles, the amalgam of races has produced a diversity of tongues and a folklore with a variety of ethnic elements. The Iberians and other pre-Celtic races, whoever they may have been; the Celts, including Picts,[2] Gaels and Brythons; the Romans; the Angles, Saxons, Danes and Norsemen; the Normans, French and Flemings—each successive wave of immigrants has brought its contribution to the common stock; and as the various racial strains have amalgamated (although their amalgamation is by no means yet complete), so have their customs and beliefs.

In Scotland, England, Wales and Ireland, practically the same racial strains are found, but mixed in greatly varying proportions, and the predominance of a particular strain in each has co-operated with geographical, historical, economic and other factors in producing and maintaining four distinct peoples within a comparatively small area.

The racial strains in the Scottish people are roughly as follows: In the sixth century, at the time of the coming of Columba, between the Pentland (Pictland) Hills and the Pentland Firth stretched the land of the Picts; in the south-west were the Britons or Brythonic Celts (the same race as the Welsh) of Strathclyde and the Picts of Galloway; and in what is now Argyll (literally the land of the Gael) and the southern Hebrides there was a colony of Scots or Gaels, who had crossed from Ireland in the previous century. These were all Celtic peoples.[3] In the south-eastern corner—the Lothians and the Merse—there was a group of Anglian settlers of the same stock as the Northern English.[4] Subsequent additions were some small scattered Flemish settlements on the East Coast; the Norse colonies in Caithness, Orkney and Shetland, together with a few 'pirate nests' in the Hebrides and along the coasts; and a number of Norman families, who came not as conquerors, as in England, but as colonists. There were, in fact, no wholesale conquests in Scottish history such as were made by the Danes and Normans in England and Ireland; indeed it may be claimed for Scotland that she has had fewer alien intrusions than almost any other country in Europe.[5] It is true that from the time of Malcolm Canmore (1057–93) Gaelic, hitherto the national language, has steadily receded towards the North-West; but racially Scotland remains basically Celtic, though with a strong admixture of Scandinavian blood. This duality is borne out in her festivals.

The great world festivals originated, as we have seen, in the worship of the sun and the earth-powers. In Europe, there were two major festivals, which fell exactly six months apart, and each half-year was again bisected and marked with a minor festival. But the dates of these festivals were not everywhere identical; for whilst the non-Celtic peoples divided the year in accordance with the solstices and equinoxes, with Midsummer Day and Midwinter Day, or Yule, as their chief festivals, the Celtic peoples divided it in accordance with the entry of the seasons, their two principal festivals being Beltane (1 May) and Samhuinn or Hallowmas (1 November).

'We must suppose,' writes Sir James Frazer, 'that the founders of the Midsummer rites had observed the solstices or turning-points in the sun's apparent path in the sky, and that they had accordingly regulated their festal calendar to some extent by astronomical considerations.' The fire-festivals of the Celts, on the other hand, coincided neither with the solstices and equinoxes, nor, as we might have expected, with the two principal seasons of the agricultural year, the sowing in spring and the reaping in autumn; but, as Frazer points out, the dates of Beltane and Samhuinn, while they are of comparatively little moment to the European husbandman, do deeply concern the European herdsman; 'for it is on the approach of summer that he drives his cattle out into the open to crop the fresh grass, and it is on the approach of winter that he leads them back to the safety and shelter of the stall. Accordingly it seems not improbable that the Celtic bi-section of the year at the beginning of May and the beginning of November dates from a time when the Celts were mainly a pastoral people, dependent for subsistence on their herds . . . . Hence we may conjecture that everywhere throughout Europe the celestial division of the year was preceded by a terrestrial division according to the beginning of summer and the beginning of winter.'

We all know that the Scottish and English Quarter Days fall on different dates, thus:

Scottish Quarter Days[6]	*English Quarter Days*
Candlemas, 2 February	Lady Day, 25 March
Whitsun or approx.	Midsummer Day, 24 June
Old Beltane, 15 May	Michaelmas, 29 September
Lammas, 1 August	Christmas Day,
Martinmas or approx.	25 December
Old Hallowmas,	
11 November	

But few of us realise that this difference has a racial basis, and that, allowing for a slight dislocation of the calendar, Scotland follows the ancient custom of the Celtic peoples, and England that of the non-Celtic peoples of Europe.

We must not, however, draw too sharp a line between these modes of division, for even in Central Europe both May Day and its Eve (Walpurgis Night) and All Souls' Day (originally a pagan festival of the dead) at the beginning of November, are widely kept; and, conversely, the ceremonial cutting of the mistletoe, the sacred plant of the Druids, at the time of the summer and winter solstices indicates that the 'celestial' division of the year was to some extent observed by the Celts.

Besides the Celtic Quarter Days, we celebrate in Scotland both Midsummer Day and Yule, which are kept with particular zest in the Scandinavian fringes. The Beltane and Midsummer festivals have gradually merged, and Yule (which embraces Christmas and Hogmanay) has, despite the ban of the Kirk, retained its popularity up to our time.

To understand the full significance of the festivals, we must know something of their background of folklore and folk-belief. In this respect it should be borne in mind that the 'Celtic fringes' form a sort of backwater to the main stream of European life and thought, and that whilst throughout Europe those archaic ideas which underlie the civilisation of the remote past have been largely submerged, the Celt has preserved a vast corpus of legend and lore which reveals a conception of life and nature undreamed of in the philosophy of the ordinary educated man of our own times.

Let us look first at the religion of our forebears, the Picts and Scots.

THREE

The Druids

Before the coming of Christianity, the religion of Scotland was Druidism,[1] a form of sun-worship peculiar to the Celtic peoples. Like all sun-cults, it was based upon a universal doctrine regarding the two states of existence—the one in the visible world where the Sun-god reigns by day, and the other in the invisible or lower world into which he disappears at night, the relation between light and darkness symbolising the relation between life and death. This conception is the basis of all the Mysteries.[2]

Although the Order of Druids was probably a Celtic institution, Druidism itself appears to have been the aboriginal faith of Britain, its basic principles being adopted by the Celtic invaders, who grafted upon it their own mythology.[3] Caesar, writing of the Druids he encountered in the course of his Gallic campaign, says, 'It is believed that their rule of life was discovered in Britain and transferred thence to Gaul, and to-day those who would study the subject more accurately journey, as a rule, to Britain to learn it.'[4]

There is evidence, says Mr Lewis Spence, that to the peoples of antiquity Britain was an *insula sacra*, the seat of a cult of peculiar sanctity and mystical power. The arcane tradition which flourished there was, he maintains, akin to that which developed in Egypt and the East, and derived from the same source—the Cult of the Dead, which the pre-Celtic invaders known variously as Iberian and Mediterranean carried to Britain as they did to Egypt. The tradition lingered in Britain after it had perished elsewhere, and has affected the entire process of British mystical thought down to our own time.[5]

Although, like all pagan religions, a form of nature-worship, Druidism was already groping towards a spiritual interpretation of the universe when it was overthrown by the domination of Rome in Southern Britain and by the subsequent introduction of Christianity beyond the Roman pale.[6]

Unfortunately we know far less about Druidism than about some of its contemporary cults, for it was esoteric, hidden, and most of its written doctrine and ritual disappeared with the last of the ancient priesthood.

EVIDENCE OF CLASSICAL WRITERS

By far the most valuable evidence is that of Julius Caesar, who came into direct contact with the cult in the course of his Gallic campaigns.

'Throughout Gaul,' he writes, 'there are two classes of persons of definite account and dignity . . . One consists of druids, the other of knights.[7] The former are concerned with divine worship, the due performances of sacrifices, public and private, and the interpretation of ritual questions; a great number of young men gather about them for the sake of instruction and hold them in great honour. In fact, it is they who decide in almost all disputes, public and private,[8] and if any crime has been committed, and there is any dispute about succession or boundaries, they also decide it, determining rewards and penalties.

'. . . Of all these Druids, one is chief, who has the highest authority among them . . . The cardinal doctrine they seek to teach is that souls do not die, but after death pass from one to another; and this belief, as the fear of death is thereby cast aside, they hold to be the greatest incentive to valour. Besides this, they have many discussions touching the stars and their movements, the size of the universe and the earth, the order of nature, the power and majesty of the immortal gods, and they hand down their lore to the young men.'[9]

And that is virtually all he has to say on the subject.

The later writers of the classical period tell us even less. We learn from them, however, that 'the Druids make their pronouncements by means of riddles and dark sayings, teaching the people to worship the gods, refrain from evil, and quit themselves like men';[10] that they 'concern themselves with divination and all branches of wisdom';[11] and that they are regarded as 'philosophers and theologians.'[12]

'I knew one myself,' writes Cicero, 'Dividiacus the Aeduan . . . He claims to have that knowledge of nature which the Greeks call "physiologia", and he used to make predictions, sometimes by means of augury, and sometimes by means of conjecture.'[13]

Pliny, on the other hand, dismisses the Druidic lore as a mere bundle of superstitions; but, generally speaking, the ancient writers placed the Druids among those mystic philosophers who, in association with the philosophers of Greece, evolved the doctrine of the Immortality of the Soul.[14]

'The Druids had a complete doctrine of that immortality,' says M. Henri Hubert, 'with a moral system, general view of the world, mythology, ritual and funerary practices to match.'

Briefly, death was regarded as a mere changing of place.[15] The world of the dead was the world of life, and a constant floating capital of souls was distributed between the two counterpart worlds. Interest in the soul, its origin and destiny, the world of souls and the dead, and the myth of the Beyond stood in the forefront of representations, as agrarian rites stood in the forefront of ritual.

'With some notions of physics and of astronomy (applied in the construction of calendars), and some knowledge of plants and their properties (which has passed to the physicians), this stock of philosophical ideas,' continues M. Hubert,[16] 'seems to have formed the bulk of the wisdom of the Druids, which contributed in no small degree to the spiritual education of the Celts.'[17]

In modern times, Druidism has been much romanticised on the one hand and derided on the other; but in all likelihood 'those who exalt the knowledge and the philosophy of the Druids to the supreme heights of magical and mystical ascendency are obviously as mistaken as the opposing school who wish to reduce their status to that of mere witchdoctors. The probability is that they were at least the equals in scientific ability and general scholarship with the Egyptian priesthood of the closing centuries of the last pre-Christian millennium.'[18]

If their knowledge of the natural sciences was rudimentary, it is still possible that the Druids knew more, or sought to know more than the modern man of science knows, or seeks to know. As Neil Gunn puts it (in the mouth of one of his characters): 'The real Druid was after real powers; he wanted to tap the source. What he sought was—well, if the Picts had a word for it, it has long been lost, but the Melanesian word is *Mana*—the mysterious energy that comes from the hidden or ultimate source of power. It is not so occult as it sounds,' he adds; 'all profound religious experience is full of it.'[19]

SACRIFICE

In Druidism, as in all early religions, the essential rite was sacrifice at the altar in presence of the tribe. The day of the sacrificial feast was observed as a holiday, and the solemn rite was followed by the abandonment of all restraint and by indulgence of every description.

About the origin of sacrifice there are conflicting theories. The word is derived from the Latin *sacer*, holy, and *facere*, to make, and in the earliest times the object of sacrifice seems to have been simply the communion of worshippers with the deity, or, in other words, the creation of a sacramental relationship with the source of spiritual strength.

The sacrificial rite has been traced by Robertson Smith to the early totem feast. The totem is an animal (very occasionally a plant or a force of nature) which is revered as the tribal ancestor of the clan.[20] The character of the totem is not restricted to an individual animal, but is inherent in every member of the species. The sacrificial animal is identified by this authority with the totem animal. The god, the victim, and the totem group belong, he considers, to the same kin, and sacrifice is, in the first instance, a communion established by a bond of kinship. In spite of the reverence accorded to the animal as one of the kin, it was necessary to kill it in solemn conclave at stated seasons, and to divide its flesh and blood among the members of the clan.

'The holy mystery of the sacrificial death was justified

in that only in this way could the holy bond be established which united the participants with each other and with their god. This bond was nothing else than the life of the sacrificial animal which lived on in its flesh and blood and was shared by all the participants by means of the sacrificial feast.'

In the course of time, the relation of the sacrificial animal to the totem was forgotten, and the sacrifice came to be regarded as propitiatory—as an offering to the deity in order to induce his favour and protection.[21] But contact with the deity is no longer direct. He is now so exalted above man that he can be approached only through a priest as intermediary. At the same time there emerge god-like kings who transfer the patriarchal system to the state. The king or tribal chief, on whom his office confers divinity, becomes the sacrificial victim, whose life is to be given for the benefit of his people. At a later stage, some one of high rank is appointed in his stead, royal powers and privileges being conferred upon him until his death. Later still comes a volunteer, who also receives temporary royal power; then comes a criminal—as in Gaul in Caesar's time—and finally an animal victim—the stage reached at the time of the medieval witch-cult. With agriculture came vegetable sacrifice—the offering of the first-fruits to the nature spirits or lord of the soil.[22]

Caesar notes the survival of human sacrifice in the Druidic religion, and Suetonious alludes to 'the barbarous and inhuman religion of the Druids in Gaul'. It should not, however, be inferred that the Celts were more cruel and sanguinary than their contemporaries. Sacrifices to the gods were made in the same spirit in which Abraham was prepared to offer up Isaac. In Rome itself, even in Caesar's time, there were isolated instances of human sacrifice, and it is highly questionable whether the sacrifices of the Druids were as 'barbarous and inhuman' as the treatment meted out by Imperial Rome to the unfortunate Gauls who had the courage to resist her domination.

The truth is that the Romans opposed Druidism not upon either religious or humanitarian, but upon political grounds, because of the power possessed by the Druids and the strength of their resistance to Rome.[23] The rebellion of

Vercingetorix resulted in the break-up of the inter-tribal system and the loss of status in the priestly caste.

'Under the specious pretext of abolishing human sacrifice,' says Gibbon, 'the emperors Tiberius and Claudius suppressed the dangerous powers of the Druids; but the priests themselves, their gods and their altars, subsisted in peaceful obscurity until the final destruction of paganism.'[24]

ORGANISATION

The Druidic priesthood was a pan-Celtic institution, cutting across the divisions of tribes and states, and the journeyings and assemblies of the Druids developed a strong sense of unity among the Celtic peoples.

The religion had three orders—the Bards, the Seers (Vates), and the Druids proper, or priests. 'The Bards,' says Strabo, 'are singers and poets; the Seers, diviners and natural philosophers; whilst the Druids, in addition to natural philosophy, study also moral philosophy.' The Druids were not merely priests, but administrators of justice with formidable religious sanction behind their decrees. Initiation was preceded by a long course of instruction and meditation—sometimes, according to Cicero, as much as twenty years.

The Druids had neither images nor formal temples, for 'they thought it absurd,' says Tacitus, 'to portray like a man[25] or circumscribe within the walls of a house the Being who created the immensity of the Heavens.'[26] Their rites were performed out of doors, usually within a grove, or on some high spot in view of the sun. We do not know whether oak-groves were used in Scotland and Ireland as they were in Gaul; but the fact that some of the early Christian churches and monasteries were built in oak groves suggests the traditional sanctity of the oak in the British Isles.[27] The stone circles—Callanish in the Island of Lewis, the Standing Stones of Stennis in Orkney, the Clava Circles in Inverness-shire, and the rest, were not built by the Druids, but eventually came to be associated with their worship.

In Montfaucon's splendid work there is an engraving of two Druids (apparently copied from Auberi's *Antiquities d'Autun*). They are bearded men with flowing robes draped plaidwise and fastened on the shoulder with a brooch. They are bare-footed. One wears a coronet of oak-leaves and carries a mace, or wand,[28] whilst the other carries a crescent, or first quarter of the moon.[29]

Among the Celts, women seem all along to have exercised certain priestly functions. We cannot be sure whether the Druidesses of Gaul and Ireland actually belonged to the college of Druids, or got their name merely by analogy, on account of their gifts in magic. The nuns who guarded the sacred fire at Kildare were the successors of the Virgin Guardians of the earlier faith, who appear to have been priestesses of a cult that was taboo to men.

THE DRUIDS IN SCOTLAND

Of the Druids of Scotland and Ireland our knowledge is comparatively scanty. It is certain, however, that they held a position of great authority.[30] The names of many of them survive—Cathbadh, for instance, the Druid of Conchobar MacNessa and the instructor of Cuchulain; Abaris, a hyperborean Arch-Druid, who visited Athens in or about 350 AD on a diplomatic mission, and who is described by Himerius as 'a seeker after truth, a philosopher, an accomplished scholar, and an ardent friend, who would trust nothing to fortune, but would weigh everything in the balance of prudence and common sense'; and Broichan, Chief Druid at the Court of King Brude, whom St Columba encountered at Inverness in 565.[31]

Toland and others surmise that the 'winged hyperborean temple'[32] to which Abaris was attached was Callanish, in the Isle of Lewis, which is oval in shape, with a double line of stones running out to the north and single lines running east and west, constituting wings. Be that as it may, there is a tradition that Druidism 'breathed its last' in Lewis, which remained a stronghold of the cult long after the advent of the Christian faith.

Another reputed retreat of the Druids is Iona, where St Columba established the mission that was to give its death-blow to the cult in Scotland.[33]

In Druidical times, the people of Scotland were organised

in tribes, each under a chief, and the chiefs themselves were (at least nominally) under the district *righ*, or king, who ruled a petty independent state.

'It would appear,' writes Sir Thomas Innes of Learney, 'that each of the tribes had its own "Druids", respectively priest, sennachie, and dempster or judge of the tribe, but the Druids regarded themselves as an Order and Hierarchy, and just as the chiefs formed a nominal group under their Ard-righ, so the Druids appear to have been organised in what one might call a hierarchy or college, evidently under the presidency of the Chief Druid of the Pictish High King.'[34]

With the advent of the Christian religion, the Druid priests gradually disappeared; but, as the same authority points out, 'the bardic and sennachiedal branch survived in two forms: (a) the Royal Heralds; (b) the tribal bards. It would be difficult to say that the second of these is even yet extinguished. They subsisted in many of the greater clans down to the middle of the eighteenth century. The office of Righ-sennachie . . . passed down into the "Principal Herald" of our medieval history, for heraldry, "as pertaining to" the sennachie's office, was added to his duties, so that the chief of the sennachiedal branch of the "Druids" evolved into the Lord Lyon King of Arms, whose "brethren heralds", pursuivants, and macers, comprising the college of seventeen individuals, preserved the form of the primitive bardic incorporation.'

And elsewhere he writes,

'Much of the Lord Lyon's peculiar importance in Scotland is due to his incorporating the pre-heraldic Celtic office of Chief Sennachie of the Royal Line of Scotland, and, in this capacity, as guardian and preserver of the Royal Pedigree and Family Records, his certification was requisite for the coronation of each Scottish king—whose genealogy it was his duty at each coronation as "Official Inaugurator" to declaim in Gaelic—latterly for seven generations, but originally through all the Scottish kings back to Fergus Mac Earc, founder of the Royal Line.

'. . . . In ceremonial matters and grants of honour, Lyon's function can also be traced to origins only explainable by reference to the Sennachie's position as a pagan priest, and the primitive principle that it was "geiss" (taboo) for a king to speak in the presence of his Druid . . . . Lyon thus appears in Scots history, not as a mediaeval invention, but with all the authority attaching to an ancient institution of the Celto-Pictish regime, in which he exercised high administerial functions, sacred in the ante-Christian era, and subsequently of secular importance in a country where succession and civil rights depended on Patriarchal principles.

'. . . . Not only in functions, but even in the manner of appointment, the senachiedal custom continued into the Middle Ages, when the Lord Lyon's symbol of investiture was a gold cup, which had likewise been the symbol of in-auguration of a High Sennachie.

'. . . . In the early records of the Anglo-Normanised kings, it is naturally difficult to find, except at coronations, a continuing trace of the High Sennachie, who, like the Judex and the Deemster, might have slipped into oblivion, had it not been for the rise of "Chivalry", which so powerfully in-fluenced the mediaeval nobility, an elaborate social and legal code, confined to the *noblesse*, and for which special officers and courts were evolved . . . . In Scotland no chivalric offi-cial required to be created, for the High Sennachie, supreme judge in genealogies and family representation, remained with the glamour of a long and ancient past behind him. Already complete with court and judicial status, he forth-with became, in mediaeval terminology, "King of Arms of Scotland", and like other kings of arms, was endowed with the Sovereign's tabard, though the judico-priestly robe has continued, emphasising Lyon's pre-heraldic functions as a judge and officer of state. In accordance with chivalric prac-tice he was named after his Sovereign's "beast", and many of his privileges were hence explained from his being, in his Sovereign's tabard, the King's Lieutenant, appointed for skilled exercise of the chivalric, heraldic, and genealogical sections of the Royal Prerogative.'[35]

It is noteworthy that the Lord Lyon's two special courts are held on 6 May and 6 November—dates which ap-proximate to those of the two principal Druidic festivals and retain their names—the Beltane and the Samhuinn court.

In Ireland, the judicial powers of the Druids passed to the order of *filidh* (bards), which lasted until the great break-up of Gaelic society in the seventeenth century. The *filidh*, again, in succession to the Druids, founded schools that were handed over to the Celtic Church and survived through the Middle Ages. In the Schools of Scotland and Ireland much of the old teaching was maintained along with classical learning and Christian doctrine, Latin learning being known as legend (reading), to distinguish it from the oral learning of the *filidh*. Many of our traditional Gaelic runes and proverbs derive, in all probability, from this source.[36]

SURVIVALS OF DRUIDICAL BELIEFS AND PRACTICES

The influence of the Druids persisted long after their religion was formally abandoned. 'The Culdees,' writes Mr Lewis Spence, 'are generally supposed to have been a caste of Christian priests or monks of early British origin, unfriendly to Roman authority and discipline. But there are many circumstances connected with them which seem to show that, if they practised a species of Christianity, their doctrine still retained a large measure of the Druidic philosophy, and that, indeed, they were the direct descendants of the Druidic caste.'[37]

In his *Druidism Exhumed* (1871), the Rev. James Rust, minister of the parish of Slains, Aberdeenshire, recounts the steps taken by the Church of Scotland in the seventeenth century to 'uproot the remains of druidical superstition and sorcery'. He quotes the minutes in the Kirk Session Register of Slains referring to an inquisition made by the ministers and elders of Slains into druidical practices and places within the parish, when several persons were 'delayit' or summoned before the Kirk Session for practising pagan rites in connection with hallow fires and refusing to till the ancient druidical fields—those dedicated spots to which people resorted for the working of charms and spells. There were no fewer than three places within the parish that were dedicated to the 'Good People', or fairies, and these, incidentally, remained uncultivated until the beginning of the nineteenth century.

The same conditions obtained elsewhere. From various Presbytery records we learn that in the seventeenth century bulls were surreptitiously sacrificed in the remoter Highlands and oblations of milk poured on the hills. In short, the incredible fact emerges that more than a century after the Reformation the General Assembly of the Church of Scotland was persuaded that Druidism was still practised all over the country, and was determined to take measures to put it down.

'As most of these superstitions, they said, proceeded from ignorance, they resolved that the most strenuous efforts should be made throughout Scotland for bringing education to the doors of all, even of the poorest, by the erection and extension of Parochial Schools, and by urging that Bibles should be possessed in every family, and the inmates taught to read them.'

Besides this, they appointed a commission to deal with the problem.[38] The 'gudeman's crofts'[39] were ordered to be cultivated under severe penalties, and such Druidical customs as the bonfires of Beltane, Midsummer, Hallowe'en and Yule were ordered to be abolished. These measures appear to have succeeded outwardly among the old, but the youths in many places kept up the old customs as a ploy long after their origin and significance was forgotten.

Traces of the old Druidical reverence for the sun linger in the Hebrides to this day.

'In my father's time,' Dr Carmichael was told by Isabel MacNeill, of Barra, towards the end of the nineteenth century, 'there was not a man in Barra but would take off his head-covering to the white sun of the day, nor a woman in Barra but would incline her body to the white moon of the night. Old men in this countryside do so still. I myself do so at times, though the children make fun of me. I think myself that it is a matter for thankfulness, the golden bright sun of virtues giving us warmth and light by day, and the white moon of the seasons giving us guidance and leading by night.'

Some fragments of sun runes were obtained by Dr Carmichael in South Uist and Mingulay. One runs:

The eye of the great God,
The eye of the God of Glory,
The eye of the King of Hosts,
The eye of the King of the Living,
> Pouring upon us,
> > At each time and season,
> Pouring upon us,
> > Gently and generously.

Glory to thee,
> Thou glorious sun,
Glory to thee, thou sun,
> Face of the God of life!

And here is one of the many moon runes:

When I see the new moon,
It becomes me to lift mine eye,
It becomes me to bend my knee,
It becomes me to bow my head.

Giving thee praise, thou moon of guidance,
That I have seen thee again,
That I have seen the new moon,
The lovely leader of the way.

Many a one has passed beyond
In the time between the two moons,
Though I am still enjoying earth,
Thou moon of moons and of blessings![40]

The custom of placing earth and salt on the breast of a corpse for the repose of soul and body has not yet died out in the Highlands; and when we 'dook' for apples on Hallowe'en, decorate the house with evergreens at the time of the winter solstice, kiss under the mistletoe and eat plum pudding, we are performing rites that originally pertained to Druidical worship.

FOUR

The Gods

Although Druidism was the official religion of early Britain, there is no evidence of a homogeneous Celtic faith. The first Christian missionaries encountered several pagan cults, and there was also a body of popular superstitions and magical practices of still earlier origin.

The mythology of the Celts has a strong affinity with the Græco-Roman on the one hand and the Nordic-Teutonic on the other. They derive, indeed, from the same source.

We know that the so-called Aryan tribes who in pre-historic times left their homes in Central Asia to colonise Europe brought with them their own primitive mythology, which took root alike on the Baltic, the Atlantic, and the Mediterranean shores. This mythology came, in time, to take on the colour of its surroundings, and the character of the gods and heroes changed, just as the character of the people changed, under their physical environment and the modes of life it engendered. Naturally the myths that matured in the harsh, invigorating North contrasted in many respects with those of the mild, indolent South. In both, the earth was regarded as a female divinity, 'the fostering mother of all things'; but in the North, where life was a constant struggle for existence, she appears as Rinda, hard and frozen, whereas in the South, where life was easy, we find her in the genial goddess, Demeter (Ceres). The Northern peoples, again, looking up at their dark, wintry skies, descried in the storm-tossed clouds the white-maned steeds of the Valkyries, and in the flashing of the Aurora Borealis the glitter of their spears; whilst the Greeks saw in the gentle cloudscapes of the Mediterranean shores the white flocks of Apollo guarded by Phaetusa and Lampetia.

Whence, we may ask, did the primitive mythology of the

European peoples spring? The answer is, from the play of
human fancy or imagination upon the natural phenomena it
encountered.

'When we try to conceive the state of mind of primitive
man,' writes Lowes Dickenson, 'the first thing that occurs
to us is the bewilderment and terror he must have felt in
the presence of the powers of nature. Naked, houseless,
weaponless, he is at the mercy, every hour, of this immense and incalculable Something so alien and so hostile
to himself. As fire it burns, as water it drowns, as tempest
it harries and destroys . . . What is it, then, this persistent,
obscure, unnamable Thing? What is it? . . . The Greek
at last, like other men under similar conditions, only with
a lucidity and precision peculiar to himself, makes the reply, "It is something like myself." Every power of nature
he presumes to be a spiritual being, impersonating the sky
as Zeus, the earth as Demeter, the sea as Poseidon; from
generation to generation, under his shaping fingers, the figures multiply and define themselves; character and story
crystallise about what at first were little more than names;
till at last, from the womb of the dark enigma that haunted
him in the beginning, there emerges into the charmed light
of a world of ideal grace a pantheon of fair and concrete per-
sonalities. Nature has become a company of spirits; every
cave and fountain is haunted by a nymph; in the ocean
dwell the Nereids, in the mountain the Oread, the Dryad
in the wood; and everywhere, in groves and marshes, on
the pastures or the rocky heights, floating on the current
of the streams or traversing untrodden snows, in the day
at the chase and as evening closes in solitude fingering
his flute, seen and heard by shepherds, alone or with his
dancing train, is to be met the horned and goat-footed, the
sunny-smiling Pan.

'Thus conceived, the world has become less terrible because more familiar. All that was incomprehensible, all that
was obscure and dark, has now been seized and bodied forth
in form, so that everywhere man is confronted no longer
with blind and unintelligible force, but with spiritual beings moved by like passions with himself. The gods, it is
true, were capricious and often hostile to his good, but at

least they had a nature akin to his; if they were jealous, they might be appeased; the enmity of one might be compensated by the friendship of another; dealings with them, after all, were not so unlike dealings with men, and at the worst there was always a chance for courage, patience and wit.

'Man, in short, by his religion had been made at home in the world.'[1]

THE CELTIC GODS

'Celtic religion,' says Canon MacCulloch, 'is, in the main, a cult of the powers of growth and fertility, perhaps because the poetic temperament of the people kept them close to the heart of nature. . . . The cult of nature-spirits preceded and outlived that of the anthropomorphic gods.'[2]

Unfortunately we have no clear picture of the Celtic pantheon such as we find of the Greek in Homer and of the Norse in the *Edda*; but although the hierarchy cannot be codified, we have a certain amount of fragmentary knowledge. As in other mythologies, the principal deities are those which personify the elements. Foremost amongst them is the British or Brythonic *Don* or Gaelic *Dagda*, whose attributes are clearly consistent with sun-worship. He is, indeed, 'the deified sun, the heavenly eye who has observed the doings of countless ages of men.'[3] Broadly, Don may be equated with Zeus (Jupiter) and Odin (Wodin), the deity of the sky and air and the father of the gods.

The British *Llyr* or Gaelic *Lir* corresponds to Poseidon (Neptune) and to the Nordic Aegar, the old king of the sea; and the British *Ludd* or *Nudd*—the Gaelic *Nuada*—to Aides (Pluto), ruler of the Underworld; for although Nudd is to some extent a sea-god, he is more probably the ruler of the Land-under-the-Waves, which is one conception of the Celtic Otherworld.

The lesser British gods are divided into two groups or clans—'the Children of Don' and 'the Children of Llyr'. The Gaelic pantheon is similarly divided into the *Tuatha dé Danann*, the people or children of the goddess *Danu* (known also as *Anu* or *Ana*), who are symbolic of light and fruitfulness and akin to the children of Don; and the Fomors or Formorians, 'the Beings of the Underseas', who are akin to the Children of Llyr.

The British *Llew* or Gaelic *Lug* (Luga Lamfada)—'a young champion, tall and comely, with a countenance as bright and glorious as the setting sun'—resembles both Phoebus Apollo and the Norse Baldur, the radiant sun-god.

The British *Manawyddadan*, son of Llyr, or the Gaelic *Manannan mac Lir*, may be identified with Mercury. He is a god of sea and wind, and the possessor of a marvellous steed called Enbarr of the Flowing Mane, who is as swift as the cold keen wind of spring and who travels with equal ease on land or sea. Manannan is the messenger of the gods and the guide of the dead to the spirit world.

Bran, another son of Llyr, has been equated with the Gallic horned god, *Cernunnos*, a divinity of the Otherworld who himself appears to be akin to the Greek god Pan.

The British *Camulos* or *Teutates*, or the Gaelic *Neith*, corresponds to Ares or Mars and to the Nordic Tyr or Tiu, the god of storm and war.

The British *Brigantia* or the Gaelic *Bridget* (*Bride*) has affinities with Pallas Athene or Minerva, the moon goddess; with Hera or Juno, goddess of the hearth and home; and with Persephone or Proserpine in her character of goddess of spring or the Corn-Maiden.

The British *Branwen*, on the other hand, resembles Aphrodite or Venus, and the northern Freya, for she, too, is a daughter of the sea-god and a flouter of the marriage law.

The Gaelic *Oengus* or *Angus*, son of the Dagda, is in one aspect a sun-god and in another, Eros or Cupid.[4] His brother is *Ogham*, the patron of letters and historic annals, whose name was given to the Ogham alphabet.

Lastly we have the British *Keridwen*, goddess of Nature, who possesses a magic cauldron with three properties—inexhaustibility, inspiration and regeneration—symbolising the reproductive power of the earth. In the Book of Taliesen we read how the Brythonic Arthur journeyed to the Welsh Hades (Annwn), where he gained possession of the magic cauldron which furnishes inexhaustible food, though it will not boil the food of a coward. This cauldron is the pagan Celtic type of the Holy Grail.[5]

The Celtic deities were very numerous, for they were mainly tribal gods, those of one tribe or group of tribes closely resembling those of another, but differing in name. Some forty of these names have survived, and we have a clue to their identity in the votive inscriptions found on both Gaulish and British monuments, where the name of the Roman deity appears beside the local Celtic equivalent. In Gaul, we repeatedly find the name of Belinus-Apollo; in Bath, there is an inscription to Sul-Minerva; and on the Roman Wall between the Forth and the Clyde there are several to Mars-Camulos, to mention only a few.[6]

In Ireland there is a wealth of legend concerning the *Tuatha dé Danann*. Originally nature divinities, the *Tuatha* appear in the medieval tales as the *Side*, or fairy hosts. They are not, however, regarded as ordinary fairies, but rather as 'the gentry of the fairy world', who, in Canon MacCulloch's words, 'enjoy a sort of god-like existence in the land of promise'. In the eleventh-century Irish documents, the Otherworld is still the world of divine beings, though they are beginning to assume the traits of fairy folk.

In the earliest Welsh writings, too, the gods have fallen from their high estate and appear as kings, champions and magicians, whilst the myths have been resolved into heroic tales. Belinus, the sun god, for instance, appears in the pages of Geoffrey of Monmouth as a mere mortal conqueror—his name survives in Shakespeare's Cymbeline—and Llyr as a British king, the precursor of Shakespeare's King Lear; whilst Camulos, the war-god, emerges as Old King Cole. The British Arthur[7] and the Gaelic demi-god, Cuchulain, are believed by some writers to be re-incarnated sun-deities, and it is probable that many gods fought in the guise of heroes under Arthur's banner. Again, Bran, son of Llyr, is identified with Bran the Blessed, who became a convert to Christianity whilst a hostage in Rome, and on his release (runs the legend) introduced the new faith to Britain; and *Manannan* appears in Irish legend as a fairy chief who deserts his bride, *Fand*.

Bishop Carswell, writing in 1567, laments the love of

the Highlanders for 'idle, turbulent, lying, worldly stories concerning the Tuatha Dedenans'. Their vogue in Scotland is attested by the fact that many of them are commemorated in our place-names, although these do not always derive directly from the god, but sometimes from a king or hero who bore the god's name.

PRE-HISTORIC TEMPLE ON THE CLYDE

New light on the science and religion of pre-historic Scotland has been shed by the discovery, in 1937, of the remains of a unique timber-built temple at Knappers Farm, Kilbowie, Dunbartonshire, seven miles north-west of Glasgow, on a spot overlooking some of the great shipyards of the Clyde.

For some five thousand years this site has remained undisturbed and intact save for the wasting of the timber superstructure. The turf has now been bared over a wide area and reveals a structure circular in form, with a radius of not less than eighty-six feet. The rows of socket-holes, with the remains of wooden posts, indicate in outline the huge wicker erections, and reveal a very precise and symmetrical arrangement involving circles, ellipses, and a number of serpentine figures.

The very uniqueness of the find makes it impossible to place it as one would place a Greek or Egyptian ruin, and archaeologists are far from agreed as to its significance. The excavators themselves[8] surmise that the temple was built to commemorate, by means of symbolic figures, an eclipse of the sun—probably a total one—that was seen in the West of Scotland about the year 3000 BC.[9] The more cautious archaeologists, however, will allow no more at present than that the site is an ancient burial-ground.

Adjoining the temple is a cemetery with over fifty burials, both cremated and inhumed, with grave furnishings and stone settings, many of them of an unusual character. Vessels of pottery placed beside the dead were found to have a deposit of carbonised matter which analysis shows to have been a kind of porridge. (It is known that cereals were cultivated in Scotland before the close of the Stone Age.) The custom of leaving food for the dead was once general in both hemispheres. Besides the sepulchral pots, symbolic relics were placed beside the body. Some of these, say the excavators, appear to be related to Manannan or the Mercury planet-god, who was believed to convey the soul to the abode of the dead, whilst inscriptions on headstones found in the graves they interpret as prayers addressed to the Moon and Manannan on behalf of the departed soul. It will take time, however, to sift fact from surmise.

THE GODS COMMEMORATED IN PLACE-NAMES

Darnaway (Gael. *Taranaich*) in the county of Moray, 'is probably from *taran* or *tarnach*, thunder,' says Lachlan Shaw, historian of Moray, 'because there Jupiter Taranis might have been anciently worshipped . . . Taranis,' he adds, 'was the name of a Pictish king, and is to be equated with Taranis, the thunder god.' Similarly the name *Aengus*, or *Oengus*, which survives in Angus, or Forfarshire, was borne by Oengus, son of Fergus, who in 729 won a great victory over Nectan, King of the Picts; and tradition identifies Camulos (in its Gaelic form *Cumhal*, pronounced Coo-al) with Coel Hen (c. 400 AD) whose family ruled in Ayrshire and Galloway independently of the Kings of Strathclyde,[10] and whose name is preserved in the Ayrshire division, Kyle (the birthplace of Burns).[11] Again, Annan, in Dumfries-shire, derives from *Anu* or *Ana*, the mother of the gods.[12]

From *Manau* is derived (the Isle of) Man, which, during the Norse occupation, was linked with the Hebrides. Manau was also a district near the head of the Firth of Forth, where we find Slamannan (the Moor of Mannan) and Clackmannan (the Stone of Mannan)—the Stone being conspicuous in the centre of the town. Dalmeny, of which the old spelling is Dunmayn, may, Professor Watson thinks, have had a similar origin.

The various ancient names of Ireland are found in those parts of Scotland where there were settlements of Irish Gaels. Amongst them are the names of three dé Danann queens—Eire, Fodla, and Banba, of which the first is borne by the Irish Free State. In Perthshire we have Strathearn (*Srath Eireann*) and Lochearn (*Loch Eireann*), and in

Moray, Auldearn (*Allt Eireann*, *allt* meaning a burn). Fodla survives in Atholl (*Ath Fodhla*, *New Ireland*), and Banba in Banff, on the Deveron, and Bamff, near Alyth.

Many of our rivers bear the names of river goddesses. Thus the Dee is the *Deva*; the Tay, *Tatha*; and the Clyde, *Clotha*—whence the cluthas or river-boats of pre-War days.

In fact, 'it is not too much to say,' writes Professor Watson, 'that the feeling of divinity pervades and colours the whole system of our ancient nomenclature.'[13]

FIVE

The New Faith

I am the Light of the World: he that followeth me shall
not walk in darkness but shall have the light of life.

St John VIII, *12*

THE DEATH OF PAN

At the moment of the Nativity, the legend goes, the cry
rang through the pagan world, 'Great Pan is dead.' Pan
died because he had lost his innocence, and this is how
it came about.

To primitive man, the most mysterious thing in the
world was the reproduction of life, which he observed
everywhere about him, from the germinating seed to the
human family, and the religion of the pagan world was based
on the worship of the two mysterious sources of life, the Sun
and the Phallus.[1] The worship of the Sun appealed to the
enlightened few; that of the Phallus to the unenlightened
multitude, who found in the functions of the human body a
simpler and more intelligible symbolism than in the motions
of the heavenly bodies.[2]

In the primitive world, the worship of the mystical
power symbolised in the Phallus was spontaneous and rever-
ent, and we may assume that the fertility rites which at a
more advanced stage of civilisation seemed indecent were
performed by the mass of worshippers with complete purity
of heart; but with sophistication, phallic worship degenerated into sheer licentiousness and depravity, and eventually
led to the downfall of ancient civilisation.

'Pagan civilisation had indeed been a very high civilisation,' writes G. K. Chesterton, 'the highest humanity
ever reached. It had discovered its still unrivalled arts of
poetry and plastic representation; it had discovered its
own permanent political ideal; it had discovered its own

clear system of logic and language. But above all, it had discovered its own mistake . . . the mistake of nature-worship
. . . What was the matter with the whole heathen civilisation was that there was nothing for the mass of men in the
way of mysticism except that concerned with the mystery
of the nameless forces of nature such as sex and growth
and death. In the Roman Empire, too, long before the end
we find nature-worship inevitably producing things that are
against nature.

'. . . The truth is that people who worship health cannot
remain healthy. When man goes straight he goes crooked
. . . and that in accordance with something much deeper
in human nature than nature-worshippers could ever understand. It was the discovery of that deeper thing, humanly
speaking, that constituted the conversion to Christianity.
There is a bias in man like a bias in the bowl, and Christianity was the discovery how to correct the bias and therefore hit the mark.'[3]

THE NEW FAITH

Long before the new teaching had spread westwards from
Palestine, philosophers, and especially the Stoics, had continuously denounced in the schools the superstition and
moral bankruptcy of the age, and had inculcated high principles as well as great truths. But the appeal of philosophy
is to the intellect, and because it failed to touch the level of
the ordinary man, it proved as ineffectual as the old gods in
curing the ills of society.[4] Christianity, on the other hand,
was not a philosophy, but a faith; not a way of thinking,
but a way of living. Its appeal was to something deeper than
reason.[5] It taught that not man, but God, is the centre of the
universe,[6] and that the more completely a man subordinates
his will to the divine will, or, in other words, 'when he is
most aware of himself as the open channel through which
God's power flows into the world,' the greater his power of
achievement.[7]

A spiritual worship and the abnegation of self-love im-
plied an idea of personality hitherto uncomprehended.[8] Its
perfect expression is love—love of God and of one's neighbour. This conception lifted the imagination of humble folk

far above the sordid details of their everyday lives; it solaced them with a sense of 'a pitying, loving, infinite Presence';[9] and it gave them courage and confidence in facing whatever dangers and difficulties life might offer them. All Christians were brothers, irrespective of rank or race; all obeyed the few simple rules concerning the Fatherhood of God and the Brotherhood of Man which Christ had taught to be the laws of the Kingdom of Heaven.

Yet on its intellectual side—that is, as a theological system—Christianity too often failed to commend itself to thinking men, who could feel little edified by the tortuous reasonings of some of the Christian Fathers in their efforts to make dogma pass for truth; by their readiness to suppress or distort the facts of history to suit their own ends; and by their unenlightened view of the pagan gods, whom they regarded not as creatures of fancy, but as demons. But despite their shortcomings, we owe an incalculable debt to the men who by their faith and works infused into a moribund society[10] new and glowing life.

As the early Christian missions took root, the ecclesiastical organisation developed naturally on lines parallel to the social and political organisation of their respective geographical areas. The most notable development took place in Rome after the Church had been taken under the wing of the Emperors,[11] when there began the process of 'imperialisation'—that is, the organisation of the Church of Rome as the ecclesiastical counterpart of the Imperial Roman Government, headed by the Pope, corresponding to the Emperor, and sustained by a hierarchy of cardinals, archbishops and bishops, corresponding to the legates and pro-consuls of the Empire.[12]

Meanwhile the Church in Gaul had retained the patriarchal and pastoral character of the Eastern Church,[13] which was admirably suited to the tribal organisation of the Celtic peoples; and even after the bishops of the 'imperialised' Church had been planted in Gaul, the native Church clung to its old ways. These ways were adopted in Britain, both north and south of the Solway.

How and when Christianity first reached Britain is not precisely known. The first authentic fact we have concerning the British Church is that three of its bishops were present at the Council of Arles in 314. The Church they represented, however, was confined to Southern Britain, and although the new teaching had already penetrated to Strathclyde, there was no organised Christian mission in what is now Scotland until the end of the century, when St Ninian established his *muinntir* or brotherhood among the Picts of Galloway.

THE PICTISH CHURCH

St Ninian was the third of three noted fourth-century Celtic evangelists, his predecessors being St Hilary[14] and that great soldier-saint, Martin,[15] whose memory is honoured in the festival of Martinmas. These two laboured in Gaul. St Martin, who did pioneer work for monasticism in that province, owed much to St Hilary, and Ninian, in turn, was one of 'Martin's men'. Ninian was himself a Briton, his traditional birthplace being the shores of the Solway Firth, where he was eventually to establish his mission. After visiting Rome,[16] he went on to Tours. It was at Tours, under St Martin, that he learned his missionary methods; it was on the religious settlement at Tours that he modelled his own foundation; and it was to St Martin of Tours that that foundation was dedicated. In short, whilst the Pictish Church established by St Ninian was connected by a common faith and doctrine with the rest of Western Christendom, its organisation, discipline and missionary methods were those of the Church of Celtic Gaul before it was absorbed by the Roman organisation.

The site on which St Ninian erected his monastery, Candida Casa (the White Hut)[17]—so called from its white-washed stone walls—was in the peninsular 'isle' of Whitehorn, close to the sea, with the wild mountains of Galloway in the distant background. From this base, which was situated outwith the frontiers of the Roman Empire, he proceeded to organise small ecclesiastical 'families' or brotherhoods called *muinntirs*, each under a chief or 'father', who was known first by the Greek name of *Papa*,[18] and later by the Syrian name of *Ab*. These *muinntirs* were the ecclesiastical counterpart of the family and tribal system of the people. The control of the family was patriarchal and the life of the community was supervised by the Tribal Council. On these councils, Ninian sought to substitute Christian councillors for the pagan 'Wise Ones'.

The Celtic Church was monastic in form, but its monasteries were not destined for recluses, although they had their anchorites. They were rather religious settlements where men were trained for the missionary work that the times demanded. There were three orders in the ordained ministry—deacons, presbyters and bishops. The Celtic bishops, however, do not correspond to those of the Roman Catholic, Greek Orthodox, or Protestant Episcopal communions. They had no diocese, but were appointed simply for the purpose of ordaining deacons and priests in their respective monasteries; and although the office was an honoured one, they were members of their *muinntirs* and subject to the jurisdiction of the Ab.[19] Occasionally, the Ab was himself a bishop, as was Ninian; but some of the greatest Abs—among them Columba—were simple presbyters.

Besides being a great ecclesiastical centre, Candida Casa became, like its prototype in Gaul, a far-famed educational centre and training-school for missionaries. Women as well as men were among its pupils, and 'ministering women' played their part in the evangelisation of Scotland. Agriculture, too, was taught and seeds distributed, for the Celtic monks, like their successors of the Roman Church, gave the people all the practical as well as all the spiritual guidance in their power.

The *cillean* or 'cells' built by the missionaries in the course of their peregrinations were quite small, holding a mere handful of worshippers.[20] Work and worship were conducted chiefly in the open air.

The precise limits of St Ninian's activities are still a subject of dispute, but it is certain that he and his followers covered the southern, central, and a considerable portion of the eastern half of Scotland. It seems likely that they made use of the line of Roman roads and camps, for the saint's name is commemorated at many points along that route.

After Ninian's death, the work was carried on by a stream of missionaries trained at Candida Casa or one of its daughter-houses, and notably by workers from St Mungo's settlement at Cathures (now Glasgow). But on the far side of the disputed Dorsal Range of Scotland (*Dorsi Montes Brittanici*) the Picts remained in contented paganism, and it was not from Candida Casa, but from Iona that they were to receive the gospel of Christ.[21]

THE COLUMBAN CHURCH

Amongst Ninian's younger contemporaries was a Briton named Patrick, whose birthplace is believed to have been Dumbarton on the Clyde,[22] though it is also claimed for Wales. The son of Christian parents, he was carried off, as a lad, into captivity in Ireland. A few years later he escaped to the Continent, and after a period of wandering returned to Britain. An ancient Irish poem records that he was baptised in manhood by St Caranoc, a pupil of Candida Casa, who later succeeded St Ninian there as Ab. In 431, the year before St Ninian's death, Patrick went back to Ireland to lay the foundation of the Irish Church.

A century later, a certain Colum, a man of kingly blood, left Ireland for Scotland, where he was to confirm his fellow-Scots of Dalriada (Argyll and the adjacent Isles) in the Christian faith, and complete and consolidate the work of St Ninian among the Picts.[23] In 563, St Columba, as he is best known, landed with twelve followers on the island of Iona, in the Inner Hebrides, where he founded a monastery, and whence, after a period of preparation, he set out to attack Druidism in its stronghold at the court of King Brude MacMaelchon, the Pictish Ard-righ in Inverness. Having secured the king's support, he summoned his missionaries from Iona and sent them up and down the country.[24] Cormac, the sailor-monk, went as far north as Orkney and Shetland; others went as far south as the Firth of Forth, the southern boundary of Pictland.[25] South of the Forth and Clyde another great saint was at work—Kentigern, better known as Mungo, the loved one, who had been trained by St Serf (Servanus) at Culross in Fife. (His biographer, the monk Jocelin, describes his meeting with St Columba and the exchange of their pastoral staves in token of their mutual love of Christ.) The places visited and churches founded by St Columba are too numerous to mention. Daughter monasteries arose, but Iona remained the citadel and retreat of all his followers.

The task of the Christian missionaries appears to have been relatively easy, for the mystical nature-worship of the Druids was much less incompatible with Christianity than were the polytheistic systems of non-Celtic Europe.[26] The contest between the Druids and the emissaries of Christianity was keen, but the 'roving clans and savage barbarians' (as Dr Johnson described them) of the North, unlike their 'civilised' contemporaries, showed no tendency to fanaticism and violence, and left no record of martyrdoms such as stain the later history of the Church.[27]

ROMANISATION

St Columba died in June, 597, a few months before St Augustine[28] landed in Kent. By that date the Christian faith was established virtually all over Scotland except among the recent Norse settlers in Orkney and Shetland and the Angles of Lothian and the Merse; the British Church flourished in Wales and in the Celtic west of England; but Anglo-Saxon England was still pagan. When St Augustine died in 604 or 605, his great enterprise was hardly more than initiated; but his successors, like Columba's, carried on, and from Lindisfarne (a daughter-house of Iona) in the north and Canterbury in the south there flowed two streams of missionary work that eventually covered the whole land.

When in due course the Celtic and Roman missionaries came into contact, a controversy arose regarding the diversity of certain practices in the two churches. In 664, a council met at Whitby to settle these differences, and the Northumbrian king, Oswi, was called upon to choose his allegiance: St John and Iona, or St Peter and Rome. Hitherto Oswi, who had been educated in Iona, had favoured the Celtic Church, but when the astute Wilfred, speaking for the Roman delegation, impressed upon him that it was St Peter who kept the keys of Heaven, the worthy king decided to run no risks. This incident ended the supremacy of the Columban Church in northern England and virtually established there the Roman see.

It should be borne in mind that the Celtic Churches were separated by no schism from the rest of Western Christendom, and had not the Anglo-Saxon invasion, following on the Roman evacuation of Britain, thrust a barrier of paganism between the Christians of the British Isles and those of the Continent, it can hardly be doubted that, like their mother-church in Gaul, they would have accepted Papal Supremacy. But the fact remains they had not done so.[29] They had retained the loose organisation of the early apostolic Church, and now were as little anxious to exchange it for the elaborate ecclesiastical system of Rome as a man used to going about in easy-fitting homespun tweeds would be to exchange them for a Savile-Row suit of broadcloth. But the *Zeitgeist* was against them. The best work of the Celtic Church had been done as a missionary Church; later, as civilisation advanced and the need of the times tended towards an organised religion, Iona was found lacking, and she eventually went down, almost without resistance, before the highly organised forces of Rome.

Meanwhile the conversion of the Lothians, which had been initiated by the monks of the Celtic Church working from Lindisfarne—Northumberland's Holy Isle—was completed by St Cuthbert (635–87). In his youth a shepherd on the Lammermoors, Cuthbert became Ab of the monastery of Melrose (a daughter-house of Lindisfarne). After the Synod of Whitby he went over to the Roman Church and subsequently worked hard to Romanise the Church throughout the south of Scotland. Across the bay from Candida Casa (which did not conform to Rome until the eighth century) he planted the rival church of Kirkcudbright (the kirk or church of Cuthbert). He has many dedications in the Lothians, the most notable being St Cuthbert's Church in Edinburgh, which is believed to stand on the site of an early shrine built by the saint in the shadow of the Castle Rock. His *Life* was written by the Venerable Bede.

The last part of Scotland to be Christianised, or re-Christianised, was Orkney and Shetland. Those twin archipelagoes, which lie on the northern confines of the ancient Pictish kingdom, had been colonised by the pagan Norsemen, whose keels had arrived in increasing numbers from the sixth century onwards. It may be that in some of the islands the oratory and altar of the Celtic Church were suffered to remain side by side with the pagan Hof, or temple, with its central hearth for the horse-roast that was a prominent feature of the rites of Thor and Odin; but of that we have no evidence.

According to the sagas, the conversion of the Norse settlers took place in 995, with the arrival in the earldom of Orkney of its over-lord, Olaf Tryggvason, the first Christian king of Norway, who introduced Christianity into his colonies at the point of the sword. Anchoring off Rognvald's Isle (South Ronaldsay), the King invited Earl Sigurd and his young son, Hindius, to visit him on board of one of his vessels. The unsuspecting chief readily complied.

'You are now fallen into my power,' said the King; and without beating about the bush, he commanded Sigurd to make his choice—profess Christianity on the spot, or die, together with his son and his people.

' "Truly, O King," replied the Earl, with much mildness, "I cannot be induced, either by choice or fear, to prostitute the religion of my fathers, or to deny the established worship of the gods; for I am not conscious of being more clearsighted than my ancestors, nor do I know in what respect that adoration which you demand excels my own." '

Olaf's reply to this obduracy was to seize the lad and raise his sword. Sigurd capitulated, and with the whole of his people, submitted to baptism.

'The king then left ministers of the divine word, with other holy men, to give the proselytes further instructions, and, taking with him Hindius as a hostage, he set sail, with pious delight, to communicate his success to his good people of Norway.'[30]

In the circumstances, it is not altogether surprising to learn that 'the light of Christianity was at first feebly opposed to the phantoms of Scandinavian mythology', and that the temples at Unst and elsewhere in the islands long retained their influence over the popular mind. Sir Walter Scott, who visited Orkney and Shetland in 1814, found that the name of Odin had not yet passed out of currency. And nowhere in the British Isles, as we shall see, has the pagan festival of Yule been preserved with the same degree of integrity as in Shetland, where up to our own time it has remained unidentified with Christmas.

The Romanisation of the Scottish Church was not accomplished in a day. As late as the eleventh century, Queen Margaret, wife of Malcolm Canmore, found in the land of her adoption more non-conformity than she relished,[31] including 'masses in I know not what barbarous rite',[32] and worked hard to establish complete conformity with Rome.[33] The introduction of a modified feudal system brought with it the establishment of a corresponding ecclesiastical system of dioceses (the equivalent of the feudal lordships) and parishes, with diocesan bishops and a territorial clergy. New monasteries arose; the cathedrals of St Andrews, Glasgow, Elgin and Kirkwall, among others, were erected, together with many splendid abbeys—notably Holyrood, Melrose, Dryburgh, Jedburgh and Pluscarden. In addition we owe three of the four Scottish Universities to the zeal and enterprise of the Roman Scotic Church, those of St Andrews (1411), Glasgow (1451) and Aberdeen (1495) being established by Papal Bull. (The University of Edinburgh (1582) is, of course, post-Reformation.)

In 1188, to put a stop to the repeated attempts of the English Church to control the Scottish one, the latter had been declared by Papal Bull to be 'the special daughter of Rome'; and a loyal, though not uncritical daughter she proved until her loyalty was forfeited by the abuses which, with other causes, led to the Reformation.[34]

REFORMATION

In Scotland, the Reformers set themselves with zeal, if not always with judgment, to the task of clearing away the accumulated trappings of dogma and ritual which had long obscured the simple basic teaching and usages of the early Christians,[35] and proceeded to organise themselves as an independent national Church.[36] In spite of the subsequent purification of the Church of Rome from within, the *Zeitgeist* was now with the Reformers. Ideas were changing, education was spreading; there was less

concern for authority and more for a living, personal faith.[37]
In Scottish worship, the pendulum swung violently from the
elaborate Roman ritual to a Puritan austerity, and in place
of the Mass, the preaching of the Word became paramount
in worship.[38]

But four centuries have elapsed, and we have again
reached the end of an era.

'The social impetus that sprang from the Renaissance
and moulded the Reformation has spent itself,' writes one
of the contemporary leaders in the Church of Scotland.
'The vast course of our material achievement has reached
and over-topped its zenith while the prophetic function of
the Church swings at its nadir.'

No medieval pattern, he maintains, can be reconstructed,
nor can we hark back to nineteenth-century evangelism.
(He speaks, of course, from the Protestant view-point.
The position of the Roman Catholic Church remains basically unchanged.) 'It behoves us, instead, to do for our day
what the Reformers, with much searching of heart and many
a false step, but with a fundamentally sure instinct did for
theirs: bit by bit, to create, regardless of their immediate
past, such channels and such disciplines that the eternal
gospel might flow again, in all its pristine richness, into
the souls of men. That is all that matters in any age.'[39]

'THE CHRISTIAN MYTH'

In these days of intellectual freedom there are an increasing number of people who reject *in toto* what they call 'the
Christian Myth'. Of those who adhere to Christianity, some
look on 'liberal thought', 'the higher criticism', or whatever
one likes to call it, as a sort of big bad wolf come to
blow the house down; others readily admit the debt of
Christianity to paganism, but do not discard its borrowings
on that account; and there are still others who believe that
Christianity would be definitely strengthened by being divested of all pagan accretions, and, above all, the element
of myth.[40] Yet many whose reason rejects the myth are in
their hearts reluctant to part with it. Is this reluctance due
to mere sentiment or to a sound instinct?

Myth has been described as 'the poetry of religion', as

something that touches the deepest desires and the highest aspirations of man.[41] Although it is not truth in the sense of fact, it is nevertheless a method—possibly the only satisfactory method—of expressing a truth that is inexpressible in terms of fact.[42] What is called 'the Christian Myth' is for multitudes of human beings the vessel containing the Water of Life which alone satisfies the spirit of man. The trouble is that men find it so much easier to revere the lovely chalice than to quaff the strong draught it contains—a draught so bitter at first taste, yet so sweet towards the dregs:

> Thou shalt love the Lord thy God with all thy heart,
> and with all thy soul, and with all thy strength, and
> with all thy mind, and thy neighbour as thyself.

Yet it becomes increasingly clear that man must drink this draught—or perish.

THE CHRISTIANISING OF THE FESTIVALS

Whilst 'the lamp whose flame lighted pagan Europe' burned steadfastly in Iona, the western world was turning slowly from paganism to Christianity. Freed from her old obsession, Europe was now ripe for intellectual and spiritual adventure. In her monasteries her more scholarly and liberal-minded men pored with wonder and delight over the manuscripts brought thither by the monks who had fled from Constantinople on its sack by the Turks. 'Fire kindleth fire', and these resurrected treasures of classical literature were to inspire that remarkable burgeoning in art and letters we know as the Renascence.

Many, however, viewed the revival of learning with misgiving. In *The Cloister and the Hearth*, Charles Reade depicts with humour the clash between these two perennially conflicting types, the puritan and the humanist. The puritan, Jerome, exhorts his fellow-Dominican, Colonna, to give up his vain pagan lore and study the lives of the saints.

'Blot out these heathen superstitions from thy mind, brother, as Christianity has blotted them from the earth.'

To which Colonna replies with heat:

'The heathen blotted out! Why, they hold four-fifths of the world. And what have we Christians invented without their aid? Painting? Sculpture? These are heathen arts, and we are but pygmies at them. What modern mind can conceive and grave so godlike forms as did the chief Athenian sculptors? . . . Is it architecture we have invented? Why, here, too, we are but children. Can we match for pure design the Parthenon . . . . and, for grandeur and finish, the theatres of Greece and Rome, or the prodigious temples of Egypt?'

Jerome observed that these were material things. True greatness was in the soul.

'Well, then,' said Colonna, 'in the world of mind, what have we discovered? Is it geometry? Is it logic? Nay, we are all pupils of Euclid and Aristotle . . . . Is it poetry? Homer hath never been approached by us, nor hath Vergil, nor Horace . . . . Would you compare our little miserable mysteries and moralities, all frigid personification and dog Latin, with the glories of a Greek play?'

'What then have we invented? Is it monotheism? Why, the learned and the philosophical among the Greeks and Romans held it; even their more enlightened poets were monotheists in their sleeve . . . . Their vulgar were polytheists; and what are ours? The Pagan vulgar worshipped all sorts of deified mortals, and each had his favourite, to whom he prayed ten times for once to the Omnipotent. Our vulgar worship canonised mortals, and each has his favourite, to whom he prays ten times for once to God. Call you that invention? . . . . The Pagan vulgar in these parts made their images, then knelt before them, adorned them with flowers, offered incense to them, lighted tapers before them, carried them in procession, and made pilgrimages to them just to the smallest tittle as we their imitators do . . . . Our infant baptism is Persian, with the font and the signing of the child's brow. Our throwing three handfuls of earth in the coffin, and saying dust to dust, is Egyptian. Our incense is Oriental, Roman, Pagan; and the early Fathers of the Church regarded it with superstitious horror, and died for refusing to handle it. Our holy water is Pagan. . . . . Their vulgar, like ours, thought drops of it falling on the body would wash out sin, and their men of sense, like ours, smiled or sighed at such credulity . . . . Thou seest the heathen were not *all* fools. No more are we. Not *all*.'

He passed to the Christian festivals.

'We celebrate the miraculous Conception of the Virgin on the 2nd of February. The old Romans celebrated the miraculous Conception of Juno on the 2nd of February. Our feast of All Saints is on the 2nd of November. The Festum Dei Mortis was on the 2nd of November. Our Candlemas is also an old Roman feast; neither the date nor the ceremony altered one tittle. The patrician ladies carried candles about the city as our *signoras* do now. At the gate of San Croce our courtesans keep a feast on the 20th August. Ask them why! The little noodles cannot tell you. On that very spot stood the Temple of Venus. Her building is gone, but her rite remains.'

And so he went on, until Jerome could endure it no longer.

'Know, profane monk,' he cried, 'that but for the powerful house that upholds thee, thy accursed heresy should go no further, for I would have thee burned at the stake.' And he strode out, white with indignation. Colonna ran and halloed joyfully after him.

'And that is Pagan. Burning men's bodies for the opinion of their souls is a purely Pagan custom . . . .'

Here Jerome slammed the door.

The primitive church had actually very few festivals, and in the first century celebrated only Sundays, Easter, and Pentecost. In the second century the fast of Lent was instituted. In 170, the Nativity of Christ is mentioned by Theophilus, Bishop of Antioch, in his Paschal Epistle, but though it apparently began to be recognised towards the end of that century, it was not universally celebrated until about the sixth century.

The worship of saints and the consequent institution of saints' days began about 317, and Eusebius quotes Plato in an exhortation to the Christians to do for their martyrs what the pagans did for their heroes and demi-gods—honour them, pray to them, and make vows to them.[43] The response was only too gratifying, for in the course of time, we hear, 'The vast multitudes and the continual accumulation of saints and festivals gave much offence to the pious and rational at an early age.'[44] The Council of Carthage condemned the multitude of martyrs. In the list of public grievances presented to Charles v by the Germans, in 1522, there is a complaint of the mischiefs done to industry and morality by the excessive number of festivals.[45] Erasmus censures this excess, and Cardinal Campegio, in 1524, proposes a considerable reduction.

The saints' days, however, were a minor matter. What gave the early Church grave concern was the fact that nothing would induce the people to give up their pagan festivals. This was hardly surprising, for their roots went back to the dawn of human existence. In the end the Church decided upon a compromise: the festivals should remain, but they should be pagan no longer: they should each and all be invested with a Christian significance. At Yule, which corresponds with the Roman Saturnalia, people should no longer worship the material sun, but the Sun of Righteousness, and the winter solstice should be celebrated as the birthday of Christ: and Midsummer Day, which in the north had been dedicated to Baldur, should be re-dedicated to St John the Baptist.

Similarly with the Celtic festivals: Bride, the Celtic goddess of Spring, gave place to St Bride of Kildare, and the first day of February (St Bride's Day) became Candlemas Eve, the eve of the Purification of the Virgin; Beltane was associated (with small success) with the Holy Cross; Lammas continued to celebrate the grain harvest, but the rites were Christianised, a loaf being presented at church; and Samhuinn, the ancient festival of the dead, became the Christian Hallowmas.

The conquest of paganism by the Christian religion was not accomplished in a day, nor yet in a millennium; for new and nobler conceptions of man's life and destiny come only as surface waves on the ocean of human consciousness, beneath which, in the race, as in the individual, there lies a vast, sub-conscious region to which such ideas penetrate slowly. How slowly, there is plenty of evidence, as we shall see, in our magic lore, in the fairy faith, in the witch cult, and in the surviving rites and ceremonies that pertain to our national festivals.

SIX

Magic

I keekit owre the warld's rim,
  The warld's rim, the warld's rim,
I keekit owre the warld's rim,
  And saw a ferlie there:
A gulf o' glamour gey grim,
  Gey grim, gey grim,
A gulf o' glamour gey grim,
  Fu' o' unco gear.
     Lewis Spence: *The Camstairie*[1]

'Magic,' says Pliny, 'flourished in the Gallic provinces down to a period within our own memory . . . . At the present day, Britain is still fascinated by magic, and performs its rites with so much ceremony that it almost seems as though it was she who had imparted the cult to the Persians.'[2]

What is magic? It is not very easy to define. 'A rudimentary religion,' says one writer; 'a bastard science,' says another; and although neither definition is complete, together they convey the undoubted truth that magic, in its origins, has affinities with both religion and science. Magic is not religion,[3] but magic and religion have developed by similar processes from primitive thought and ritual; magic is not science, but magic, alchemy and science form a direct sequence.

Virtue of some sort was attributed by our forefathers to every natural object and phenomenon, and above all, to the elements—air, earth, fire and water. In the course of time there was evolved from this belief a kind of magical science which was ultimately codified into rites and formulas.

There were two schools of magic—benevolent or 'white' magic, which is productive of love, health, fertility, success in one's undertakings, protection from misfortune, and good luck generally; and malevolent or 'black' magic, which is the reverse of white magic, and includes necromancy (the raising of spirits), and 'fascination' (worked by envious praise, or ill-wishing, or the evil eye). There is also prognostic magic, which includes divination, soothsaying and prophecy.

Although most anthropologists take a rationalistic view of magic, the medieval view is by no means abandoned.

'Magic,' writes Dr Evans Wentz, 'apart from mere jugglery and deception of the senses, is, according to the wisest ancients, nothing more than the controlling of daemons, shades, and all sorts of secondary spirits or elementals by men sufficiently trained for that purpose.'[4]

The psychologists, however, make short work of the magician's world. In Freud's words, 'Spirits and demons were nothing but the projection of primitive man's emotional impulses: he personified the things he endowed with effects, populated the world with them, and then re-discovered his inner psychic processes outside himself.'[5]

THE PRACTICE OF MAGIC

In concrete terms, the magician's task was to produce marvellous results with the aid of the hidden forces of nature. Magic was always a very practical affair: it had to bring rain to the crops, fish to the nets, a loved one to the lover's arms, a child to the barren womb; to protect from misfortune, avert the evil eye, or bestow victory in battle.

There are two elements in the magical act—the Spell and the Rite. The spell is the uttering of words according to a formula; the rite is the accompanying set of actions by which the spell is conveyed to the object it is desired to affect. The sprinkling of water on the ground, for instance, is the rite for rain, and the leaping of the dancers in a field is the rite for making the corn grow high. The spell, which is of major importance, was known only to the esoteric circle of practitioners; the rite was public.

The Druid is the *magus* or magician *par excellence*, and, magic being of the very fabric of Celtic religion, it is not surprising that we find in Scotland innumerable traces of

these world-wide beliefs and rites, notably in the cult of
wells, trees, and stones, and in our age-old festivals.

THE AIRTS

The Caledonians paid a superstitious reverence to the sun,
and practically every religious festival began with the ceremony of walking thrice *deiseil*, that is, in a sunwise direction, round the circle, cairn, altar or bonfire that marked
the site, the object of the rite being to aid the sun by virtue
of mimetic magic.

The seasons are associated with the cardinal points as follows: spring, east; summer, south; autumn, west; and
winter, north. The sun's daily journey is from east to south
and so round the circle. Thus the movement of the sun is the
same as that of the seasons, or, in other words, the sun leads
the seasons round in a ring. It is possible, however, that the
deiseil movement had originally a stellar significance, for the
constellation of Ursa Major or the Great Bear (known also
as the Plough and the Farmer's Clock) points with its 'tail'
or 'pole' eastward in spring, southward in summer, and so
round the circle.

Deiseil, the sunwise movement or the right-hand turn,
has always been regarded as the way of good, the lucky
way, and *tuaithiuil*, widdershins, or wrang-gaites,[1] which is
the contrary movement, as the way of evil, the unlucky way.
The Druids walked *deiseil*; the witches danced *tuaithiuil*.
In ancient times, as we learn from our Gaelic tales, warriors
approaching a fort indicated whether they were friend or
foe according as they advanced *deiseil* or *tuaithiuil*. Until
comparatively recent times, expectant mothers went thrice
round a church in order to ensure an easy delivery; fire was
carried thrice round an infant before baptism to save it from
the fate of a changeling; at a wedding, the company went
thrice round the house before entering; sick persons thrice
circulated a holy well before drinking the healing waters;
boats putting out to sea thrice rowed about sunwise in order
to ensure a safe passage or a good catch; even coffins were
carried thus to the grave.[2] The custom of going *deiseil* is far
from having died out in the Highlands and Islands.

An old rhyme pertaining to the airts runs thus:

Shut the north window,
And shut quickly the south one,
And shut the window to the west;
Evil never came from the east.[3]

THE QUARTER DAYS

The great seasonal festivals of the Celtic peoples were held at Samhuinn (Hallowmas), Oimelc or Imbolc (St Bride's Day), Bealltan (Beltane or May Day), and Lugnassad (Lammas), which fell respectively on the first day of November, February, May, and August, and marked the entry of the four seasons or quarters of the year. These festivals were primarily religious assemblies, but were also partly judicial in character, and with them were associated fairs, with games and races.

The Quarter Days being holy days, occult influences were believed to be more potent and magical rites more effective than at other times. Hence the ritual kindling of the need-fire, the supreme protective against disease, disaster, and the powers of evil; the saining of cattle and crops, boats and buildings; the visits of the sick, the maimed, and the barren to the holy wells; the divination rites; and the baking and dedication of the sacrificial cakes. They were also lucky days for setting out on a journey, for a new undertaking, and for drawing lovers together.

On the Quarter Days, those who were skilled in the use of charms and spells were careful to rise before the sun was up. Many used their powers solely for good, but there were always some who desired to benefit themselves at their neighbours' expense, and wise folk took no risks. Thus it was dangerous to give fire (in the form of a kindling) out of the house, even to a neighbour whose fire had gone out, for this gave her the means of taking the *toradh*, the substance or benefit, from the cows; or, if one did give it, one took the precaution of throwing a piece of burning peat into a tub of water as soon as the neighbour had left, to counteract any evil intention. To give rennet was equally injudicious. Indeed, loans of any sort were to be avoided, lest the luck of the house should go with the thing lent. This applied not only to the Quarter Day, but to the first Monday of the Quarter.

> The first Monday of the Quarter,
> Take care that luck leave not thy dwelling![1]

Another rite used by the unscrupulous to increase his own supply of milk at his neighbour's expense was to gather the dew off the pastures where his neighbour's cows fed and with this to rinse his own milk-vessels. To prevent one's cows from being thus 'forespoken', one drew water from the well before sunrise, poured it into a cogue or pail over a new silver coin, and gave the 'silvered' water to the animals to drink.[2]

In the Island of Lewis, a girl noted carefully the name of the first male she met on the Quarter Day, for his surname would be that of her future husband.[3]

The first Monday of the Quarter, being dedicated to the Moon, was believed to share the influences of the Quarter Day itself, and was reckoned a day of good omen. In order to propitiate any evil spirits that might be lurking about, it was once customary in the Highlands and Islands for the first person who rose in the morning to thrust a living creature outside and shut the door on it. The animal was usually a cock, a hen, a drake, a duck, or a cat. The awaiting spirits (if there were any about) were believed to seize the propitiatory offering, and neglect of the rite might lead to mishap or disaster.

THE FRITH

The first Monday of the Quarter was also considered the most auspicious day for making the *frith*, a form of magic horoscope which still lingers in the Outer Isles. The *frith*, which is akin to the *frett* of the Norseman, was a species of divination which enabled the *frithir*, or augurer, to see into the unseen, in order to ascertain the whereabouts and the condition of the absent or the lost, whether man or beast.

Immediately before sunrise, the augurer, fasting, his head and feet bared and his eyes closed, went to the door of the house and stood on the threshold with a hand on each jamb. He began with an incantation or 'a prayer to the God of the Unseen to show him his quest and grant him his augury', and then, opening his eyes, looked steadfastly in front of him. From the nature and position of the objects within sight, he divined the facts of which knowledge was sought. The possible signs were very numerous. For instance, a man standing meant health or recovery; a man lying down meant sickness; a woman standing, some untoward event; a woman passing or returning, a fairly good sign. A woman with red hair was unlucky; a woman with black, lucky; a woman with brown, still luckier. A bird on the wing was a good omen, particularly the lark or the dove; but the crow and the raven were exceptions. A cat was good for Mackintoshes, Macphersons, Cattenachs, and all other members of Clan Chattan; a pig or a boar, though a good omen for everybody, was particularly good for Campbells;[1] and generally, the totem animal was good for all members of the clan with which it was associated.

A variation of the ceremony is recorded in South Uist. 'The *frithir*,[2] or seer, says a "Hail Mary" . . . and then walks *deiseil* or sunwards round the house, his eyes being closed till he reaches the door-sill, when he opens them, and looking through a circle made of his finger and thumb, judges of the general character of the omen by the first object on which his eye has rested.'[3]

Many men in the Highlands and Islands were famous augurers, and tales of their powers are still told.

THE QUARTER CAKES

The baking of the Quarter Cakes, which served originally as a sort of communion bread between men and the earth powers, has survived as a household custom up to our own time. Each has its distinctive name. The *bonnach Bride*, or bannock of Bride, was baked for the spring festival; the *bonnach Bealltain*, or Beltane bannock, for the summer festival; the *bonnach Lunastain*, or Lammas bannock, for the autumn festival; and the *bonnach Samhthain*, or Hallowmas bannock, for the winter festival.

A large cake was made for the family and smaller cakes for the individual members. The people repaired to the fields, glens, and corries to eat their quarter cakes. When

eating them, they threw a piece over each shoulder, alter-
nately, saying 'Here to thee, wolf, spare my sheep; there
to thee, fox, spare my lambs; here to thee, eagle, spare
my goats; there to thee, raven, spare my kids; here to
thee, martin, spare my fowls; there to thee, harrier, spare
my chickens.'[1]

On the eve of the Quarter Days, the fairies were believed
to flit from one fairy hill to another, and were visible to those
who had the second sight. These, too, were the dates of the
witches' 'sabbaths'. The belief lingers in the countryside
that a witch may be detected by observing her chimney on
the first Monday of the quarter, when the smoke invariably
goes *against* the wind.

MOON MAGIC
Our forefathers had a firm belief in the sympathy between
man and the planets, and in the power of the moon to shape
events. The moon, Plutarch tells us, is fertile in its light and
is kindly to the young of animals and to the new shoots of
plants;[1] and even Bacon expresses the view that observations of the moon with a view to planting and sowing and
grafting of trees are 'not altogether frivolous'.[2]

In Scotland, as elsewhere, the phase of the moon was
always observed when certain kinds of work had to be
done. The crescent moon was believed to encourage growth
in substances, and was the time for sowing and planting—an
exception being made of such plants as onion and kail,
which tended to run to seed if sown in increase.

'The men of old would not kill a pig nor a sheep nor a
goat nor an axe-cow at the wane of the moon,' said an old
man in Eigg. 'The flesh of an animal is then without taste,
without sap, without plumpness, without fat. Neither would
they cut withes of hazel or willow for creels or baskets, nor
would they cut trees of pine to make a boat, in the black
wane of the moon. The sap of wood goes down into the
root, and the wood becomes brittle and crumbly, without
pith, without good. The old people did all these things at
the waxing or at the full of the moon. The men of old were
observant of the facts of nature, as the young folk of to-day
are not.'

In Moray, withes of woodbine were cut down in the increase of the March moon, twisted into wreaths, and preserved until the following March, when children sick of fever and consumptives were made to pass thrice through them as a means of cure.

The crescent moon was propitious for setting out on a journey and for any new undertaking. Until recent times, marriages in Orkney always took place under a waxing moon.

The waning of the moon was propitious for ploughing, reaping, and the cutting of peat, for only then would the natural juices depart and drying be expedited. Eggs laid in wane were used in hatching, rather than those laid in increase, and birds hatched in increase were believed to be difficult to rear. Animals were gelded in wane. In some parts of the country it was held that the cow sought the bull only in the first and third quarters of the moon and never at neap tide. Another belief was that if the cow was served by the bull in the first quarter, a bull calf resulted; if in wane, a cow calf.

At one time everybody, old and young, kept in his pocket a coin known in Gaelic as *peighinn pisich*, the lucky penny, which was turned thrice in the pocket at the first glimpse of the new moon. Many of us, of course, still turn a coin—preferably a silver one—on the same occasion, 'for luck'.

A superstitious regard for these observances still persists in the remoter parts of the country.

Moon worship, in pagan religions, was second only to sun worship. The Standing Stones of Stennis, in Orkney, include a Circle of the Sun and a smaller Semi-Circle, or Crescent, of the Moon. On tombstones at Luss, Stobo, Paisley, and many other places in Scotland we find a curious device—two crescents set back to back, representing the last quarter of the old moon and the first quarter of the new. This is an ancient Pictish symbol of immortality: the moon died and was re-born every month.

All animals with curved horns were sacred to the moon deity on account of the affinity of shape with the crescent moon, and bulls were sacrificed to obtain his help in cases of sickness, blight, and murrain, and in the initial stages of the after-life. Among the grave-furnishings at the prehistoric temple on the Clyde are fetish stone relics resembling horned bovine heads—to attract and propitiate the moon deity his symbols were deposited with the dead body—and 'there are satisfactory reasons for believing,' say the excavators, 'that young bulls with curved horns (symbolic of the new crescent moon) carried the bones in panniers to the final place of burial.'

The moon-title Ra, or one of its many variants, is found in several languages, and survives in Celtic speech as Ur, Er, and Ara. In Scotland, we have the form Mo-Urie or Mourie. Mourie appears to have become identified in the course of time with Maol Rubha (640–722), an Irish monk who, next to Columba, is the most famous saint of the Scoto-Irish Church. In 673 Maol Rubha founded the monastery of Apurchrosan (now Applecross) in a sheltered spot on the Ross-shire coast, looking over to Skye and Raasay.[3] Here he died, and his grave is still revered. The person who takes earth from it before travelling is, it is said, ensured a safe return. 'The common oath of the country,' says Pennant, 'is by his name;' and he is commemorated in many place-names throughout the Highlands.[4]

It is recorded that in 1678 Hector Mackenzie, in Mellon of Gairloch, together with his son and grandson, sacrificed a bull on St Mourie's Isle (Isle Maree), in Loch Maree,[5] 'for the recovery of Christine Mackenzie, who was formerly sick and valetudinarie'; and again we read in the records of the Presbytery of Dingwall that in 1695 the inhabitants of the surrounding districts were discovered to have been in the habit of sacrificing bulls on the feast-day of the saint (25 August), with 'other idolatrous customs', including the circumambulation of the chapels associated with the saint's memory and the practice of divination rites.

Here, obviously, reverence for the saint is merged in the earlier moon-worship, and Maol Rubha himself in the moon-god.

EARTH MAGIC

'Everywhere,' says Mrs Macleod Banks, 'the earth itself or the power connected with it has commanded the reverence of man . . . As parent of life and controller of fate, it was seen to hold beneath its surface the secret of growth and renewal and the mystery of decay; it was, as we know, the centre of the most ancient faiths.'[1]

In times past, people swore by the earth. When the hero in the Gaelic tale related on his return how he had been insulted and ill-treated by his enemies, his companions lifted a little piece of earth and shouted, 'Vengeance!'—that is, they swore by what was most sacred to them. In the Outer Hebrides there used to be in every township a *constabal baile*, constable of the hamlet, whose duties were to direct the work of gathering peats, to select new peat grounds, to see to the repair of mountain paths, to represent the crofter in dealing with the factor, and so forth. When he accepted office, he took off his shoes and stockings so that he should be in direct physical contact with the earth from which he had sprung and to which he should return; then, raising his bonnet and lifting up his eyes to heaven, he vowed fealty to his trust.[2]

The close kinship between man and the earth is apparent in many of our spring-time and harvest customs. On the Quarter Days, as we shall see, a libation of the produce of the soil was made to the earth powers. At both birth and death the bond is symbolised in our folk-customs. Pennant records that Highland midwives gave new-born babes a small spoonful of earth as their first food, and we know that it was customary to place earth and salt on the breast of the dead, the earth symbolising the corruptible body, and the salt, the immortal spirit.

Earth mounds that were once regarded as sacred spots are to be found all over the country. Regular assemblies were held round them, when religious rites were performed, new laws made, and law-breakers punished. The courts of the Brehons (judges) were usually held on the side of a hill, where they were seated on green banks of earth.

The Lord of the Isles made his grants of land to his vassals sitting on Dundonald, a moot hill—actually the 'judgment seat' at the roadside between the hotel and the churchyard at Kilmachumaig, near Crinan.[3]

In the parish of Kilmaranock, in Dunbartonshire, the Marmaers or Dukes of Lennox had formerly a judgment seat called Cathair. The name survives in Catter, and here (says the *Old Statistical Account*) there is a large artificial mound of earth, where in olden times courts were held. Nearby was the place of execution.

In Barra one may still see traces of the mound where MacNeill sat among his people dispensing justice. The traditional place of punishment is, as usual, close at hand.

Probably the most revered of these sacred mounds is the ancient Moot Hill at Scone. Scone was the capital of the kingdom long before the annexation of the Lothians, and Sir Thomas Innes of Learney, Lord Lyon King of Arms, declares that 'The Moot Hill of Scone is still the constitutional centre of Scotland'.[4] To this spot, according to well-established tradition, when a King was crowned at Scone each chief or noble brought soil from his own domain, and on this he stood while swearing allegiance to his sovereign, thus imparting peculiar sanctity to his vow.[5]

Some of the judgment seats were originally burial mounds, and were later identified with the 'fairy hills'.

After the introduction of Christianity, the sacred lands of the Druids with the lands adjoining them were taken over as Church lands. The Gaelic name for Church lands, sanctuary or sacred grove is *neimheadh* (pronounced approximately nevay) the name anciently given to a Druidical grove in which there was a stone shrine, a magic tree or well, or a fairy mound. The word survives in many of our place-names, usually in the form of *nemet* or *navity*. The Nemeta, says Professor Watson, were holy places, and were used as meeting-places for purposes of judgment. Later they remained the objects of superstitious reverence, and sometimes became the sites of Christian churches.

Duneaves, in the parish of Fortingall (Perthshire), derives from *Tigh-neimh* (for *neimhidh*), 'house of the nemed', and the great yew of Fortingall, says the same authority, may well have been a sacred tree connected with the nemeton.

Roseneath, on the Gareloch, is *Ros-neimhidh*, and among other place-names are Nevay (formerly Nevyth), a parish in Angus; Navidale, in Sutherland, where there was a traditional sanctuary; Creag Neimhidh (the rock of the Nemet) in Glenurquhart; Dalnavie (*Dail Neimhidh*) in Ross-shire; Navitie in Fife; and Navity in Cromarty.[6]

Some navities were islets, such as Neave, near the Kyle of Tongue; Isle Maree in Loch Maree; and, it is said, the islet lying off Harris which is commemorated in Barrie's play, *Mary Rose*.

Centuries after the introduction of Christianity, the navities were regarded as sacred to the fairies.

> He that tills the fairies' green
>   Nae luck again sall hae,
> And he that spiles the fairies' ring,
>   Betide him want and wae;
> For weirdless days and wearie nichts
>   Are his till his deein' day.
>
> He that gangs by the fairy ring
>   Nae dule nor pine sall see,
> And he that cleans the fairy ring
>   An easy death sall dee.[7]

THE GUDEMAN'S CROFT

Akin to the Navity was the Gudeman's Croft, known also as Halyman's Rig, Cloutie's Croft, or The Black Faulie. This was a small piece of land dedicated variously to the earth powers, the fairies, the witches, or the 'Gudeman' (the Devil of the witches), which neither spade nor plough was permitted to touch. There were two kinds of 'croft'. First we have the traditional open sites, visible from a distance, and long venerated as places of sepulture and worship. Then there were the small private 'crofts', one of which was found on practically every estate, usually on the Mains or home farm, and, in some districts, on every farm.

> The moss is saft on Cloutie's craft,
> And bonnie's the sod o' the gudeman's taft.[1]

There are numerous allusions to the Gudeman's Croft

in the Presbytery records. At Elgin, in 1602, some men were brought before the Kirk Session to give a reason 'quhy (why) they reserved a peise land to the devill callit the Gudeman's'. They explained that it was an offering to the devil, that he might abstain from blighting or otherwise harming their crops or animals. A Forgue farmer confessed that it was because his goods were falling away and he hoped to arrest the decline that he had dedicated a corner of his field.

The procedure was to enclose the selected spot, and, probably repeating some form of words, promise to let it lie untilled. In token of this promise, some stones were cast over the enclosing dyke.

The practice of laying off a gudeman's croft continued beyond the middle of the nineteenth century. Sir James Simpson, the discoverer of chloroform, tells (in 1861) how a relative of his had bought a farm near Edinburgh a few years previously, and how one of his first acts was to enclose a small triangular corner with a stone wall.

Sir Walter Scott compares the Gudeman's Croft to the Temenos of the Greek temple—a piece of land marked off from common uses and dedicated to the god.

FIRE MAGIC

The most sacred form of fire was the need-fire,[1] or virgin flame, which is produced by the violent friction of two pieces of wood. The ritual kindling of the need-fire was one of the main ceremonies at the great fire-festivals. It was the most potent of all charms to circumvent the powers of darkness, and was resorted to in any immanent or actual calamity, or to ensure success in any important undertaking.

There are various methods of creating the need-fire. The simplest is to use two sticks, one furnished with a point, and the other with a hole to fit it. The stick with the hole is laid flat on the ground and the point of the other is inserted. The operator holds the pointed stick in an upright position, and twirls it rapidly between his hands until the friction produces first a spark and then a flame.[2] This primitive method was employed in the islands of Skye, Mull and Tiree. In some parts of the mainland, a square frame of green wood was used, with an axle-tree or wimble in the centre, and as soon as any sparks were emitted, a species of agaric—a fungus that grows on old birch trees and is very combustible—was applied.

A more elaborate method is described by Frazer:

'Two poles were driven into the ground about a foot and a half from each other. Each pole had in the side facing the other a socket into which a smooth cross-piece or roller was fitted. The sockets were stuffed with linen, and the two ends of the roller were rammed tightly into the sockets. To make it more inflammable, the roller was often coated with tar. A rope was then wound round the roller, and the free ends at both sides were gripped by two or more persons, who by pulling the rope to and fro caused the roller to revolve rapidly till through friction the linen in the socket took fire. The sparks were immediately caught in tow or oakum and this was waved in a circle until it burst into a bright glow, when straw was applied to it, and the blazing straw used to kindle the fuel that had been stacked to make the bonfire. Often a wheel—sometimes a cart wheel or even a spinning-wheel—formed part of the mechanism: in Aberdeenshire it was called the 'muckle wheel'; in the island of Mull the wheel was turned from east to west over nine spindles of oakwood . . . . Sometimes it was necessary that the two persons who pulled the rope which twirled the roller should be brothers, or at least bear the same baptismal name; sometimes it was deemed sufficient if they were both chaste young men.'[3]

The wheel was, of course, a symbol of the revolving sun.

Still another method is described by Martin Martin, who collected the material for his *Description of the Western Isles* in 1695:

'The inhabitants did also make use of a fire called *tinegin*, i.e., a forced fire, or fire of necessity, which they used as an antidote against the plague or murrain in cattle; and it was performed thus: all the fires in the parish were extinguished and then eighty-one[4] married men, being thought the necessary number for effecting this design, took two great planks of wood, and nine of them were employed by turns, who by their repeated efforts rubbed one of the

planks against the other until the heat thereof produced
fire; and from this forced fire each family is supplied
with new fire, which is no sooner kindled than a pot full
of water is quickly set on it, and afterwards sprinkled upon
the people infected with the plague, or upon the cattle that
have the murrain. And this they all say they find successful
by experience. It was practised in the mainland, opposite to
the south of Skye, within these thirty years.'

There were various rules, as Frazer notes, about the
kind of men who should make the need-fire.

'In North Uist, the nine times nine who made the fire
were all first-begotten sons, but we are not told whether they were married or single . . . In Caithness, they
divested themselves of all kinds of metal. If after long
rubbing of the wood no fire was elicited, they concluded
that some fire must still be burning in the village; so a
strict search was made from house to house, any fire that
might be found was put out, and the negligent householder
punished or upbraided.' Again, 'if any of them (those preparing the need-fire) had been guilty of murder, adultery,
theft, or other atrocious crime, it was imagined either that
the fire would not kindle, or that it would be devoid of its
usual virtue.'

Long after the Reformation, belief in the magical properties of the need-fire persisted in the Highlands.

'On Mull, in 1767,' it is recorded, 'in consequence of a
disease among the cattle, the people carried out a sacrifice
of this type in an elaborate way, though they thought it
wrong to do so. They carried to the top of a hill a wheel
and nine spindles of wood. After extinguishing every fire
within sight of the hill, the wheel was turned from east to
west, long enough to produce fire by friction. If the fire
was not produced before the moon, the incantation had no
effect. A heifer was then sacrificed and the diseased part
burned. They then lighted their own hearths from the fire,
and feasted on what remained of the heifer. An incantation
was repeated by an old man from Morven during the whole
time the fire was being raised.'⁵

When collecting material in the Hebrides for his *Carmina
Gadelica* (published in 1900), Alexander Carmichael

talked to several men who had helped to make the need-fire. A relative of Professor Simpson, of chloroform fame, offered up a live cow to arrest an outbreak of murrain within twenty miles of Edinburgh;[6] Miss Gordon-Cumming recalls a similar incident on her father's estate at Dallas, in Moray, about 1850;[7] and 'I know one farmer's wife,' says Mr J. Spence, of Peterhead, writing at the end of the nineteenth century, 'who actually offered a calf as a burnt sacrifice to stay a plague that had broken out among her cattle.'[8]

The saining of crops, cattle, fishing-boats and unchristened infants by carrying torches around them in a sunwise direction persisted until quite recent times. 'Lowin' cinders'—aisels or embers—had occult properties which were lost in crossing water. 'Who steals one's fire steals one's blessing,' says the proverb; and it was always risky to give out kindling—which was often asked for in the days when flints were rare and matches unknown—though one could counter any ill intentions by dropping an ember into a stoup of water as soon as the applicant had left with the kindling.

A curious fire rite known as the *Beannachadh na Cuairte*, the Blessing of the Circle, has survived to within living memory. It was used for a sick or dwining child, to counteract the 'evil eye' that was responsible for its condition. An iron hoop was procured—often the hoop that encircled the wash-tub—and round it, but leaving a space at each side of a diameter for the hand to grasp, the wise woman of the district wound a *siaman*, or straw rope. Then, having saturated it with paraffin oil, she set it on fire. The hoop was held vertically by two other women, and the 'wise woman' passed the child through the blazing circle, using the appropriate incantation.

WATER MAGIC

The custom of visiting certain wells on the Quarter Days or on the days of the saints to whom they were dedicated may be traced to a pagan water-cult of pre-Druidic origin.

'Wells, springs, streams and pools have been accredited with healing powers wherever man has had ailments to cure,' writes Mrs Macleod Banks, 'and Scotland with its numerous mountains and glens was famed more than many other lands for healing waters. Long before the Christian era, springs endowed with magical virtue were regarded as bringers of health from the heart of the earth, or as forces able to work destruction in overflow and flood; both hope and dread urged the adoption of ceremonial visiting rites.'[1]

There are said to have been at one time over six hundred holy wells scattered over the country—north to south from Yelaburn in Unst (the most northerly of the Shetland Isles) to the Co Well at Kirkmaiden in Galloway, and west to east from the Well of Youth in St Kilda to the Coryvannock Well in Angus. The majority have fallen into oblivion; a few are visited to this day. One of the most ancient and famous is the Well of Youth in Iona.

The magic or holy wells of Scotland were originally the shrines of local deities. Wherever there was a spring, there was life; wherever there was life, there was a spirit; and each river and loch, each burn and tarn, each bubbling spring had its own deity. In some instances, this primitive guardian deity is found in animal form. Martin mentions a well at Kilbride, in Skye, with only one trout in it.[2] 'The natives are very tender of it,' he says, 'and though they may catch it in their wooden pails, they are very careful to prevent it from being destroyed.' In the well at Kilmore, in Lorne, there used to be two fishes that were revered by the folk as *Iasg Sianta*, holy fishes.[3]

The wells were in due course Christianised and 'denominat of sancts'. In the sixth century, St Columba sanctified a noxious well in the province of the Picts. He approached the well fearlessly, says his biographer, whereat the Druids, whom he had often vanquished and confounded, greatly rejoiced, for they believed that he would suffer seriously if he touched the baneful waters. 'But he, first raising his holy hand with invocation of the name of Christ, washes his hands and feet; then, with his companions, drinks of the same water he had blessed. And from that day the demons departed from that spring.'[4]

Martin, writing a thousand years later, describes the dedication of a holy well in the Island of Eigg:

'In the village on the south coast of this isle, there

is a well called St Katherine's Well; the natives have it in great esteem, and believe it to be a catholicon for diseases. They told me that it had been such ever since it was consecrated by one Father Hugh, a Popish priest, in the following manner: he obliged all the inhabitants to come to this well, and then employed them to bring together a great heap of stones at the head of the spring, by way of penance. This being done, he said mass at the well, and then consecrated it; he gave each of the inhabitants a piece of wax candle, which they lighted and all of them made the dessil (*deiseil*), of going round the well sunways, the priest leading them; and from that time it was accounted unlawful to boil any meat with the water of this well.

'The natives observe St Katherine's Anniversary; all of them come to the well, and having drunk a draught of it, they make the dessil round it sunways: this is always performed on the 15th day of April.'[5]

These holy and healing wells were thought to be particularly potent on the Quarter Days, but, owing to the cold weather, were seldom visited at Candlemas or Hallowmas. In many places there was an annual pilgrimage at Beltane, and a 'holy fair' was held in the vicinity.[6]

Whilst some of the wells were visited on the first day, many were visited on the first Sunday, and others, again, on the first Monday in May, these days of the week being dedicated to the Sun and the Moon. Pilgrimages were also made on the day of the saint to whom a well was dedicated. These local pilgrimages were, indeed, a favourite form of recreation in the Middle Ages. Great companies of people, 'bairleged and bairfutit', arrived in the vicinity of the well between midnight and dawn. Many were bent on revelry, and the scene was like a fair, with greetings, badinage, and gossiping groups.

'Perhaps there are here relics of the old nature festivals,' comments the Rev. J. M. McPherson, 'celebrated in the old licentious way, thus inciting the wrath of the Church.'

Certain rites had to be performed by those who had come to seek health or good fortune. The pilgrim first walked thrice sunwise round the well; before drinking, he 'silvered' the water, i.e., he threw in a silver coin (often,

in later times, a crooked sixpence); as he drank, he formulated his wish; and before his departure, he left either
a rag, a pin, or a fragment of his clothing at the tree or stone
that was at one time commonly associated with the well and
thought to share its influence. By this last act he cast off his
cares or ills, and anyone who stole or removed a rag fell heir
to all the troubles of its original possessor. Above all, the
ceremony had to be performed in strict silence and in the
absence of the sun—indeed the pilgrim was careful to be
out of sight of the well before sunrise.

The same ritual was observed when a pool was visited,
the pilgrim 'silvering' the water before entering the pool
and wishing his wish as he bathed.

Certain wells are still associated with an adjacent tree
or a standing stone. At Loch Shiant, in Skye, 'there is a
small coppice near to the Well, and there is none of the
natives dare venture to cut the least branch of it, for fear of
some signal judgment to follow.'[7] In Easter Ross, there is a
Well of the Yew, but the yew tree was cut down long ago.
The most famous of these trees is the aged oak—known as
the wishing-tree—that grows beside the healing well in Isle
Maree, one of the lovely wooded islets in Loch Maree.
Hither the insane were brought from far and wide. Before
landing, the boat made the sunwise circuit of the islet,
during which the patient, with a rope tied round him,
was thrice thrown into the sea and hauled out again. After
he had drunk the healing water of the well, an offering was
fixed on the tree, either a coin being driven in edgewise or
a rag nailed on.[8]

Another place to which the insane were brought for
healing is the Holy Pool of St Fillan, near Tyndrum,
Perthshire.[9] The pool lies in the stream known as Fillan
Water (which lower down broadens into the Tay), opposite the little church of St Fillan, where the stream sweeps
round a high, projecting rock. This rock divides the pool
almost in two. The upper part is called *Poll nam Ban* (Pool
of the Women), and the lower, *Poll nam Fear* (Pool of
the Men). The patient was led thrice sunwise round the
pool, first in the name of the Father, then in the name of
the Son, and lastly in the name of the Holy Spirit. He was

then immersed in the pool in the name of the Holy Trinity. This ordeal over, he was led to St Fillan's Church, stretched with his back to the ground, placed between two sticks, and bound in a simple, ingenious way. If he extricated himself before morning, he was expected to recover; if not, there was no hope.

The wells dedicated to St Mary had a special attraction for barren women who desired motherhood—notably those at Whitekirk, in East Lothian, and on the Isle of May. St Mary's Well in the Island of Mull has given its name to the town of Tobermory (*Tobar Mhoire*, the Well of Mary). Since St Mary's Day (15 August) falls close to Lammas Day, O.S., and shares the associations of the Quarter Day, Lammas pilgrimages were frequently made to the wells dedicated to the Virgin. St Mary's Well at Orton, near Fochabers—the most famous in the province of Moray—used to draw crowds from far and near.[10]

A glimpse of the age-old rites at these fertility wells is given us by John R. Allan, who when a boy on an Aberdeenshire farm in the 'twenties, got it from an old man whose 'head was full of rituals'. For a barren wife, old Ronald explained, there was nothing better than that she should go to a well that had 'a po'er o' nature for married women'.

' "There was siccan a well on Willie's Muir when I was a laddie," he said. "Aye, there was a hollow at the heid o' the muir and a spring o' clean cauld water that came out atween the stones in the middle o' a lythe place wi' auld whin bushes round it. The barren wives used to gang there in the midsummer's week, three or four o' them that were tired o' waiting, and some auld wife went with them. As to what happened there I can tell ye the order o't, for I once hided in the whins and saw it when I was a laddie. There were four o' them, the three barren women and the auld auld wife, and they came into the hollow wi' many's a look over their shoulders in case they'd been seen. The auld wife went doun on her knees on the flat stone at the side of the spring and directed the women. First they took off their boots, and syne they took off their hose; and syne they rolled up their skirts and their petticoats till their wames were bare. The

auld wife gave them the sign to step round her and away
they went, one after the other, wi' the sun, round the spring,
each one holding up her coats like she was holding herself to
the sun. As each one came anent her, the auld wife took up
the water in her hands and threw it on their wames. Never
a one cried out at the cold o' the water and never a word was
spoken. Three times round they went. The auld wife made
a sign to them. They dropped their coats to their feet again,
syne they opened their dress frae the neck and slipped it off
their shoulders so that their paps sprang out. The auld wife
gave them another sign. They doun on their knees afore her,
across the spring: and she took up the water in her hands
again, skirpit on their paps, three times the three. Then the
auld wife rose and the three barren women rose. They put
on their claes again and drew their shawls about their faces
and left the hollow without a word spoken and scattered
across the muir for hame."

'. . . . I asked, "Did it work?"'

'He said, "Capital; ye see the well had a power o'
nature." ' [11]

At least a dozen wells were dedicated to St Bride. They
lie scattered between Wigton and Aberdeen. St Bride's Well
at Pitlochry was famous for the cure of consumptives.

Near the old dovecot in the park of Glamis Castle is
the Nine Maidens' Well. The Nine Maidens lived in the
eighth century. They were the daughters of one Donald
or Donevaldus, whose home was in the glen of Ogilvie,
through which a burn runs down from the Sidlaws to the
village of Glamis. Their missionary labours, conducted from
Abernethy, earned them an honoured place among our early
saints. [12] Throughout Angus and Aberdeenshire we find
traces of chapels and wells dedicated to the Nine Maidens,
the most northerly being in Buchan, where, on the sands
near Pitsligo Castle, there once stood a Nine Maidens
Chapel, with a well in the vicinity.

In the sixteenth century, the most famous well in the
Lowlands was Our Lady of Loretto's, at Musselburgh.
It has disappeared along with the chapel, but the site is
marked by the boys' school that bears its name. Other
holy wells in the vicinity of Edinburgh are St Anthony's,

where Edinburgh lasses still convene on Beltane morning to drink and 'wish a wish', St Bernard's in Stockbridge, and St Catherine's (the Balm Well) near Liberton, which was believed to heal cutaneous complaints. The nuns of Sciennes used to make an annual pilgrimage to this well. In 1617 it was visited by James VI, who had it properly enclosed; in 1650 it was destroyed and filled up by Cromwell's soldiers; but it was subsequently re-opened and repaired, and is still in a state of preservation.

On Soutra Hill, in the Lammermoors, there once stood the hospital built by Malcolm IV about 1164 for the reception of wayfarers, and dedicated to the Trinity. Near the site is the spring known locally as Trinity well, which was formerly visited for its healing virtues.

It is said that a spring near Ayr cured Robert Bruce of his leprosy.

Among the many healing wells in the Border country is the Leper Well, which lies in a dark wood near Earlston. It is encircled with rank growth and with the mounds and hollows where once huddled the miserable shelters of these stricken folk. In striking contrast is the Fairies' Well, which lies in a spot of great natural beauty in the woods near the old mansionhouse of Ferniehurst, formerly a seat of the Kerrs (the family of the Marquis of Lothian), and now a Youth Hostel.

The power of foretelling life or death is said to have been conferred by the Brahan Seer upon the Dripping Well at Avoch, in Ross, which was frequented for deafness; 'Whoever he be that drink of the water henceforth shall, by placing two pieces of straw or wood on the surface, ascertain whether he recover or not. If he is to recover, the straws will whirl round in opposite directions, but if he is to die soon, they will lie motionless.'

St Andrew's Well, in Lewis, had the same property. A tubful of water was brought from the well to the patient's room (care being taken not to let it touch the ground on the way) and a wooden bowl was set afloat in it. If the bowl moved sunwise, the omen was favourable, and vice versa.

At Yelaburn (the Burn of Health), in Shetland, the islanders used to go to the head of the stream and throw in three stones to the Water Trow (troll), walk thrice round the pool sunwise, and in silence, then fill their cupped hands with water and throw it over their heads.

The well of Beothaig, in the Isle of Gigha, off Kintyre, was reputed to have command of the winds. It was protected with stones, and when a fair wind was required the stones were removed, the well cleaned out with a wooden bowl or a clamshell, and the water thrown three, or sometimes nine times in the direction from which the wind was desired to blow.

Water was sometimes drunk at the holy wells from the horn of a living cow—possibly, it has been suggested, because of some vague notion that life from the animal might be thus communicated.

A few wells have a more or less ornamental stone covering—St Margaret's Well in the Queen's Park, Edinburgh, for instance, St Michael's, Linlithgow, and St Ninian's, Stirling. The great majority, however, remain untouched in their natural setting—small inconspicuous springs bubbling out of the rock.

In pre-Reformation times, it was customary in some districts to dress the wells (as also the Mercat Crosses) with flowers on the day of the local saint. On St Margaret's Day (20 July) well at Dunfermline that bore her name was thus decorated, and 'a procession of monks and religious inhabitants visited (the) well, in joy, praise, and song'.[13] Other holy wells in the district were garlanded with flowers on their saint's days, and visited by hundreds of people 'with song-singing and superstitious awe' until about 1649, when the kirk sessions interfered and put an end to the 'holywell annuals'.

In post-Reformation times, civil as well as ecclesiastical authorities were resolutely opposed to these pagan practices.

'It was customary,' says Chambers, 'for great numbers of persons to go on a pilgrimage, bare-footed, to Christie's (Christ's) Well in Menteith and there perform certain superstitious ceremonies "to the great offence of God and scandal of the true religion". In May, 1624, the Privy Council issued a commission to a number of gentlemen in the district, enjoining them to post themselves at the well and apprehend all such superstitious persons and put them into the castle of Doune.'[14]

St Fittack's Well, near the old Church of St Fittock's, on the Bay of Nigg, was the favourite resort of the citizens of Aberdeen. In 1630, 'it was ordainit be the haill session in ane voce that quhatsomever inhabitant within this burgh beis find going to Sanct Fiacke's Well in ane superstitious manner, of seiking health to thame selffis or bairnes, sall be censured in penaltie and repentance in such degrie as fornicatours ar efter tryall and conviction.'[15]

In 1840, there were old folk in Stirling who in their younger days had regularly visited St Corbet's Well, at the summit of the Touch Hills, on Beltane morning. 'They describe the gatherings at the anniversaries as having been splendid. Husbands and wives, lovers with their sweethearts, young and old, grave and gay, crowded the hill-tops in the vicinity of the well long before dawn, and each party on their arrival took copious draughts of the singularly blessed water. It is reported that St Corbet, after a lapse of years, deprived the well of its life-preserving qualities in consequence of the introduction of 'mountain dew' of a less innocent nature into these annual festivals.[16]

A remarkable survival is the annual pilgrimage to the ancient well in the birchwood above Culloden House, near Inverness. It is known variously as *Tobar Ghorm* (the Blue Well), *Tobar na h'Oige* (the Well of Youth) and St Mary's Well; but nowadays it is popularly known as the Cloutie Well—a name derived from the 'clouts' or rags which are customarily nailed on to the surrounding bushes by the 'pilgrims'.

'The practice of visiting Culloden Well on the first Sunday in May,' says a press report of 1934, 'judging by the number of pilgrims who made the journey yesterday, is growing despite declamation and the protests of Highland ministers. It is an age-old custom in the Highlands, and has been described as pagan and superstitious. Buses heavily laden were run from Inverness almost every hour yesterday, and there were motoring parties from all parts of the North. Most of the visitors had a drink from the well and observed the old custom of dropping a coin into the well and silently expressing a wish for good luck in the future. Others placed a piece of cloth on the adjoining trees, also an ancient custom which has given to the spring the name of Cloutie Well.[17] County policemen regulate the traffic, and the money dropped into the well is distributed among Highland charities.'[18]

Nor is the Cloutie Well unique. Of St Bennet's Well, on the southern shore of the Moray Firth, just outside the Cromarty Firth, D. A. Mackenzie notes that its overhanging bush 'is still fluttering with rags in the year 1934'.

The tenacious hold of the holy wells on the imagination of the people is illustrated in the anecdote of one Jock Forsyth, who, after performing the solemn rites, 'rose and said, "O Lord, Thou knowest that well would it be for me this day an I had stooped my knees and my heart before Thee in spirit and in truth as often as I hae stoopit them afore this well. But we maun keep the custom o' our faithers." And he slipped aside and fixed an offering to the briar bush.'[19]

Magical power was attributed not only to wells, but also to certain river pools, such as St Fillan's, and notably to those at a ford or a bridge 'over which the dead and living pass'—i.e., over which bodies were carried for burial. Water from such a pool was used to counteract the influence of the 'evil eye'.[20] It had to be carried home in complete silence, and particular care was taken that the vessel should not touch the ground—i.e., there must be no contact between earth and water. A wooden ladle containing a piece of silver was dipped in and the victim was given three sips of the 'silvered' water. The remainder was then sprinkled over and around him.[21]

The water of streams 'flowing to meet the sun', or, in other words, south-running, had also power to bless and heal. A march stream, too, was 'lucky'.

A bargain made over running water was indissoluble. It is the old calling of water as a witness. Lovers who desired to plight their vows with peculiar solemnity repaired to a burn, stood on opposite banks, dipped their fingers into the water, clasped hands across the stream, and so exchanged their vows. It was thus that Burns plighted his troth with Highland Mary.

Another mode of betrothal was for the lovers to lick the thumbs of their right hands and press them together, vowing fidelity.

> There's my vow, I'll ne'er beguile thee,

runs the old song. To break such a vow was regarded as perjury.

To this day, farmers, before shaking hands over a bargain, spit in their loofs, and school-boys lick their thumbs when bargain-making.

Ordeal by water, or 'dooking' for apples, on Hallowe'en, is, as we shall see, the survival of a Druidic rite. Water was also used as a witness in the witch trials. Among the numerous pools where the water-ordeal was carried out are the Witches' Pool in St Andrews Bay and the lochan known as the Order Pot, near Elgin. If the witch sank, she was innocent; if she floated, she was guilty; thus the ordeal too often decided nothing more than whether the unfortunate creature was to die by fire or by water.

In Orkney, sea-water was used in a rite to bring butter. The skeely woman, or charmer, went to the shore with a pail and waited until nine waves had rolled in. At the reflux of the last, she took three gowpens of water (a gowpen is as much as can be held in cupped hands) and carried them home in her pail. The water was put into the churn with the milk, and ensured a good supply of butter.

To the Druids, the most sacred of all water-forms was dew, and particularly the dew of Beltane morning. The tradition of its potency has come down through the centuries, and all over Scotland young girls still rise before dawn on the first of May in order to lave their faces in the dew.

MAGICAL OBJECTS

Magical objects were very numerous. They were frequently worn either as talismans, to transmit their qualities, or as amulets, for protection.[1] Some were chosen for their shape; others for their colour. The wheel, for instance, symbolises the sun, and the small discs of metal or wood found in Britain and Gaul are Celtic amulets that bring the wearer under the protection of the sun-god; whilst the cowrie shell, which is the shape of 'the portal of life', is used among many races to promote fertility.

Red, being the colour of blood—the essence of life—is the supreme magical colour. In Scotland, necklaces of red coral or red rowan-berries, strung on red thread, were worn as amulets. As late as 1885, it was still a common practice in the North-East to tie two rowan twigs crosswise with red thread—a characteristic combination of pagan and Christian symbolism—and place them above the door of the byre to protect the cattle.

Amber or 'lammer' beads strung on red silk were frequently worn as an amulet by women of the upper classes.[2] Amber has a colour link with urine, which also had hidden virtues. Horses and cattle were sprinkled with it (the human variety) on the eve of every Quarter Day, and the same rite was carried out by the midwife on the lying-in woman to ensure a safe delivery.

Blue thread was also used as a charm, and was worn as a preventive by women liable to ephemeral fevers while suckling infants. These threads were handed down from mother to daughter and were esteemed on account of their age. Witches had their 'blue clews' to aid their necromancy, and 'Winning the Blue Clew' is a well-known Hallowe'en rite.

In Shetland, a sprain was cured by means of the healing or wresting thread—a thread spun from black wool, on which were cast nine knots. This was tied round the affected limb, the 'wise woman' intoning:

> The Lord rade,
> And the foal slade;
> He lighted,
> And he righted,
> Let joint to joint,
> Bone to bone,
> And sinew to sinew—
> Heal in the Holy Ghost's name!

This is one of the numerous magical or medico-magical spells and incantations that survive in a form half pagan, half Christian.

Salt, without which we cannot live, symbolises life and good fortune. At a 'flitting', the first thing moved to the new house was commonly the salt-box, and salt was scattered 'for luck'. Again, in St Kilda, when the cattle were moved from one pasture to another, they were sained with salt, fire and water.[3]

A charm still used in the Hebrides is the *Airne Mhoire* (literally, the Kidney of Mary), or the Virgin's Nut, on which the mark of a cross is faintly discernible. These seeds are carried across the Atlantic by the Gulf stream and are occasionally cast up on the shore. Being rare, they are highly prized. In the Roman Catholic islands they are often blest by the priest. The charm is used by women in childbed, the midwife placing it in the hand of the expectant mother, who clasps it tight in the belief that it will ease her pain and ensure a safe delivery.[4]

In the Highlands, people still talk of the *sian* or charm—an amulet of tough vellum or leather which was used with a forgotten incantation called the *Fath-fidh* to make persons or things invisible, or to hide them in a magic mist.[5]

Silver, too, has magical properties. It is usually dipped in water (see *Water Magic*), but occasionally a silver coin serves as a charm.[6]

MAGICAL ANIMALS

Among the magical animals of Scotland are the Serpent, the Salmon and the Bull.

The Serpent, which symbolises wisdom, is probably a form of earth spirit. There are no snakes in Ireland, and there the place of the Serpent is taken by the Salmon. (This is in accordance with the recognised folk-practice of substituting some object that is locally feasible for one that is not.) In Scotland, where both snakes (adders) and salmon are plentiful, we find both symbols.

A curious serpent rite associated with the Day of Bride long survived in the Isles and is described elsewhere.[1]

When the first salmon grilse of the season is caught, the salmon fishers on certain rivers celebrate the event and make merry, as their forebears have done down the centuries. For over the springs in which the great rivers had their sources there grew, say the bards, wild hazel trees laden with red nuts which contained the knowledge of poetry and art; and when the nuts fell from the boughs and floated on the water, the salmon of the river rose to the surface and swallowed them—whence the red spots on the salmon's belly. He who first tasted the juice of the salmon as it was being cooked became wise among his fellows and had the power to foretell coming events. Hence the expressions, 'nuts of knowledge' and 'the salmon of wisdom'.

Drawings of salmon and serpents appear on many of our sculptured stones, and the bull is no less prominent. At Burghead, in Moray, six stones have been found in different spots, each with an incised outline of a bull, highly conventionalised, and ornamented with spiral curves. The design varies slightly, but all the drawings are strong and spirited. Similar stones have been discovered near Inverness, and in 1920 another was unearthed in the parish of Falkland, in Fife.

These bull-slabs indicate the survival in Scotland of an animal-worship that was once world-wide. At Memphis, a bull was worshipped by the ancient Egyptians as the soul of Osiris, and in Gaul and Germany riotous processions took place in which men were dressed in the heads and hides of animals whose flesh they had eaten sacramentally in order to achieve closer contact with their divinity. Bull sacrifices were common among the Celts, and long after the introduction of Christianity a bull was occasionally sacrificed to a saint—to St Maol Ruadh in Ross-shire, for example, and to St Cuthbert at Kirkcudbright. The masquerading in animal disguise, of which traces are still found, is obviously connected with the sacramental slaughter of a bull or mart at Martinmas. Canon Macculloch alludes to the folk-belief that St Martin was cut up and eaten in the form of an ox, the god incarnate being associated with the saint. And there are other survivals: the 'King Deil' who presided at the Witches' Sabbaths frequently assumed as his ritual attire the head and hide of a bull, and so did the leader of the Hogmanay guisers in the Highlands and Hebrides,[2] up to our own times.

MAGICAL PLANTS
'The oak, the largest and strongest tree in the North, was

venerated by the Celts as the symbol of the supreme Power, whose primary emanation, or operative spirit, seems to have been symbolised by the mistletoe which grew from its bark, and, as it were, emanated from its substance.'[1]

Although the oak was revered in Scotland and Ireland as well as in Gaul and Southern Britain, the rowan tree and the hazel appear more frequently in the Druidic rites. Possibly the oak did not grow so extensively in these countries, and mistletoe was scarce.

The reverence in which the mistletoe was at one time held is indicated by a family tradition of the Hays of Errol, who had adopted it as their badge. In the words of a member of the family:

'There was formerly in the neighbourhood of Errol, and not far from the Falcon stone, a vast oak of an unknown age, and upon which grew a profusion of the plant: many charms and legends were considered to be connected with the tree, and the duration of the family of Hay was said to be united with its existence. It was believed that a sprig of the mistletoe cut on Allhallowmas Eve with a new dirk, and after surrounding the tree three times sunwise and pronouncing a certain spell, was a sure charm against all glamour or witchery, and an infallible guard in the day of battle. A spray gathered in the same manner was placed in the cradle of infants, and thought to defend them from being changed for elf-bairns by the fairies . . . . When the old tree was destroyed I never could learn. The estate has been some time sold out of the family of Hay, and of course it is said that the fatal oak was cut down a short time before.'

The old superstition is recorded in verses traditionally ascribed to Thomas the Rhymer:

> While the mistletoe bats on Errol's aik,
>   And that aik stands fast,
> The Hays sall flourish, and their good grey hawk
>   Sall nocht flinch before the blast.
>
> But when the root of the aik decays,
>   And the mistletoe dwines on its withered breast,
> The grass sall grow on Errol's hearthstane,
>   And the corbie roup in the falcon's nest.[2]

The rowan, rodden, or mountain ash—'the mystic tree
whose scarlet berries were the ambrosial food of the Tuatha
dé Danann'—may still be seen growing hard by many of
our cairns, stone circles and other sites of pagan worship.
As a potent charm against witchcraft and evil spells, it
was used in many forms about the homestead—in fact,
an old Scots word for the cross-beam in the chimney is
rantree, a form of rowan tree, of which, as a 'lucky' wood,
it was commonly made. Rowan wood was also used for
the distaff, the churn-staff, the peg of the cow-shackle,
the pin of the plough or water-mill, and other domestic
and agricultural implements, and a rowan-tree was commonly planted at the door of the homestead to 'keep the
witches away.'

> When the days were still as deith,
> An' I couldna see the kye,
> Though I'd mebbe hear their breith
> I' the mist oot-bye;
> When I'd mind the lang grey een
> O' the warlock by the hill,
> And sit flegged, like a wean,
> Gin a whaup cried shrill;
> Though the hert wad dee in me
> At a fitstep on the floor,
> There was aye the rowan tree
> Wi' its airm across the door.[3]

'So late as 1860,' writes Dr James Napier, 'I have seen
the rowan tree trained in the form of an arch over the byre
door and in another case over the gate of the farm-yard to
protect the cows.'[4]

On the Quarter Days, a wand of rowan was placed
above the lintels of the house and out-houses, and a twig
was carried in the pocket for personal protection. It was particularly effective in conjunction with red thread, whether of
wool or of silk.[5]

> Rowan tree and red threid
> Gar the witches tyne their speed.

says the old rhyme; the Gaelic bard, Alein Dall (Blind
Allan) writes:

A tuft of rowan twig
   From the face of Ailsa Craig—
Put a red thread and a knot on it,
   And place it on the end of the sprinkler,
And though the witch of Endor came,
   Alan could manage her.[6]

Highland women twisted red silk round their finger and wore a necklace of rowan-berries as a charm. This was as efficacious as the necklace of amber beads worn by ladies of high degree and by the fisherwomen of the East Coast.

A special use of the rowan was to prevent mishap to bearing animals.

A black mare a-kicking
   Among the rocks,
A black mare a-kicking,
   And she a-running.
A handful of red rowan berries
   To safeguard her,
And she a-running.[7]

Festival cakes were baked over a fire of rowan faggots or other sacred wood. A coffin or bier was regarded with special reverence if made of rowan wood.

The elder, or bourtree, as it is more commonly known in Scotland, ranked second only to the rowan as a protective against witchcraft and evil spells. In Kirkcudbrightshire, a cross framed of the elder-tree was affixed to stables and byres. Dr Napier, writing in 1879, tells us that in his own recollection the driver of a hearse had his whip-handle made of bourtree to avert evil. But the bourtree was more than a mere protector. The green juice of the inner bark applied to the eyelids of a baptised person gave him the power of 'seeing things' (presumably on the Quarter Days), and if he stood under a bourtree near a fairy hill on Hallowe'en, he could see the fairy train go by.

'A few years ago,' wrote a mountaineer in 1938, 'when I was about to go hill-climbing in the Highlands, I watched two of the party, both Highland born, pluck a sprig of bourtree to put in their button-holes ere we set out. When

I asked why, I was told vaguely, "Flies and things don't like it." [8]

In Gaul, the Druids ate acorns in order to acquire prophetic powers. In Scotland, the hazel-nut was used for the same purpose. Young people still resort to hazel-groves in order to get a supply of nuts for use in the divination rites on Hallowe'en. The hazel was associated with the milk-yielding goddess because of the milk contained in the green nut. Children who were born in autumn were considered particularly fortunate because they could have the 'milk of the nut' as their first food, and weakly children received an elixir of this milk mixed with wild honey.

The hazel was also associated with the deity of fire, and therefore of thunder and lightning, because its wood was used to make fire by friction. Hazel rods were formerly used to detect veins of gold, lead, coal and other minerals.[9] Water diviners, of course, commonly use hazel twigs.

Apples, which figure in the Hallowe'en rites, were the fruit of life and grew abundantly in Avalon (apple-land), the Celtic paradise.

An apple branch, or sometimes a single apple, was, as we shall see, the passport to the Celtic Otherworld, or Fairyland.

> I bring you a branch of Emain's apple-tree,
> With silver twigs and crystal buds and blossoms.

Traces of the cult of the apple-tree survive in our folk-tales. When Cuchulain visited Scotland to attend the military college in Skye, he found his way across the mysterious 'Plain of Ill-luck' by rolling a wheel and throwing before him an apple, whose direction he followed; and it is told of St Servanus, an early Scottish saint, that when he flung his pastoral staff across the Firth of Forth, it stuck in the earth, rooted, sent forth branches, and blossomed into an apple-tree.

Of vaguer tradition is the druidical cult of the yew, which is believed to have existed in Iona. Professor Watson, indeed, derives the name of the island from an ancient word signifying 'yew place', and refers to the Irish tradition that

St Columba found Druids on the island and expelled them. It is significant, too, that the name Tom-na-hurich (Gael, *Tom-na-h-Iubhraich*) in Inverness, a reputed fairy haunt, signifies the 'knoll of the yew wood'. At Fortingall, in Perthshire, there is a hoary yew tree that is believed to have been in existence in pre-Christian times.[10]

Juniper, or the mountain yew, was burned by the Highlanders both in the house and in the byre as a purification rite on New Year's morning. Like all magical plants, it had to be pulled in a particular manner. The Druids, as we have seen, had considerable medical skill. They knew all that was known of botany and chemistry, and to them fell the selection of the herbs for the mystic cauldron. These were gathered at certain phases of the moon. Magical rites were employed in the culling; sexual abstinence, silence, a certain method of uprooting, and occasionally sacrifice were necessary. Long after the disappearance of the Druids, herbs found by sacred streams were used to cure wounds and bruises and other ills, and traces of the rites and runes linger in folk tradition. Juniper, for instance, to be effective, had to be pulled by the roots, with its branches made into four bundles and taken between the five fingers, whilst the incantation was repeated:

> I will pull the bounteous yew,
>   Through the five bent ribs of Christ,
> In the name of the Father, the Son, and Holy Ghost
>   Against drowning, danger, and confusion.[11]

The yarrow, the plant of power, was also pulled with mystic words, of which only four lines have been recovered:

> I will pull the yarrow
>   As Mary pulled it with her two hands;
> I will pull it with my strength,
>   I will pull it with the hollow of my hand.[12]

The trailing pearlwort (*sagina procumbens*), in Gaelic *mothan* (pronounced *mo-an*), was one of the most efficacious plants against evil spells and the wiles of the fairy woman. It was gathered with these words:

> I will pull the pearlwort,
>   The plant that Christ ordained;
> No fear has it of fire-burning,
>   Or wars of fairy women.[13]

The plant was carried on the person. When placed on the lintel of the door, it prevented the *sluagh*, or aerial host, from entering and beguiling or spiriting away any member of the household. When placed below the right knee of a woman in labour, it comforted and relieved her, and also defeated the machinations of the fairy woman who would substitute a changeling for the new-born babe. The milk of a cow that had eaten it was equally effective. If it was placed in the bull's hoof when with the cow, the milk was sained and its *toradh* or substance could not be taken away by the witches; and the calf was also sained from mishap. A cow that had eaten the pearlwort was similarly sained and its calf made secure. Sometimes, instead of 'silvering' the water from a magic well, the plant was used, its juice being pressed out.

The pearlwort was also used as a love charm. The woman who administered it went on her left knee and plucked nine roots of the tiny plant. These she knotted together so as to form a ring, and placed it in the mouth of the girl who sought her aid, 'in the name of the King of the sun, the moon, and the stars, and in the name of the Holy Three.' When the girl met the man whose love she desired, if she could induce him to kiss her while the ring was in her mouth, he became her bondman. Lovesick maidens also wet their mouths with the juice of the pearlwort to entice the loved one.

The virtues of the pearlwort are in fact (or fancy) manifold.

> I will cull the pearlwort
> Beneath the fair sun of Sunday,
> Beneath the hand of the Virgin,
> In the name of the Trinity
> Who willed it to grow.
>
> While I shall keep the pearlwort,
> Without ill mine eye,

Without harm my mouth,
Without grief my heart,
Without guile my death.[14]

Ivy was used as a protective for milk, milk products, and flocks. On the Quarter Days young girls used to pin three leaves of ivy into their night-shifts in order to dream of their future husbands. There was an old man in Uist, says Dr Carmichael, who used to swim to an islet in a loch in his neighbourhood for ivy, woodbine, and rowan. These, sometimes separately and sometimes combined, he twined into a three-ply wreath, which he placed over the lintel of his cow-house and under the vessels in his milk-house, to safeguard his cows and his milk from witchcraft, the evil eye, and murrain.

Sometimes, instead of woodbine, the bramble was the third of the trinity. This plant was much valued by the old Highlanders, who cultivated it where it was not indigenous. The berries were used as food, an infusion of the leaves as medicine, and the root as a dye.

Another magic hoop was made of milkwort, butterwort, dandelion, and marigold. It was from three to four inches in diameter, and was bound by a triple cord of lint—for lint also had magical properties—in the name of the Father, the Son, and the Spirit, and placed under the milk-vessel, to prevent the substance of the milk from being spirited away.[15]

An old rhyme runs:

> Trefoil, vervain, John's wort, dill,
> Hinders witches in their will.

St John's wort (*Hypericum pulchrum*), which according to tradition, was St Columba's favourite flower, was believed to have the power, if found unsought, to ward off fever and to prevent the finder from being 'taken' in sleep by the fairies. Its Gaelic name is *Achlasan Challum*, St Columba's axillary one, and the rune intoned in pulling it runs:

> The axillary plant Colum-Cill,
>   Unsought for, unwanted,

They will not take you from your sleep,
  Nor will you take fever.
I will pull the brown-leaved one,
  A plant found beside a cleft,
No man will have it from me
  Without more than my blessing.[16]

St John's wort was commonly used in the North of Scotland in the divination rites of Midsummer Eve.

The four-leaved clover was always in great repute as a charm against evil spells, and country lasses still consider it lucky to come across it unawares.

Another magical plant is 'The Enticing Plant', in Gaelic *Lus an Tàlaidh*, the purple orchis[17] that grows in the soft patches among heather. 'Adam and Eve' is the popular name. 'It has two roots, one larger than the other, and it is in these that its magic power consists. The larger represents the man, the lesser a woman, whose affections are to be gained. The plant is to be pulled by the roots before sunrise, with the face directed to the South. Whichever root is used is to be immediately placed in spring water, care being taken that no part of the sun's surface is above the horizon. If it sinks, the person whose love is sought will prove the future husband or wife. If the charm is made for no one in particular, the root reduced to powder and put below the pillow causes dreams of the person to be married.'[18]

'In some parts of the north,' says another writer, referring particularly to Aberdeenshire, 'the rustics believe that if you take the proper half of the root of the orchis and get anyone of the opposite sex to eat it, it will produce a strong affection for you, while the other half will produce as strong an aversion. This is probably the plant mentioned in a Highland incantation as "*Gràdh is Fuadh*" (love and hate).'[19]

It appears that when the roots of the orchis are dug up, the old root is frequently found to be exhausted, and the new root heavy. The new root is dried, ground, and secretly administered as a love potion; but love thus gained is, it is said, dissipated by marriage.

In the Highlands, the water-lily was supposed to facilitate the fairy spell and would cause one to be fairy 'struck'.

The magical plants in the Skye tradition are the mistletoe, club moss, watercress, ivy, bramble, figwort, St John's wort, and the bog violet.[20] In Buchan they include orpin (stone crop), vervain, and fern seed.[21] In the south of Scotland, the plants the witches avoided were the ivy, the bindwood, and the fern, and amongst those they favoured were the hemlock, the nightshade, and the fox-glove, whose bells are known as 'witches' thimbles'. The trees they hated were the rowan, the yew, the elder, the witch-elm, and the holly, and those they used to ride on were the broom, the thorn, and the ragweed.[22]

There is a tradition in the Highlands of nine sacred woods that were used to kindle the Druidical fires at Beltane and Hallowe'en.

An old rhyme runs:

> Choose the willow of the streams
>   Choose the hazel of the rocks,
> Choose the alder of the marshes,
>   Choose the birch of the waterfalls.
> Choose the ash of the shade,
>   Choose the yew of resilience,
> Choose the elm of the brae,
>   Choose the oak of the sun.[23]

These are possibly some of the trees used by the Druids, but other 'magical' trees include, as we know, the holly, the elder and the apple. The ash mentioned is presumably the mountain ash or rowan.

MAGICAL STONES

Our forefathers venerated not only certain animals and plants, but also certain stones, either because of the spirit believed to be resident in them, or because of some magical power inherent in them.

THE STANDING STONES

The megalithic stone structures found in the British Isles and on the Continent were erected by the pre-Celtic inhabitants of Western Europe. There are roughly three types of structure. First, we have the single upright stones known as menhirs (Celtic 'high stones') which may commemorate

some great event or personage.¹ Then there are the dolmens
(Celtic 'table stones'), which are formed of three or four
upright stones roofed with a flat stone slab, and are believed
to have represented a house or dwelling-place for the dead.
(The chamber mounds or *tumuli* are a later development of
the dolmen.) Lastly, there are the cromlechs (Celtic 'stone
circles'), which are circles of upright stones enclosing barrows or dolmens. Examples of this class—some of them
highly specialised—are Carnac in Brittany, Stonehenge and
Avebury in England, and New Grange in Ireland; whilst
in Scotland we have Callanish in the Island of Lewis, the
Standing Stones of Stennis in Orkney, the Clava Circles near
Inverness, and many more of lesser importance.

The formal religion of primitive peoples is based mainly
on the rites and practices associated with the burial of the
dead; for the spirit world as they conceived it included
both the 'nature spirit', which was inherent in sun, moon,
stars, earth, rivers, trees, and so forth, and the 'ancestral
spirit'. Being constituted after the manner of human beings, the spirits of the dead were believed to understand
and respond to human petitions; and whilst the temporal
affairs of the tribe were administered by the king or chief,
it was the business of the megalithic priesthood, or body of
'wise men'—the precursors of the Druids—to act as inter-
mediaries between the seen and the unseen worlds.

The stone circles probably surrounded places of sepulture, and they were believed to be haunted by gods,
daemons, and ancestral spirits. These ancient pagan cem-
eteries became the chief rallying-point of the tribal life, and
out of the funeral games associated with them arose the great
conventions and fairs of later times.

Callanish, which may or may not be the 'winged hyperborean temple' to which there is more than one reference
in the classics, lies on the wild Atlantic coast of Lewis. Its
shape is unique, being that of the Celtic cross—that is, the
shafts of the cross are intersected by a circle. In the centre
of the circle is a chambered cairn.

'That the position was chosen and laid down by astronomical observation,' writes Henry Callendar, 'can easily
be demonstrated by visiting the spot on a clear night,

when it will be found that by bringing the upper part of a single line of stones to bear on the top of the large stone in the centre of the circle, the apex of that stone coincides exactly with the pole-star.'[2] The Druids are believed to have offered up their sacrifices on the altar-stone at the moment the sun was visible above a certain stone. When Martin visited Callanish in or about 1695, 'I inquired of the inhabitants,' he tells us, 'what tradition they had from their ancestors concerning these stones, and they told me it was a place appointed for worship in the time of heathenism, and that the chief Druid or priest stood near the big stone in the centre, from which he addressed himself to the people who surrounded him.'[3]

The Stones of Stennis have a perfect setting of wild moorland and loch. There are two main groups—the Ring of Brogar, or Temple of the Sun, and the smaller Ring of Stennis (which is strictly a semi-circle or crescent), or Temple of the Moon. There are also traces of a third circle from which the stones have disappeared, and there are two solitary upright stones. The adjacent land is covered with burial mounds, and in the vicinity are the ruins of a broch (the Big Howe) and a holy well (Bigswell), which was once greatly venerated; whilst about half a mile distant is Maeshowe, the principal chambered mound in Western Europe. Like many other megalithic monuments, Maeshowe has its entrance facing the winter solstice, and the various alignments between the Mound, the Circles, and the two solitary menhirs appear to indicate the rising and setting sun at the date of the principal feasts of the sun-worshippers—the solstices and equinoxes, Beltane and Hallowmas.[4]

The Clava group, near Inverness, is the most important of the northern mainland circles, which are characterised by chambered cairns within the ring. The Aberdeenshire circles differ slightly in character, and the western circles, from Skye to Arran, are composed of rings or pairs of concentric rings of irregular shape.

The holding of courts at the Stone Circles (a custom known to Homer) survived in Scotland well into historic times. In 1349, the Bishop of Aberdeen held a court at the

Ring of Fiddes, where William de Saint Michael was called upon to explain the seizure of certain Church property; in 1380, the Wolf of Badenoch, the natural son of Robert II, held a court at a circle to which the Bishop of Moray was summoned in connection with his claim to certain lands in Badenoch; in the fourteenth century, the king's steward held a court at Strathearn in Perthshire; and similar courts are recorded at Crieff, in Perthshire, and at Huntly, in Aberdeenshire.[5]

The records of both the pre-Reformation and the Reformed Church show how firmly rooted in the lives of the people were the rites pertaining to the Cult of the Dead. A thirteenth-century statute of the diocese of Aberdeen decrees that neither '*choree*' nor '*turpes et inhonesti ludi*' should be permitted in church or churchyard, which indicates that the '*ludi*' formerly associated with the sacrificial ceremonies of the Druids were still carried on, and that they had been diverted from the pagan temples to the Christian church and its environment.[6]

Apart from the circles, there are many solitary Standing Stones scattered over the country. In the Isle of Skye, for instance, there are Stones to which, until fairly recent times, the islanders brought libations of milk. These are called Gruagach Stones, and are believed to be rude representations of Grannos or Gruagach, one of the many names of the sun-god of the Gaels.[7] In later times the milk was brought as an offering to the fairies.

Like the tree-trunk, the Standing Stone frequently had a phallic significance.[8]

The belief is found throughout the Celtic territories that certain Standing Stones, set in motion by the spirits which animate them, sometimes go to drink in river or lake. In Orkney, one such Stone was said to walk from the Circle to the Loch of Stennis regularly on Hogmanay, dip its head into the Loch, and return to its old position. The story goes[9] that a sailor once seated himself on the Stone some time before midnight in order to test the truth of the legend, and next morning his dead body was found half-way between the Circle and the Loch.

THE MERCAT CROSS

Linked remotely with the Standing Stone is the Mercat (Market) Cross which is possessed by every city and burgh of importance. The Cross has been for centuries the symbol and the hub of the civic or burghal life. It derives its name from the custom of presenting merchandise for sale at its base. In an age when few people were able to sign a written contract, the parties to a bargain touched the Cross and thus came under solemn obligation. The reason is not far to seek. In some places it is evident that the Cross was originally 'an upright stone or ancient pillar left standing as a centre of older local ceremony and worship and adapted to Christian usage by the inscription of a cross, occasionally of an elaborate design . . . . Royal. edicts were proclaimed from its steps, municipal injunctions were affixed to it, and officers of the burgh were chosen at its side. The powerful Gilds gave out notices and humble offenders suffered public disgrace at the same Cross. It was the centre of public festivity and rejoicing as well as of the affairs of the market. "Ridings" and the Saints' Day pageants of the Gilds all set out from the Cross.'[10]

The Mercat Cross of Edinburgh incorporates an ancient shaft. Close by is the Heart of Midlothian—a heart-shaped design of granite setts built into the causeway—which gave its name to Sir Walter Scott's romance. Occasionally a boy passing by may be seen spitting on it 'for luck'.

The Cross of Crail, an ancient and picturesque fishing-port in Fife, was said to work marvellous cures, and in the Middle Ages drew many pilgrims.

THE STONE OF DESTINY

The most famous of all the magical stones of Scotland is the Stone of Destiny, which for six centuries remained inset in the Coronation Chair at Westminster. The earlier history of the stone (that is, previous to the ninth century AD) is legendary. Identified with Jacob's pillow at Bethel, it is said to have been carried to Ireland in the ninth century BC by the invading 'Scots' or Gaels, and as the Lia Faill was revered at Tara. From Ireland it was taken to Scotland by the Gaels who migrated to Argyll in pre-Columban times,

and became the Coronation Stone of the early Dalriad kings
at Dunstaffnage. In the ninth century AD it was carried
to Scone, the capital of Southern Pictland, by Kenneth
Macalpine, under whom the Picts and Scots were united
in 844. There it remained until the end of the thirteenth
century, when its connection with Scotland was rudely
severed. This account, however, is nowadays regarded as
untenable.

As a result of modern geological investigation and anti-
quarian research, 'We are now able to confirm,' writes
Sir Thomas Innes of Learney, 'that the Stone of Destiny is a native Scottish stone, from the neighbourhood
of Scone itself, and necessarily *the sacred inaugural seat
of the Pictish monarchy of ancient Alba*—the seat of the indigenous line of Caledonian chiefs who ruled in Caledonia,
long ere the Dalriad kings set foot in Scotland—and that
our British sovereigns enthroned on this sacred piece of
rock are thus the representatives of an indigenous line of
Caledonian high chiefs, emerging from the very dawn of
our national history.'[11] The last king to be crowned at
Scone in accordance with the ancient ritual was Alexander
III, then (1249) a boy of about eight, who was lifted on
to the stone by the Earl of Fife, by virtue of hereditary
privilege. In 1296 the stone was removed to London by
Edward I of England, possibly in the hope of achieving
by magic what he had failed to achieve by force—the
sovereignty of Scotland. But nine years later Robert the
Bruce was crowned, *sans* magical rites, on the traditional spot.

There is a tradition that when the monks of Scone heard
of the depredations being carried out by Edward's army in
its northward advance in 1296, they hid the sacred stone
and substituted a block of local sandstone of the same di-
mensions. Sir Thomas Innes considers the story untenable.
'Those concerned lived into the Bruce's reign, and it is in-
conceivable that steps would have been taken in 1328 to
recover a bogus stone, or not to denounce it as such if it
had been.'[12]

An oracular verse pertaining to the Stone of Destiny
runs as follows:

> Cinnidh Scuit saor am fine,
>   Mur breug am faistine;
> Far am faighear an Lia-Fail,
>   Dlighe flaitheas do ghabhail.

'The race of free Scots shall flourish, if this prediction be not false; wherever the Stone of Destiny is found, they shall prevail by the right of heaven.'

The Latin inscription formerly on the stone is said to have been:

> Ni fallat fatam, Scoti, quocunque locatum,
> Invenient lapidem, regnare tenentur ibidem.

> 'Unless the Fates be false, and Sooth be said in vain,
> Where'er this Stone is found, a Scottish king shall reign.'

The Stone remained faithful to its trust, and in due course a Scottish King ascended the English throne.

STONE AS WITNESS

The Stone of Scone is a relic of the ancient belief that a sacred stone conveys power and that an oath taken upon it has a peculiar sanctity. The Lords of the Isles, at their installation, stood upon a stone with footmarks cut out in it, thus denoting that they would walk in the footsteps of their predecessors in uprightness and in loyalty to the Clan, and the inauguration of a Chief took place 'at the Stone', the 'sacred place' associated by long tradition with the ceremony, in the presence of the assembled tribe or clan. We find references to the 'Bear Stone' of the Forbeses and the 'Falcon Stone' of the Hays, for instance;[13] and Martin, writing of the Western Isles, tells us that the Chief of a Clan, upon his succession, took his vows standing upon a cairn of stones.

Near St Columba's Tomb, in Iona, there stood formerly one of the most ancient and sacred relics of the island—the Black Stones of Iona, so-called, not from their colour, but from the black doom that fell on any who dared to violate an oath sworn upon them. As recently as the reign of James VI, two clans who had spent centuries in bloody feud met here and solemnly pledged themselves to friendship. The last of these stones disappeared about the middle of the nineteenth century.

In medieval times, stones were erected to mark the boundaries of the clan territories,[14] and chiefs met at these boundary stones to settle their disputes. A clansman who went beyond a boundary stone did so at his own risk, and could not claim the protection of his chief.

SANCTUARY STONES

In a pass in the Ochils, overlooking Strathearn, there is a block of free stone that formed the pedestal of the celebrated Cross of Macduff. When anyone claiming kinship with Macduff, Earl of Fife within the ninth degree, committed manslaughter in cold blood and took refuge at the Cross, he could atone for his crime by the payment of nine cows and a colpindach, or year-old calf. Near the stone is a spring known as the Nine Wells, and here, according to tradition, the man seeking sanctuary at the Cross washed his hands, thereby freeing himself from the stain of blood.[15]

Another sanctuary stone is associated with the Knights of St John of Jerusalem, who in the twelfth century were a recognised order in Scotland. Their chief seat was at Torphichen, in West Lothian, where the ruins of their priory or preceptory can still be seen. A little to the west lies St John's Well, and in the graveyard is what looks like a milestone surmounted with a Maltese Cross. This is known as the Refuge Stone, and all the ground within the radius of a mile from it was a sanctuary for criminals and debtors.

HEALING STONES

Certain stones were credited with healing power.

In Brahan Wood, a few miles from Dingwall, there is a dolmen-like holed rock called the *Garadh Tholl* (pronounced Garah Howl), where divination rites were practised and children taken to be cured of divers ailments. A fire was lit; the ailing child was stripped; and first his clothing, then the child himself, was passed through the hole. If a member of the household fell ill, the woman of the house lit a fire of wood close by, made some cakes and baked them on a flat stone, and left them on the summit of the rock.[16] If the cakes were gone next morning, she

was satisfied that the child would recover; if still
there, he was in danger of death.[17]

Another much frequented stone was the Shargar Stone
at Fyvie, Aberdeenshire, beside St Paul's Well. It was supported by two uprights, through which mothers passed their
ailing children.

Child-getting stones were visited by barren wives during
the waxing of the moon. In the Chapel yard at Burghead, in
Moray, there is a gravestone on which a hollow, resembling
'cup marks', has been beaten out with a beach pebble by the
youngsters playing about. It is known as the 'cradle-stone',
because, it is said, if one strikes the hollow and immediately
puts one's ear to it, one can hear the sound of a rocking cradle and the crying of a child. The Borestone of Gask[18] was
resorted to by women of Strathearn in Perthshire, who passed their hands through the hole to ensure motherhood.

Small healing stones have been widely used up to modern
times. Adamnan describes how Broichan, the Chief Druid
at the Pictish Court in Inverness in St Columba's time, was
cured of his sickness by drinking water in which a white
pebble from the Ness had been dipped. Three stones said
to have been at one time in the possession of St Fillan were
kept for generations in the meal mill at Killin, in Perthshire,
and were believed to impart healing power to the water in
which they were steeped. Healing-stones were kept on the
altars of ancient churches, among them St Ronan's Chapel
and the Abbey Church of Iona, whilst others lay beside some
of the holy wells. Some resembled the different parts of the
human body, and were known variously as the e'e-stane, the
heid-stane, the hert-stane, and so forth. The patient took a
draught of water, then washed the part affected and rubbed
it with the appropriate stone. The usual rag, nail or button
was left behind.

Special virtue attached to the Serpent Stone (*a Chlach
Nathrach*), Adder Stone, or 'Druidical Bead', which is occasionally found among the heather. According to a Lewis
isleman, 'A number of serpents (adders) congregating at
certain times form themselves into a knot and move round
and round on the stone until a hole is worn. They pass and
re-pass after each other through the hole, which by-and-by

becomes hard. It is this slime which gives the stone the healing properties it is supposed to possess.'[19] The Serpent stone was commonly used in child-bed, as well as for general healing purposes, and as a protection from all enchantments; and it is even found as part of the gear of the distaff.

In Galloway, round flat stones, about five inches in diameter and artificially perforated, were used 'within living memory,' says Dr Charles Rogers, writing in 1869, the water in which they had been steeped being sprinkled on ailing animals; and 'to this day,' says the same writer, 'cattle are given water in which a flint arrowhead—the elf-bolt of superstition—has been dipped.'[20]

THE KNOCKING STONE

A domestic utensil once found in every home is the knocking-stone. This is a large, heavy lump of stone or rock roughly shaped on the outside and smoothly hollowed inside until it resembles a huge bowl. In this, corn was bruised with the 'beetle'—a thick stick with a heavy, rounded head. The stone was kept in the barn. Probably because it was so closely associated with the daily bread of the household, special virtue was attributed to it, and it came to symbolise the luck of the house. The knocking-stone was in many families a precious heirloom, and always accompanied a family that was obliged to 'flit'. Modern milling methods, however, have relegated it to oblivion.

FAMILY CHARM STONES

In several Highland families charm stones have been preserved as precious heirlooms. One of the most famous is the Clach-Dearg, or Stone of Ardvorlich, which is in the possession of the Stewarts of Ardvorlich. This is a rock crystal the size of an egg, in shape spherical and hog-backed, and set in four silver hoops.[21] There are two conflicting traditions concerning it—one that it originally surmounted the wand of office of an Arch-Druid, and the other that it came from the East. In the latter half of the nineteenth century, people still came from far and wide for healing water in which the stone had been dipped. Visitors to Ardvorlich still touch the stone and 'wish a wish'.

The Keppoch Charm Stone is associated with the Macdonnells of Keppoch. It is an oval of rock crystal of the size of a small egg, and is fixed in a bird's claw of silver to which a silver chain is attached. Near Keppoch is a well called Tobar-Bride (St Bride's Well) and when people came for magic water for healing purposes, the stone, suspended by its chain, was dipped into the well. The incantation that accompanied the rite has been preserved:

> Let me dip thee in the water,
> Thou yellow, beautiful gem of power!
> In water of purest wave,
> Which pure was kept by Bridget.
>
> In the name of the Apostles twelve,
> In the name of Mary, virgin of virtues,
> And in the name of the High Trinity
> And all the shining angels.
> A blessing on the gem,
> A blessing on the water,
> And a healing of all bodily ailments
>   To each suffering creature![22]

The stone is believed to have been taken to Australia by a cadet of the Macdonnells who settled there in or about 1854.

Another celebrated stone is *Clach-na-Bratach*, the Stone of the Standard, which is said to have come into the possession of the Chiefs of Clan Donnachaidh on the eve of Bannockburn (1314). When the standard was drawn out of the ground, a clod of earth adhered to it, and in this clod was embedded the crystal—a transparent globular mass the size of a small apple—the appearance of which was hailed as an omen of victory. Henceforward, when the clan was 'out', the stone was carried on the person of the Chief. Water into which the stone had been thrice dipped by the hands of Struan (Struan Robertson, as the Chief of Clan Donnachaidh was generally known) was used for healing purposes.

In Arran, Martin tells us, a green stone about the bigness of a goose egg was in the possession of a 'little family called Clan-Chattons, *alias* Macintosh'. It was said that Macdonald of the Isles had formerly carried this stone about him, and that victory was always his when he threw it among the enemy. The stone was believed to have curative powers, and

the natives used to swear their oaths upon it. Its whereabouts is now unknown.

Other charm stones include the *Leug*, or Charm Stone
of the Macleans; the *Clach-Bhuai* of the Campbells of
Glenlyon; the Glenorchy Charm Stone—a polished pyra-
mid of rock crystal in an octagonal disc of silver studded
with pearls—which is in the possession of the Marquis of
Breadalbane (Campbell of Breadalbane); the Barbreck
Bone—a piece of ivory—formerly in the possession of
Campbell of Barbreck, and now in the Scottish Museum of
Antiquities; and the Auchmeddan Stone—a black ball of
flint mounted in four bands of silver—which has been in the
possession of the Bairds of Auchmeddan since 1174. There
is one Scottish charm stone that has achieved world-wide
fame, and that is the Lee Penny, which has been immortalised by Sir Walter Scott in the *Talisman*. The stone is a
cornelian, roughly triangular or heart-shaped, set in a piece
of silver coin. It is said to have been given, along with ran-
som money, to Sir Simon Lockhart of Lee by the wife of
a Saracen chief whom he had taken prisoner in Palestine,
after accompanying Sir James Douglas as far as Spain in
1329 with the heart of Robert the Bruce. It has remained
ever since in the hands of the Lairds of Lee. The stone was
renowned far and wide for its healing properties. To impart
its power, it was drawn sunwise round a vessel filled with
water, and then dipped three times. In the reign of Charles
I, when the plague was raging in Newcastle, the stone was
hired to the city, and £6,000 was the sum pledged for its
safe return. It was also credited with the power of keeping
the cows from parting calf and the milk from changing, and
no byre within a wide surrounding district was considered
safe that had not a bottle of Lee-penny water suspended
from the rafters. So widely, in fact, was the stone resorted
to, that in 1638 the Presbytery of Lanark brought the matter
before the Supreme Judiciary.[23]

The green pebbles of Iona, which were freely used as
amulets and said to save from drowning, were believed to
derive their influence from St Columba.

Stones of rock crystal were frequently perforated and
worn as a protection against the Evil Eye. The toadstone of

the Mearns witches is legendary, and the Strathardle witches
cherished a garnet stone which is now in the Highland Museum at Fort William.

STONE OF THE BRAHAN SEER

The most famous magical stone in Highland tradition was
that of the Brahan Seer, who ranks as a prophet with
Thomas the Rhymer. Coinneach Odhar, or Kenneth Mackenzie, commonly known as the Brahan Seer, was born in
Uig, in the Island of Lewis, about the beginning of the seventeenth century. His prophetic powers, like those of the
Rhymer, were reputed to be a fairy gift. One day, the story
goes (although the versions vary in detail), the lad, weary
with cutting peats, lay down on the side of a fairy hill and fell
fast asleep. On waking, he became aware of a small stone,
white and smooth and round, with a hole in the centre, that
was lying on his breast, and on looking through the hole he
discovered that he could 'see things'—see into the future
as clearly as he could remember the past, and see men's
designs and motives as clearly as their actions. His fame
spread far and wide, and his prophecies have been recited
from generation to generation.[24]

But Coinneach's gift was to prove his undoing. After
the Restoration of Charles II, Kenneth Mackenzie, the
third Earl of Seaforth and Chief of his clan, had occasion
to visit Paris, leaving the Countess behind him at Brahan
Castle. The lady became first uneasy, then wrathful, over
her husband's prolonged absence, and at last decided to
consult his namesake. The seer obeyed her summons, but
refused to divulge what the stone revealed. Her suspicions
now thoroughly aroused, the Countess used persuasion and
threats, until Kenneth was at last obliged to admit that he
had seen the Earl in a gilded chamber making love to a fair
lady. The Countess's rage immediately turned full flood on
Kenneth. She accused him of the crime of witchcraft and
ordered him to be put to a horrible death—to be thrown
head first into a barrel of burning tar. Before his execution,
Kenneth looked through the stone for the last time and
uttered his most famous prophecy, known as the 'Doom
of the Seaforths'. 'I see into the far future, and I read the
doom of the race of my oppressor . . . . I see a Chief, the

last of his House, both deaf and dumb. He will be the
father of four fair sons, all of whom he will follow to the
tomb. He will live careworn and die mourning, knowing
that the honours of his line are to be extinguished forever,
and that no future chief of the Mackenzies shall bear rule at
Brahan or in Kintail . . . . And as a sign by which it may be
known that these things are coming to pass, there shall be
four great lairds in the days of the last Seaforth—Gairloch,
Chisholm, Grant and Raasay—of whom one shall be buck-
toothed, another hare-lipped, another half-witted, and the
fourth a stammerer. When he looks round and sees them,
he may know that his sons are doomed to death, that his
broad lands shall pass to a stranger, and that his race shall
come to an end.'

The speaker then threw the stone into a small loch
nearby, and turned to meet his fate.[25]

The prophecy made a profound impression. Towards the
end of the eighteenth century, the four 'marked' lairds duly
appeared.[26] Francis, the last Earl of Seaforth, was born in
1794. He was a normal child at birth, but in boyhood had
an attack of scarlet fever which left him deaf, and in later
life he completely lost his power of speech. These physical
disabilities, however, were offset by his remarkable mental
powers. At the beginning of the Napoleonic Wars he raised
the second regiment of Seaforth Highlanders, and became
successively a Lieutenant-General, Governor of the Barba-
does, Member of Parliament for Ross-shire (before he
entered the Lords), and Lord Lieutenant of the same
county.[27] One by one his sons predeceased him. 'Mr Morrit
can testify,' says Lockhart in his *Life of Sir Walter Scott*,
'that he heard the prophecy quoted in the Highlands when
Lord Seaforth had two sons alive and in good health,' and
he goes on to say that both Scott and Sir Humphrey Davy
were convinced of its truth, and with many others watched
the latter days of Seaforth in the light of these predictions.

After the death of his last surviving son, the broken-
hearted father lingered only a few months, his mind affected by paralysis, yet, in Scott's words 'not so entirely
obscured but that he perceived his deprivation "as in a
glass darkly".' Deeply moved by the tragedy, Scott wrote

his *Lament for the Last of the Seaforths*, of which the last
verse runs:

> Thy sons rose around thee in light and in love,
> All a father could hope, all a friend could approve;
> What 'vails it the tale of thy sorrows to tell?
> In the spring-time of youth and of promise they fell.
> Of the line of Mackenzie remains not a male
> To bear the proud name of the Chief of Kintail.

The belief in the efficacy of charm stones had not died
out in the remoter Highlands at the beginning of the present
century, and probably still lingers.

'The last specimen about which I heard about thirty
years ago,' wrote Mr D. A. Mackenzie in 1935, 'was in
Erradale, parish of Gairloch (Ross-shire). Mr Matheson,
Free Church Minister, got hold of it and took it to the pulpit one day. At the close of the service he held it up before
the congregation, remarking that the "god of Erradale" was
the smallest god of which he had ever heard or read. It was
a small piece of flint stone, three or four inches long, found
on the shore and highly polished by the action of the waves
. . . . Mr Matheson broke it in their presence, and yet no
dire results followed.'

SANCTUARY FROM EVIL

'Evil does not come from the sea,' says the proverb. In
Scottish folk belief, the 'Black Shore'—that is, the shore
below the line or roll of seaweed thrown up by the tide,
was a sanctuary from all the supernatural beings that in-
fest the night, for none dare go beyond the tide mark. Nor
could they cross a running stream. While Tam o' Shanter,
mounted on his auld grey mare, was being pursued by the
witches whom he had disturbed in Kirk Alloway, his one
thought was to reach 'the keystane o' the brig', when all
danger should be past.

When neither the black shore sanctuary nor running
water was at hand, there was another method of protection,
derived from the Druids, to whom the most sacred and perfect figure was the circle, the symbol of the sun. With his
dirk, or with the point of a young sapling, a man would draw

a circle round himself on the ground, saying, 'The Cross of Christ be upon me!' Evil spirits might dash in fury against this circle, but were unable to get beyond it.

When St Columba was engaged in converting the Scots from Druidism, he substituted the pastoral staff for the Druidical wand, and the sign of the cross for the magic circle. Yet both wand and circle linger in the folk memory. Not so long ago (and possibly still) Highland children had a game in which they took a stick, set fire to one end of it, and swung it rapidly in a fiery circle, while repeating a Gaelic incantation; and in the Islands to this day, a child who is tired of being chased in the game of tig will draw a circle round his head with his hand, saying, 'The circle of God is on my head; you can't touch me!'

THE HORSEMAN'S WORD

A curious relic of the old ritual magic still survived in north-east Scotland at the beginning of the twentieth century. This is The Horseman's Word, which gave its possessor power over horses and women, and was the proof that he had become a man.

'When the youth was at the age to be a man, he was told he must appear for initiation. The place was the barn. The time eleven on a dark night. He must take with him a candle, a loaf and a bottle of whisky. At the barn door he was blindfolded and led before the secret court. This consisted of a few older ploughmen, presided over by a master of ceremonies at an altar made by inverting a bushel measure over a sack of corn, that strong symbol of fertility. The youth was then put through a long questioning and made to repeat certain forms of words. In later days, at least, he had to suffer many indignities, some of them sexual, according to the humour of the court. At the climax of initiation, he got a shake of the Devil's hand—usually a stick covered by a hairy skin. Then he was given the horseman's word. Then at last the bread and whisky, sacramental elements of universal significance, were passed round; and the youth had become a ploughman.

'. . . But the Word—what was it? McPherson, in his book on our primitive beliefs, says it was "Both in one", meaning there would be complete harmony between the man and his beasts, whereby he would have power over them. He could reist them—that is, make them stand still so that no other person could get them to move; or he could make them come to him though he were miles away. He got a similar power over women: he had only to touch a girl and she would do his will—and as to that I do know that some young men had a strong magic.

'Even in the early days of this century the horseman's word was the token of a sort of freemasonry among ploughmen.'[1]

This description is given us by John R. Allan, who grew up on an Aberdeenshire farm and acquired much interesting lore from the older generation of country folk.

MAGIC IN THE MODERN WORLD

Magic can still work miracles; but the miracles of magic, as Malinowski points out, are always wrought in the long run by man himself. In war magic, for instance, the spells and rites are effective only in so far as they pour real bravery into the heart of the warrior, and the man who runs away and trusts the magical spell to win the fight is beaten. Magic, in short, is useful only in so far as it goes hand in hand with the utmost effort of man to do all that he could not do by his own efforts. The affirmations of magic, however, must never be allowed to encroach upon the preserve of sound knowledge, solid work, and real achievement.

Where, the same authority asks, does magic survive in our modern communities? Minor superstitions, such as the fear of ladders, of the number thirteen, of the spilling of salt, or of looking at the new moon through glass, he dismisses as having little relation to the true magical attitude. But it is found elsewhere—in certain kinds of faith-healing, for instance. Nothing corresponds more closely to a magical formula from New Guinea or Melanesia than the sentence which M. Coué advised the sick person to repeat, 'Every day and in every way I am getting better and better.' Then slightly adjust the words of a modern advertisement, make them scan and correspond to one another, and there, he asserts, you have a magical spell. 'Here, once more, the modern magic of advertisement corresponds also in its cultural setting to primitive magic. For here, also, advertising is of social value . . . in stimulating people to use improved medicines, health foods, intelligent clothing, or the best of motor cars, as long as the advertiser delivers the goods.'

The magical attitude survives, too, in modern politics— especially in the totalitarian state, with its complete control of education and its ministries of propaganda. 'Such entities as "race", "national genius", the "mystical power" of a people, drawn from some ancient figment, are used verbally in exactly the same way in which the Melanesian appeals to his spirit or to his ancestors, or his Mana, drawing from them magical strength or virtue. The power of "the leader" and his clique is impressed on the people by an endless array of spells, ritual performances, and symbols.' Whilst the aim of the totalitarian state is world conquest, real social science teaches us that in these days no one nation, however powerful, is able to dominate all others. 'Here once more we have two forces, the one magical, the other sane and scientific . . . . Whereas ancient magic was associated with sound and vital services to the community, the new magic is merely destructive. Both appeal to hope, credulity, and unreason. In olden days, when man's mastery over nature and his own destiny was in its infancy, the unreason of magic had its justification. Nowadays, magic works only for evil in the affairs of men.'[1]

The magical attitude in human affairs appears to be an unconscionable time a-dying, but if the human race is to progress, the substitution of a rational—and spiritual—attitude must become one of the major tasks of the post-war world.[2]

The Fairies

O whaten a castel is yon, ma minnie,
  That harles the hert's bluid oot o' me
And beckons me owre a warld o' watters
  To seek its weird or dee?
Yon castel braw, ma bonny bit hinny,
  It is the Scottis Glamourie;
There's a spell intil't and a well intil't,
  And the sang o' a siller bell intil't,
But the braes abune it are dowf and whinny,
  And the bracken buries the lea;
It's noo a ship wi' the haar for sail,
  And syne a strength, as ye may see,
Forbye it's a hill wi' a hollow ha',
  Whaur the fludes sough eerilie.
      Lewis Spence, *The Stown Bairn*[1]

The belief in fairies is not peculiar to the Celtic or Anglo-Celtic peoples. The nymphs and nereids of Greece and the elves of Germany and Scandinavia have much in common with the *side* (pronounced shee), the fairies of the British Isles and of Brittany, and our Scottish Queen of Elfhame is obviously sib to the Greek sirens, the German Lorelei, and the fairy leman of Sanskrit poetry. Even in Samoa, Robert Louis Stevenson found tales of fairy women who had amours with mortals such as befell Thomas the Rhymer, Tamlane, and other heroes of the Scottish ballads he had known from boyhood.

The fairies of Celtic tradition bear no resemblance to the gossamer-winged flower-sprites of the modern child's picture-books. They are of nearly normal stature, and their mode of life corresponds closely with human life; in fact, they differ from human beings only in their supernatural knowledge and power.

Where did the belief in fairies originate? Some anthropologists maintain that the whole fairy-faith has grown out of a folk-memory of a small-statured (though not genuinely pigmy) race, the Neolithic and Bronze Age folk, which at one time inhabited the British Isles and many parts of the Continent. In our Gaelic tales we read of little men who lived in green mounds, and there is other evidence of a dwarfish population, probably akin to the modern Laplanders, who are merely a stunted branch of the Finnish race.[2]

These primitive folk were scattered over the country in small communities, each with its own ruler, usually a 'Queen'. Their bee-hive houses, which were built in groups, were sunk two or three feet deep in the ground, and were roofed chiefly with turf, so that when overgrown with grass or heather, they had the appearance of hillocks. They had flocks and herds, but no crops. They were skilled workers in bronze—so much so that their weapons were coveted by the invaders—but had a superstitious horror of the new metal, iron. Their characteristic weapon was the *saighead shith*, the little flint arrow-head or elf-bolt, which is still frequently found on the moors, and is thought to bring the finder good luck.[3] They were reputed to be skilled in all the arts, notably poetry and music. (It is from the mound-dwellers that the 'fairy' melodies so prevalent in the Highlands and Hebrides derive.) Above all, they were great necromancers, and in medieval times, as we shall see, they were constantly consulted by the adherents of the witch cult as their superiors in magic. They learned to defend themselves from the incoming Celts by creating in them a superstitious fear. They came out chiefly at night, and were swift of movement, appearing and disappearing as if by magic; and thus they came to be regarded as non-human, or, in other words, as 'fairies'. Practically all we know of their religion is that once in every seven years they made a sacrifice to the god, and that they stole children from the families of their conquerors and reared them as victims.[4]

The last authentic account of 'the fairies' in Scotland occurs at the end of the seventeenth century, long after they had disappeared in England, but there are indications that as late as the eighteenth century people of dwarfish stature were living apart somewhere in Caithness, like the tinkers in our own time.

It is now generally accepted that by the Middle Ages the fairies had become identified in the popular mind with these primitive folk, but it by no means follows that the belief in fairies originated there. It goes, indeed, infinitely farther back. The evidence collected by Dr Evans Wentz throughout the Celtic territories and published in his book, *The Fairy Faith in Celtic Countries* (1911)[5] shows that the majority of witnesses regarded fairies either as non-human nature spirits or as spirits of the dead. According to Lewis Spence, they were believed to lurk in mounds awaiting reincarnation. Similarly the elves of Northern Europe were originally regarded as spirits of the dead living in hills, and more especially in barrows and burial-places. The *Erl-König* (Elf-King) in the ballad of that name is Death. Fairyland, indeed, is hardly distinguishable from the world of the dead.

To our Celtic forebears the universe consisted of two inter-penetrating parts—the visible world, as revealed to mortals through the five senses, and the invisible, which is immanent in and transcends the other, and which they called Fairyland or the Otherworld. Glimpses of the invisible world could occasionally be obtained by those who had that sixth sense we know as Second Sight.

FAIRYLAND

The Celtic Elysium was situated not, like the heaven of the hymnist, 'above the bright blue sky', but here upon earth; but, as it was a subjective world, its location was vague. Sometimes it was a subterranean land entered through a cavern or hill, and thither, as we read in the ballads, the Queen of Elfhame, mounted on her milk-white steed, carried off those mortals on whom she had cast her spell. Sometimes it was a mystic green island that drifted on the western seas. Men caught occasional glimpses of it, half hidden in a twinkling mist, but when they attempted to draw near, it vanished beneath the waves. From the island, fairy women came out in magic boats to spirit away those mortals who had won their love, or to convey a dying hero, like Arthur, to Paradise.

The Green Island has been seen in almost every latitude from Cape Wrath in Scotland to Cape Clear in Ireland. Sometimes it was identified with a particular isle of the West.

'According to Irish tradition,' says Professor Watson, 'Arran was the home of Manannan, the sea-god, and another name for it was *Emain Ablach*, Eiman of the Apples. This is, I suppose, equivalent to making Arran the same as Avalon, the Happy Otherworld.'[6] Again, it is said of St Kilda that 'the ancient Celts fancied this sunset isle to be the gateway to their earthly paradise, the Land-Under-Waves, over the brink of the Western Sea.'[7]

Whence the two conceptions, one of an island paradise and the other of a subterranean Otherworld entered through a fairy hill? One theory is that the island paradise is the earlier conception, and that after the introduction of Christianity the gods retreated to the hollow hills.[8] However that may be, the island paradise is confined to Celtic, and more particularly to Gaelic mythology, whereas the subterranean Otherworld is common to practically all European lands and races.

The heroes privileged to enter the Otherworld—whether the Avalon of the Cymbri or the Tir-nan-Og of the Gael—describe it as a realm fairer than any known to mortals: a land of eternal spring and youth, bathed in sunshine, washed by clear streams and fanned by perfumed breezes. Its meadows are 'clad in flowering clover all bedewed with honey'; its trees are melodious with bird song and bending with mellow fruit.

In the Ossianic tales handed down through the centuries by word of mouth, there are many references to the 'fairy hills' of Tir-nan-Og, and the ineffable beauty of this land-of-heart's-desire is still sung in the Hebrides. Its ruling deity is Aengus, who, like the Brythonic Arthur, is in one aspect a sun-god. Aengus has a harp of gold with silver strings, and is attended by bright birds, his own transformed kisses, whose singing arouses love in the hearts of youths and maidens.

To enter this Otherworld before the appointed hour of death, a passport was necessary. This was a silver branch of the mystic apple-tree, laden with blossom or fruit—though sometimes a single apple sufficed—and it was given by the Queen of Elfhame or Fairy Woman to that mortal whose companionship she desired. It served not only as a passport, but also as food; and it had the property of making music so entrancing that those who heard it forgot all their cares and sorrows.[9]

Of the hero Bran the legend runs:

'One day Bran heard strange music behind him as he was alone in the neighbourhood of his stronghold; and as he listened, so sweet was the sound that it lulled him to sleep. When he awoke, there lay beside him a branch of silver so white with blossom that it was not easy to distinguish the blossom from the branch. Bran took up the branch and carried it to the royal house, and when the hosts were assembled therein, they saw a woman in strange raiment standing on the floor . . . . And as they all beheld her, she sang . . . to Bran:

> A branch from the apple-tree of Emain
> I bring, like those one knows:
> Twigs of white silver are on it,
> Crystal buds with blossoms.
>
> There is a distant isle,
> Around which white sea-horses glisten:
> A fair course against the white-swelling surge—
> Four pedestals uphold it.

The next day, with the fairy spell upon him, Bran begins his voyage towards the setting sun.[10]

In another Gaelic tale, *Cormac's Adventure in the Land of Promise*, there is a magic silver branch with three golden apples upon it. 'Delight and amusement to the full was it to listen to the music of that branch, for men sore wounded, or women in childbed, or folk in sickness, would fall asleep at the melody when that branch was shaken.'[11]

The same talisman appears in the Border ballad, *Tamlane*:

> Ae fatal morning I gaed out,
>   Drieding nae injurie,
> And thinking lang, fell fast asleep
>   Beneath an aipple tree.

> Then by it cam the Elfin Queen
>   And laid her hand on me;
> And frae that time syne e'er I mind,
>   I hae been in her companie.

It is uncertain how far the pre-Christian Celts distinguished between the land of the gods and the heroes who had not passed from this world by death and the region to which mankind at large went after death. The Greeks called the former the Isles of the Blest, the Hesperides, or the Elysian Fields, and the latter Hades—a dark and woeful region. The Norse heroes passed similarly to Valhalla, but those who died in their beds passed to Hel—a bleak and hunger-stricken abode. The Celtic Otherworld, however, was a very different place from the gloomy land of shades that was Hades or Hel. The Land of the Dead was in reality the Land of the Living (*Tir nam Bèo*), a place where life was freer and more abundant than on earth, and where the sensuous joys of human experience were spiritualised. Nearly all mythologists speak of two separate places of reward and punishment, and it is perhaps only in the idea of Fairyland, as Mr Lewis Spence points out, that they become fused.

Although one also hears of Ifrinn, the cold and gloomy island where the wicked were doomed to wander, it must be remembered that this is a late conception, introduced, as the name indicates, from Christian teaching, for *Ifrinn* is simply a Celticised form of the Latin *Infernum*. The true Celtic Otherworld was beyond good and evil.

THE SECRET COMMONWEALTH

We possess in Scotland a remarkable book dealing with the Fairy Faith. This is *The Secret Commonwealth of Elves, Fauns, and Fairies*, written in 1691 by the Rev. Robert Kirk, Minister of Aberfoyle.[12] The work has been described by Andrew Lang as 'a kind of metaphysic of the Fairy World'.

'Having lived through the period of the suffering of the Kirk,' he comments, 'the author might have been expected to neglect Fairyland altogether, or to regard it as a mere appanage of Satan's Kingdom. . . . Yet Mr Kirk of Aberfoyle, living among Celtic people, treats the land of faery as a mere fact in nature, a world with its own laws, which he investigates without fear of the Accuser of the Brethren . . . as if he were dealing with generally recognised physical phenomena.'

'There be many places called "Fairy-hills",' writes Mr Kirk, 'which the Mountain People think impious and dangerous to peel or discover, by taking Earth or Wood from them; superstitiously believing the Souls of their Predecessors to dwell there.'

The Fairies, he says, are distributed in tribes and orders.

'They are said to have aristocraticall Rulers and Laws, but no discernible Religion, Love, or Devotion towards God, the blessed Maker of all; they disappear whenever they hear his Name invoked, or the Name of Jesus, nor can they act aught at that Time after hearing of that sacred Name . . . . 'Tis ane of their Tenets that nothing perisheth, but (as the Sun and the Year) everything goes in a Circle, less or greater, and is renewed or refreshed in its Revolutions.'[13]

The Fairies were also known as the Good People, 'it would seem to prevent the Dint of their ill Attempts (for the Irish used to bless all they feel Harme of), and are said to be a midle Nature betwixt Man and Angel, as were Daemons thought to be of old; of intelligent studious Spirits, and light changeable Bodies, like those called Astral, somewhat of the Nature of a condensed Cloud, and best seen in Twilight. These Bodies be so pliable through the Subtilty of the Spirits that agitate them, that they can make them appear or disappear at Pleasure.

'. . . They are sometimes heard to bake Bread, strike Hammers, and do such-lyke Services within the little Hillocks they most haunt. They remove to other Lodgings at the Beginning of each Quarter of the Year. Their Chameleonlyke Bodies swim in the Air near the Earth with Bag and Bagadge; and at such Revolution of Time, Seers, or Men of the Second Sight (Faemales being seldom so qualified) have terrifying Encounters with them, even on High Ways.

'. . . What Food they extract from us is conveyed to their Homes by secret Paths, as some skilful Women do the Pith and Milk from their Neighbours' Cows into their own Chies-holde through a Hair-tedder, at a great Distance by Airth (Earth) Magic, or by drawing a Spicket fastened to a post, which will bring Milk as far as a Bull is heard to roar.[14]

'. . . The method they take to recover their Milk is a bitter chyding of the suspected Inchanters, charging them by a counter Charm to give them back their own in God or their Master's Name. But a little of the Mother's Dung stroakit on the Calf's Mouth before it sucks any, does prevent this Theft.

'. . . Their Apparell and Speech is like that of the Countrey under which they live; so are they seen to wear Plaids and variegated Garments in the Highlands of Scotland, and Suanochs therefore in Ireland . . . . Their Women are said to Spine very fine, to Dy, to Tossue, and Embroyder: but whether it is a manuall Operation of substantial refined Stuffs, ... or only curious Cobwebs, impalpable Rainbows, and a fantastic Imitation of the Actions of the more terrestrial Mortalls . . . I leave to conjecture as I found it.'

A seventh son, Kirk was born with the faculty of second sight,[15] without which, according to tradition, no mortal is able to see the fairies.

'The Men of the Second Sight,' he says, 'do not discover strange Things when asked, but at Fits and Raptures.' They must be in 'a Rapture, Transport, and sort of Death'. And he proceeds to give us a description of the extraordinary ceremony of initiation:

'There be odd Solemnities at investing a Man with the Priviledges of the whole Mistery of this Second Sight. He must run a Tedder of Hair (which bound a Corpse to the Bier) in a Helix (?) about his Middle, from End to End; then bow his Head downwards, as did Elijah, 1 Kings, 18, 42, and look back through his Legs until he sie a Funerall advance till the People cross two Marches; or look thus back through a Hole where was a Knot of Fir. But if the Wind change Points while the Hair Tedder is ty'd about him, he is in Peril of his Lyfe.

'The usuall Method for a curious Person to get a transient Sight of this otherwise invisible Crew of Subterraneans (if impotently and over-rashly sought) is to put his (left Foot under the Wizard's right) Foot, and the Seer's Hand is put on the Inquirer's Head, who is to look over the Wizard's right Shoulder (which has ane ill Appearance, as if by this Ceremony ane implicit Surrender were made of all betwixt the Wizard's Foot and his Hand, ere a Person can be admitted a privado to the Airt); then will he see a Multitude of Wights, like furious hardie Men, flocking to him hastily from all Quarters, as thick as Atoms in the Air.'

If the initiate was struck speechless and breathless through fear, the Seer would defend the lawfulness of his skill by quoting instances of apparitions in the Bible—Zacharias (Luke I, 20); Elisha (II Kings, VI, 17); Peter (Acts V, 9); Elisha (II Kings V, 26); Paul (II Corinth. XII, 4) and others. 'Hence,' says Mr Kirk, 'were the Prophets frequently called Seers, or Men of the 2nd or more exalted Sight than others.' Finally he quotes Matt. IV, 8, where 'the Devil undertakes to give even Jesus a Sight of all Nations, and the finest Things in the World, in one Glance, they in their natural Situations and Stations at a vast distance from other . . . . whence it might seem that extraordinary or Second Sight can be given by the Ministery of bad as well as good Spirits to those that will embrace it.'

'This, I suggest,' writes Mr Lewis Spence, 'is an account not of something imaginary, but of the long-preserved ritual of a hereditary cult whose members actually or professedly were able to communicate with and enter some other plane resembling that *Annwn* of which Taliesen's mystical poem speaks, a long-descended Keltic rite of occult potency, recognised as practicable by men living only 237 years ago.'[16]

POPULAR BELIEFS ABOUT FAIRIES

Dr Carmichael quotes a typical description of a fairy—'The slender woman of the green kirtle[17] and the yellow hair, wise of head and deft of hand, who can convert the white water of the rill into rich red wine and the threads of the spider into a tartan plaid, and bring from the stalk of the fairy reed the music of lull and repose'; whilst Cromek refers to the fairies of Nithsdale and Galloway as 'of small stature,[18] but finely proportioned; of a fair complexion, with long yellow hair hanging over their shoulders and gathered above their heads with combs of gold. They wear a mantle of green cloth, inlaid with wild flowers; green pantaloons, buttoned with bobs of silk; and silver shoon. They carry quivers of "adder slough" and bows made with the ribs of a man buried where three lairds' lands meet; their arrows are made of bog-reed, tipped with white flints and dipped in the dew of hemlock; they ride on steeds whose hoofs "would not dash the dew from the cup of a harebell".'[19]

In the Highlands, the red deer were spoken of as the fairies' cattle, and were believed to supply them with milk.

In the Hebrides we find the belief that the fairies were originally fallen angels. 'On certain nights,' an old Barra man told Dr Carmichael, 'when their *bruithain* (bowers) are open and their lamps are lit and the song and the dance are moving merrily, the fairies may be heard singing lightheartedly:

> Not of the seed of Adam are we,
> Nor is Abraham our father,
> But of the seed of the Proud Angel,
> Driven forth from Heaven.[20]

The fairies were never allowed abroad on Thursday, that being St Columba's day.

> God be between me and every fairy,
> Every ill-wish and every Druidry;
> To-day is Thursday on sea and land,
> I trust in the King they do not hear me.

In the Lowland tradition, the fairies are divided into two classes—the 'gude wichts' and the 'wicked wichts'; otherwise the 'seely court' and the 'unseely court'.

> Meddle and mell
> Wi' the fiends o' hell,
> And a weirdless wicht ye'll be;
> But tak' and len'
> Wi' the fairy men,
> And ye'll thrive until ye dee.[21]

The good fairies readily helped human beings with their work in the home or in the barn, and were well disposed towards those who propitiated their favour. The 'wicked wichts', on the contrary, were always ready to inflict skaith or injury upon mortals, and all sorts of precautions were taken to keep them at bay, especially, as we have seen, on the Quarter Days, when their power was at its height.

THE FAIRY HILLS

It is doubtful if there is a parish in Scotland which did not once possess at least one fairy hill, although these are being gradually forgotten; and in addition there was in every region a larger hill where fairies from far and wide foregathered on the eve of the Quarter Days and other high occasions. Among the most famous are Tom-na-hurich in Inverness; the Fairy Hill of Aberfoyle; the Calton Hill, in Edinburgh; and the Eildon Hills, in the Borders, whither Thomas the Rhymer was lured by the Fairy Queen; and if ever our Scottish fairies held a National Mod, the site was surely that Grampian peak, Schiehallion (Gael. *Sidh Chailleann*), the Fairy Hill of the Caledonians.

'The whole site of the Calton,' says Mr Lewis Spence, 'was almost certainly a Druidic centre, and that it was "the hill situated between Edinburgh and Leith" alluded to in Sinclair's *Satan's Invisible World Discovered*, as the site of the legend of the Fairy Boy of Leith, cannot be questioned.'

A certain sea-captain whose ship came in to Leith harbour somewhere about the middle of the seventeenth century tells how his hostess drew attention to a strange youth who drummed on the table, assuring him that the lad was of the tribe of elfin. When spoken to and asked if he was a drummer, the lad admitted that he was 'in the habit of beating all points to a sort of folk' who gathered beneath the Calton Hill every Thursday in a palatial mansion, where they pleasured themselves with dancing and feasting.

Another of the many 'fairy boys' of tradition is the Rannoch herd (Perthshire), whose business it was to make music for the little people; and in Inverness-shire they still tell the tale of the two Strathspey fiddlers who performed the same office for the fairies of Tom-na-hurich.

Tom-na-hurich, the Inverness Mound, which is reputed to have been the chief resort of the fairies in the Northern Highlands, is now one of the most beautiful churchyards in Scotland.

There is an age-old connection between fairy hills and burial mounds. The Rev. Robert Kirk, it will be recalled, stated that the Highlanders 'superstitiously believe the souls of their predecessors to dwell (in the fairy hills)', and he adds, 'for that end, say they, a Mote or Mound was dedicate beside every Churchyard, to receive the souls till their adjacent bodies arise, and so become as a Fairy Hill.'

Andrew Lang, however, points out that 'the tumuli are much older than the churches, which were no doubt built beside them because the place had a sacred character'; and he instances Dalry and Parton, in Kirkcudbrightshire, where 'the grassy knowes are large and symmetrical, and the modern Presbyterian churches occupy old sites; at Parton are the ruins of the ancient Catholic church.'[22]

'About a mile beyond the source of the Forth,' writes Martin Martin, 'above Lochcon, there is a place called Coir-shian or the Cove of the Men of Peace, which is still supposed to be a favourite place of their residence. In the neighbourhood are to be seen many round, conical eminences; particularly one, near the head of the lake, by the skirts of which many are still afraid to pass after sunset.'

In Eigg there is a fairy hill called Cnoc-na-piobaireachd, the Knoll-of-piping. 'In my young days,' says Kenneth Macleod, who was a native of the island, 'and in the days of the ones before me, all the lads of the island used to gather on the beautiful moonlight nights, and, bending an ear to the knoll, it was tunes they would get, and tunes indeed—reels that would make the Merry Dancers themselves go faster, and laments that would draw tears from a corpse.'[23]

Sometimes a man passing by a fairy hill was tempted by the sounds of revelry to find his way inside. He would stay for a night, as he thought, but on returning would find that he had been gone for seven years, and mourned as dead.

The fairies often played tricks on mortals who courted their favours. There is the story of Robin Og (young Robin), for instance, who, passing one night by a *sithean*, or fairy hill, overheard enchanting music, and, flinging his knitted bonnet towards the spot, called, '*Is leat-sa so; is leam-sa sin!*' (This is yours; that's mine!) There fell at his tiny feet a tiny set of bagpipes. He placed them carefully in his pocket; but, when he reached home, all he found was a puff-ball and a crumpled fragment of willow-reed.

Similarly a gift of fairy gold turned proverbially into withered leaves or horse muck.

FAIRY GIFTS

But not all fairy gifts were worthless. In old Highland families there are several treasures of reputed fairy origin. The Black Chanter of Clan Chattan is said to have been given to a gifted Macpherson piper by a fairy woman who loved him; the Macrimmons, hereditary pipers to Macleod of Macleod, cherished the Silver Chanter of the Fairy Woman; and the Mackays have a flag said to have been a fairy gift to one of the clan.

But the most famous of all is the Fairy Flag preserved by Macleod at Dunvegan Castle, in Skye. The story is that the Lady of Macleod, as she sat in the hall, spinning, heard sweet singing issuing from the sleep-chamber of her infant son, and, approaching the spot, was startled to see a little woman in a green kirtle, who was smoothing over the child a silken banner of many colours, and lulling him to sleep.

'God sain us!' exclaimed the lady; and at the sacred name the little woman vanished, leaving behind her the banner and (in the listener's memory) her song.[24] The banner brought victory to the Clan at the battle of Glendale in 1490, and again at Waternish in 1580; and, according to the legend, has the power to bring it once again.

One of the most gifted song-writers of the Hebrides is Mairi Nic Iain Fhin (Mary, daughter of Fair John), who was bardess to MacNeill of Barra in the sixteenth century, and is said to have received her gift of song from her fairy lover.[25] Their trysting-place, close to Castlebay and near the mouth of the burn that flows down to Ledaig, is still pointed out.

THE 'TAKING' OF MORTALS

There are numerous references in song and story to the 'taking' of mortals by the fairies. The most famous abduction is that of Thomas the Rhymer,[26] a thirteenth century poet and seer, who was said to owe his prophetic gifts to his intercourse with the Queen of Elfhame.[27]

> True Thomas lay on Huntlie bank;
>   A ferlie spied he wi' his e'e;
> And there he saw a ladye bricht
>   Come riding doun by the Eildon Tree.
> Her skirt was o' the grass-green silk,
>   Her mantle o' the velvet fyne;
> At ilk tett o' her horses' mane
>   Hung fifty siller bells and nine.
>
> 'Harp and carp, Thomas,' she said;
>   'Harp and carp alang wi' me;
> And if ye daur to kiss my lips,
>   Sure o' your bodie I will be.'
> 'Betide me weel, betide me woe,
>   That weird sall never daunton me.'
> Syne he has kissed her rosy lips,
>   All underneath the Eildon Tree.
>
> She's mounted on her milk-white steed,
>   She's ta'en True Thomas up behind;
> And aye, whene'er her bridle rang,
>   Her steed gaed swifter than the wind.[28]

Through the heart of the Eildon Hills True Thomas was carried to Fairyland,

> And till seven years were come and gane,
>   True Thomas on earth was never seen.

Four hundred years later we have the celebrated case of the Rev. Robert Kirk, who is thought to have been removed because he knew too much. Mr Kirk, Andrew Lang tells us, 'died (if he did die) in 1692 . . . His tomb was inscribed: Robertus Kirk, A.M. Linguae Hiberniae Lumen.

The tomb, in Scott's time, was to be seen in the east end of the churchyard at Aberfoyle; but the ashes of Mr Kirk *are not there*. His successor, the Rev. Dr Grahame, in his *Sketches of Picturesque Scenery*, informs us that, as Mr Kirk was walking on a *dun-shi*, or fairy-hill, in his neighbourhood, he sank down in a swoon that was taken for death. 'After the ceremony of a seeming funeral,' writes Scott, 'the form of the Rev. Robert Kirk appeared to a relation, and commanded him to go to Grahame of Duchray. "Say to Duchray, who is my cousin as well as your own, that I am not dead, but a captive in Fairyland; and only one chance remains for my liberation. When the posthumous child, of which my wife has been delivered since my disappearance, shall be brought to baptism, I will appear in the room, when, if Duchray shall throw over my head the knife or dirk which he holds in his hand, I may be restored to society; but if this is neglected, I am lost for ever." True to his tryst, Mr Kirk did appear at the christening, and "was visibly seen"; but Duchray was so astonished that he did not throw his dirk over the head of the appearance, and to society Mr Kirk has not yet been restored . . . . Neither history nor tradition has anything more to tell about Mr Robert Kirk, who seems to have been a man of good family, a student, and, as his book shows, an innocent and learned person.'[29]

In his lovely poem, *Kilmeny*, the Ettrick Shepherd describes the 'taking' of a Border maiden:

> Bonny Kilmeny gaed up the glen,
> But it wasna to meet Duneira's men.
>
> It was only to hear the yorlin sing,
> And pu' the cress-flower round the spring;
> The scarlet hypp and the hindberrye,
> And the nut that hung frae the hazel-tree;
> For Kilmeny was pure as pure could be.
> But lang may her minny look o'er the wa',
> And lang may she seek i' the greenwood shaw,
> Lang the Laird o' Duneira blame,
> And lang, lang greet or Kilmeny come hame.
>
> In yon green wood there is a walk,
> And in that walk there is a wene,

And in that wene there is a maike
That neither has flesh, blood, nor bane;
And down in yon greenwood he walks his lane.
In that green wene Kilmeny lay,
Her bosom happed wi' flowerets gay;
But the air was soft and the silence deep,
And bonny Kilmeny fell sound asleep.
She kenned nae mair, nor oped her e'e.
Til wak'd by the hymns o' a far countrye.[30]

In Clackmannanshire they tell the story of the Miller of Menstrie, who lost his wife thus and who used to hear her singing (she herself being invisible):

O Alva woods are bonnie,
   Tillicoultrie woods are fair,
But to think o' the bonnie woods o' Menstrie,
   It maks my hert aye sair.

After several vain attempts to win her back, the miller was one day riddling corn at the mill-door when he unconsciously assumed a posture of enchantment, and his wife fell into his arms.

Then there is the story of the blacksmith of Tullibody, whose wife was carried up the chimney as he was busy at work, and who overheard the abductors singing:

Deidle linkum doddie,
We've got drucken Davie's wife,
The smith o' Tullibody!

New-born children were in especial danger, and young mothers would not go out after dark until the christening was over, when the fairy power became ineffective. Iron was placed above the bed; mother and child were given milk from a cow that had eaten the *mothan* (trailing pearlwort); and other protective rites were carried out. Without them, the child might be spirited away, and in its place would be left a puny, peevish changeling, which would slowly dwine away and die.

THE CHANGELING

The belief in changelings is connected with the age-old conception of life and sacrifice, and with the custom of the aboriginal pre-Celtic peoples to kidnap the children of their conquerors as victims and leave the sickly in their place.

'It was common rumour that Elphin Irving came not into the world like other sinful creatures of the earth, but was one of the kain-bairns of the fairies, whilk they had to pay to the enemies of man's salvation every seventh year. The poor lady-mother—a mother's aye a mother be she Elve's flesh or Eve's flesh—hid her elf-son beside the christened flesh in Marion Irving's cradle, and the auld enemy lost his prey for a time . . . . And touching this lad, ye all ken that his mother was a hawk of an uncanny nest, a second cousin of Kate Kimmer of Barfloshan, as rank a witch as ever rode on ragwort.'[31]

The fairy woman appears in many of our Gaelic lullabies. One of the best-known is *An Coineachan* (The Sweet Little One), which is sung by a sorrowing mother whose baby has been 'taken'. She follows the trail of the mountain mist, of the swan on the lake, of the brown otter, but finds no trace of her child.

All over Scotland, the fairy tradition is preserved in legend and song.

THE TROLLS

The elves and trolls (called trows in Orkney and Shetland) of Scandinavian tradition differ considerably from the fairies of the Celtic tradition. The latter are chiefly women, 'wondrously fair, with their long pale faces and flowing hair like red gold;[32]' whilst the dwarfish northern elves are chiefly men, and, in Sir Walter Scott's words, 'spirits of a coarser sort, more laborious vocation, and more malignant temper, and in all respects less propitious to humanity than the fairies . . . (who) were the invention of the Celtic people and displayed that superiority of taste and fancy which, with the love of music and poetry, had been generally ascribed to their race.'[33]

In Shetland, there lingers a tradition of a race called

the 'peerie (little) hill-men', who inhabited the islands before either Pict or Norseman. They are thought to have been akin to the Lapps or 'Yaks' (Esquimaux), and 'from these,' says Mrs Saxby, the Shetland folklorist, 'comes without doubt our tradition of Trows.' Later came the 'Mukle Maisters', the Finns and Picts. The Finns are said to have had magical gifts, including the power to transform themselves into otters and seals. Hence, doubtless, the tradition of the 'Children of Lochlann', the seal-folk of Hebridean folklore.

In Orkney and Shetland, the fairy hours were noon to midnight, when the trows rode through the air on bulrushes. If a trow chanced to be above the grass when the sun rose, he was day-bound, and was obliged to remain upon the earth in sight of man until sunset.

On Midsummer Eve, the trows held high festival.[34] Again, seven days before Yule, they were released from the underworld and throughout the Merry Month of Yule were free to work mischief on those who had neglected to protect themselves with adequate saining rites. Like the fairies, the trows 'took' mortals. On Up-helly-aa, which marked the end of the midwinter festival, they returned to the underworld.

TUTELARY BEINGS

The close association of the fairies with the spirits of the dead is illustrated in the use of the anglicised Gaelic name, banshee (*bean sidh*), which means literally 'fairy woman', but is commonly applied to the spirit of some dead ancestress who has become the guardian spirit of one of the great families. The banshee occupies a middle position between mortals and the fairies: she is, in fact, regarded as a mortal who has been put under enchantment and given a fairy nature. In the Highlands, she is known as the *Glaistig*, or *Glaistig Uaine*, from her wan looks and green garments, or as *Maighdeann Uaine*, the green-clad maiden. Elsewhere in Scotland she is known as the Green Lady.

> Wild fawn, wild fawn,
> Hast seen the Green Lady?
> The bird in the nest,

> And the child at the breast,
> They open wide eyes as she comes down the dawn—
> The bonnie Green Lady,
> Bird and child make a whisper of music at dawn,
> Wild fawn, wild fawn![35]

The Green Lady was always regarded as having been in life a woman of honourable position, usually a former mistress of the house whose precincts she haunted, and she might be seen at dusk, gliding noiselessly through the grounds towards the castle or mansion-house, or wandering through its corridors and rooms, where she could be heard putting things in order.

When any great happiness or any great misfortune was about to befall the family, the event was heralded by her cries of rejoicing or lamentation. Sir Walter Scott writes of 'the fatal Banshi's boding scream'; but 'it was not a scream,' writes J. G. Campbell, the Highland folklorist, 'only a wailing murmur (*torman mulaid*) of unearthly sweetness and melancholy.'

Besides the house-haunting *Glaistig*, there was another kind that lingered about the cattle-fold, sheep-pen and dairy. If the herd fell asleep and neglected his task, she tended the cattle herself, and at night she would keep the calves away from their dams and preserve the substance in the milk. But she expected a *quid pro quo* for her services, and would beat with a small wand those who neglected to propitiate her with a daily offering of milk.[36] (It is probable that the libation was originally made to the earth-powers.)[37]

In Tiree, Skye, and elsewhere, the tutelary spirit of both castle and cattlefold is called the *Gruagach*, and in Skye, *Gruagach* stones, where libations were formerly left, are still pointed out. One of these is at Sleat, formerly the residence of the Lords of the Isles, and the Gruagach attached by tradition to the Castle is said to have been frequently seen in the vicinity of the stone.

At one time few of the great houses of Scotland lacked their tutelary spirits (although many of these properly abandoned their old haunts on the advent of a horde

of industrial and financial magnates of alien extraction).
Amongst the most widely known are Dunstaffnage Castle,
near Oban, a seat of our early kings; Dunolly Castle, the
seat of the Macdougalls, in the same district; Breacacha
Castle, the seat of Maclean of Coll; Ardnacallich, the
seat of MacQuarrie of Ulva (visited by Dr Johnson and
Boswell); the Island House of Tiree; and the seat of
the chiefs of Glengarry, in Strathglass. Hugh Miller tells
of a Green Lady in Banffshire, 'tall and slim and wholly
attired in green, with her face wrapped up in the hood of
her mantle', who haunted the grounds of the castle where
she had once been mistress. Another is associated with
Ardblair, a property given to the Blairs by William the
Lyon.[39] Stonehaven, too, has a Green Lady of its own.[39a]

'Some Green Ladies were so common,' says D. A. Mackenzie, 'that people became quite accustomed to them, remarking, "There she goes again." '

Occasionally the banshee appears as a kind of tutelary
deity of the hills. In Aberdeenshire there are two hills where
travellers used to propitiate the banshee by placing barley
cakes on a well near each hill. If the offering were neglected,
the traveller was in danger of death or dire calamity.[40] These
banshees of the wild were associated with solitary places.
They would wander at dusk through the woods, or by the
banks of some river, or close to some waterfall or ravine, and
lure the traveller to his doom. The domestic banshee, on the
other hand, was benevolent, and inspired little or no fear.

Another form of banshee is the *caoineag*, the weeping
one, who is heard wailing in the darkness on the hillside.
It is said that she was heard on several successive nights before the massacre of Glencoe. 'This roused the suspicions of
the people,' says Dr Carmichael, 'and notwithstanding the
assurance of the peace and friendship of the soldiery, many
of the people left the glen and thus escaped the fate of those
who remained.'[41]

> Little caoineachag of the sorrow
> Is pouring the tears of her eyes,
> Weeping and wailing the fate of Clan Donald,
> Alas, my grief! that he heeded not her cries![42]

Of the same class is the *Bean-nighe*, the Washer at the
Ford, an uncanny being who is sometimes seen at midnight washing with skeleton fingers the shrouds of those
about to die.

> A shadowy shape of cloud and mist, of gloom and dusk,
>   she stands,
>   The Washer at the Ford.[43]

He who comes across her at her task knows that the
shroud she is washing is either his own or that of some one
dear to him. While she washes, she sings a dirge.[44] In one
instance the dirge is spoken of as the *Song of the Macleans*,
from which it seems likely that she sang a dirge appropriate
to the clan of the doomed one. If he is fated to die in battle
or by the sword, the ghostly shroud is stained with blood.

The washing of the shroud may have been an early
purification rite, and must have been part of the regular
funeral rites of those who had been slain in battle.

> Where the winds gather
>   The souls of the dead,
> O Torcall, my father,
>   My soul is led!
>
> For a river is here,
>   And a whirling Sword—
> And a Woman washing
>   By a Ford![45]

There was hardly a district in the Highlands where the
Washer had not her haunt. 'I know of such a haunted burn
in my own native parish,' says J. M. McPherson; and another minister-folklorist writes:

'I knew people who, though not seeing her, heard her
plying her work of "slac, slac", pounding her wash. Once a
man passing such a ford heard the refrain of her song, "'*Si
do leine, 'si do leine ta mi nigheadh*"—"'Tis thy shroud, 'tis
thy shroud that I am washing"—which he told on going
home. Not long afterwards, the same man, crossing by the
stepping-stones at the same place on a dark night lost his
footing, and, being alone, was drowned.'[46]

Associated with the tradition of the Washer of the Ford

is the divination rite, Dipping the Sark Sleeve, performed on Hallowe'en by maidens who desire to see the wraith or fetch of their future husband.

THE SLUAGH

In the Hebrides one still hears tales of the *Sluagh*, or aerial hosts. These are the spirits of mortals who have died. They travel about in the air after fall of night, and particularly about midnight. 'You'd hear them going in fine weather against the wind like a covey of birds,' one man described them. Another said, 'They fly about in great clouds up and down the face of the world like the starlings, and come back to the scenes of their earthly transgressions. No soul of them is without the clouds of earth, dimming the brightness of the works of God, nor can any win Heaven till satisfaction is made for the sins of the earth.'[47]

A minister long resident in North Uist[48] told the present writer the following story:

'One day an old man in North Uist was walking along by the seashore when he was impelled to look up, and what should he see approaching him through the air but a great spirit-host; and in the forefront were shades of men, hawk on wrist and hound straining at the leash, whom by the beauty and nobility of their countenance he knew to be Oscar and Finn and the great heroes of old; and they were moving swiftly westward towards Tir-nan-Og. The old man stood spell-bound until the vision had passed, and even after he reached home, he could not for a time find speech, so overcome was he by the wonder of what he had seen.'

The Sluagh may not be unrelated to a natural phenomenon—a whirlwind that raises dust on the roads and is known in the North-East as 'a furl o' fairies' ween' ' (a whirl of fairies' wind).

'In this climate,' writes J. G. Campbell, 'these eddies are among the most curious of natural phenomena. On calm summer days they go past, whirling about straws and dust, and as not another breath of air is moving at the same time, their cause is sufficiently puzzling. In Gaelic the eddy is known as "the people's puff of wind" (*oiteag sluaigh*) and its motion "travelling on tall grass stems" (*falbh air chuiseagan treòrach*). By throwing one's left shoe at it, the fairies are made to drop whatever they may be taking away—men, women, children or animals. The same result is attained by throwing one's bonnet, saying, "This is yours; that's mine!" (*Is leat-sa so, is leam-sa sin!*) or a naked knife, or earth from a molehill.'[48]

TRACES OF ANIMISM

Besides the fairies, the trolls, the banshees, and the sluagh, there are many supernatural beings in Scottish folklore. Traces of the old animism linger in the tales of the Fomorians (Gael. *Famhairean*), the giants whose seats are certain mountain peaks,[50] and who fling boulders at one another, and the Cailleachan or storm-hags, who together represent the elemental forces of nature, particularly in a destructive aspect; in the names 'Nimble Men' and 'Merry Dancers', given to the darting streamers of the Aurora Borealis; in the legends of river spirits; and in the tradition of the Blue Men of the Minch.

Many a mountain has its Cailleach. The *Cailleach nan Cruachan*, for example, dwelt on the summit of Ben Cruachan. 'When anything ruffles her temper, she gathers a handful of whirlwinds and descends in a tempest, steps across Loch Etive at a stride, lashing it into fury, and prevents all passage at Connel Ferry.'[51]

Many a river, too, has its spirit. 'Glen Cuaich, in Inverness-shire,' writes Professor Watson, 'is—or was till lately—haunted by a being known as Cuachag, the river sprite. The tutelary sprite of Etive is Eiteag; a man of my acquaintance declared that he knew a man who had met her in Glen Salach—after a funeral. . . . In Ross, "*Cailleach na h-abhann*", the river-hag, was dreaded at the fords of the river Orrin.'[52]

'The Blue Men of the Minch' were believed to cause the restlessness of the strait that separates the Shiant Islands from the Island of Lewis. The Blue Men went swimming up and down, trying to sink the boats and ships that passed that way; but they were poets, and spared the lives of those seafarers who could complete the half-verses they shouted to them in order to try their skill.

The 'Blue Men', who are not mermen, are peculiar to Scotland.

THE MERFOLK

The merfolk—almost invariably mermaids—appear chiefly in the traditions of the North-East. Sea-faring men believed that they inhabited the caves along the coasts. Hugh Miller, writing in 1857, speaks of a mermaid well-known to the people of his native Cromarty 'less than fifty years ago'.[53] She was seen by moonlight sitting on a rock in the sea a little to the east of the town. Sir Hugh Reid, writing in 1870, says that 'In the village (in Buchan) there lived a man who had seen and conversed with a mermaid under a great cliff off the Bullers of Buchan'; and 'Some old men,' says another writer,[54] 'remember a mermaid pitching upon the bow-sprit of a small vessel belonging to Peterhead, which was driven among the rocks near Glamis Castle, and all hands perished save the man who bore the tidings to land.'

It is said that a mermaid was once captured on the west coast of Ross-shire by a boat-builder called Roderick Mackenzie. She begged for freedom, which he granted on condition that no one should ever be drowned from any boat he should build. The promise was made and kept. 'It is possible,' says the narrator,[55] 'that some of his boats are still defying the stormy winds and waves of the west coast.'

Galloway, too, had a mermaid, who frequented the shore of the Solway Firth adjoining the mouths of the Nith and the Orr.

The ballad of the Mermaid in *The Minstrelsy of the Scottish Border* (edited by Sir Walter Scott) is founded on the traditional Gaelic tale of MacPhee of Colonsay and the Mermaid of Corryvreckan.

In Shetland, the merfolk are known as sea-trows.

Like the sirens, the mermaids lure men to their destruction.

> A wumman cam' up frae the blae deepths o' the sea,
> And 'I'm Jeannie MacQueen,' she said, lauchin', to me.
> But it's 'Gi way wi' your oyster-shine, lassie, gi way'
> —For she'd a different colour in the nail o' each tae.[56]

This mermaid has discarded her tail, but not her nature.

The mermaid is to be distinguished from the seal-woman, who casts off her skin in the moonlight and assumes human form. There are many tales of marriages between the seal-women and the young fishermen of the islands.

In Orkney and Shetland, the seal-folk are known as selkies.

SPIRITS OF THE FOREST

Chief amongst the spirits of the forest is the Urisk (Gael. *Uruisg*),[57] which is described by Dr Carmichael as 'a monster, half human, half goat, with long hair, long teeth, and long claws', which haunted glen, corries, reedy lakes, and sylvan streams; and by Sir Walter Scott in a note to *The Lady of the Lake*, as 'a figure between a goat and a man; in short, precisely that of a Greek satyr'. His haunts were shunned after nightfall; but although he might be seen at dusk sitting motionless on the top of a rock, gazing at the passer-by, he would rarely molest him. In summer-time he stayed in the high solitudes, but on the approach of winter he would descend to the strath and the farm lands, sometimes taking up his abode in the nearest mill, or paying it nightly visits.

An urisk was said to haunt Ben Doran, on the confines of Argyll and Perthshire, and according to the legend was encountered and banished by St Fillan, who lived in a neighbouring strath. Near Tyndrum there is a waterfall known as *Eas na h-uruisg*, the Urisk's waterfall, the reputed winter headquarters of the Urisk of Ben Doran. Ben Loy, in the same district, also had its Urisk, who came down in winter to the farm lands of Glenorchy. Others were associated with Strath Duisg, near Loch Sloy, at the head of Loch Lomond; the 'Yellow Waterfall' in Glen Maili, Inverness-shire; and the Coolins of Skye. 'Breadalbane,' says Professor Watson, 'was specially noted for its uruisg tribe, chief of whom was *Peallaidh*, whose name is preserved in *Obar Pheallaidh*, anglicised as Aberfeldy . . . . His footprint is to be seen in a rock in Glenlyon, and the wild burn of Inbhir-inneoin, near the foot of the glen, was a favourite haunt of his. A cataract on it is called *Eas Pheallaidh*.'[58] Then on the slopes of Ben Venue, above Ellen's Isle, is the famous *Coire nan Uruisgean*, Corry of the Urisks.

> By many a bard, in Celtic tongue,
> Has Coir-nan-Urisken been sung.

This is said to have been the site of the solemn stated meetings of all the Urisks in Scotland.

In the folklore of Lochlomondside and the Trossachs, which is rich in the traditions of urisks, they are remembered as a distinct race—a kind of wild men of the woods—who made terrible depredations on the peace-loving dwellers in the glen, with ravaging, butchery, and arson; and who yet, when friendly relations were established, were capable of complete loyalty and devoted service to these same people.[59]

'His undulled savage instincts,' writes Miss Eve Blantyre Simpson, 'allowed him to foresee coming events, so he was credited with repaying his patrons by giving timely warning. He worked hard for small reward, for the wage he craved for most was the milk of human kindness. He was easily offended and strong in his likes and dislikes.'[60]

In due course it became the fashion for the great houses to encourage an urisk to attach itself to them. The wife of an urisk was nurse and foster-mother to an infant chief of the Macfarlanes. The Grahams of Morphie, in Angus, have a tradition of an urisk who served an ancestor as a drudge; Maclachlan of Maclachlan, in Strathlachlan, had a faithful attendant called Harry—possibly the 'hairy one'; MacNeill of Taynish had another, and so had the Frazers of Abertarff, with many other Highland houses. The last two remembered in the eastern Highlands were associated with the ancient family of Tullochgorum in Strathspey. They were male and female—probably husband and wife. The male was said to be of a jocose and humorous disposition.

The female, who was known as Mag Mulloch, or Hairy
Meg, owing to a superabundance of hair, was reputed to
be an honest, faithful, and highly competent housewife, but
unpopular with the servants, whose neglect of duty and
other shortcomings she faithfully reported to her mistress.

Another name for the urisk is the *Ciuthach*, anglicised
as kewach. Kenneth Macleod 'distinctly remembers two old
people in Eigg talking about "the *ciuthach* who once lived in
the cave".'

The Bòcan or bogie is also an urisk.

A form of urisk found on the East Coast is the Shelly-coat,
described by Scott as a water-spirit covered with shells and
other marine products, whose clattering announced his approach. A shelly-coat, says D. A. Mackenzie, used to haunt
a rock on the shore of Leith, and the boys used to run three
times round him, singing,

> Shelly-coat, shelly-coat, gang awa hame,
> I cryna your mercy, I fearna your name.

It was said to seize and thresh those who offended it.[61]

THE BROWNIES

There is a considerable affinity between the Urisk and
the Brownie, although they appear to have been entirely
different in origin.

So far from being a spirit of the forest, the brownie
was a friendly, domesticated spirit which frequented the
houses and farm steadings and helped both farmers and
housewives in their tasks. We know that the family cult
of the dead centred on the hearth, and the brownie, like
the *lares* of Roman tradition, appears to have been in origin
a sort of domestic tutelary spirit.

'The brownie, lurking in the daytime in some obscure
recess of the house to which he was attached, came forth
at night to perform any laborious office which might be
beneficial to the master and other inmates of the household.
He was meagre, shaggy, taciturn, and had a genuine love of
his midnight labours. When the inmates of the kitchen sat
too late round the fire, he appeared at the door and warned

them off—"Gang aff to your bed, sirs, and dinna put oot the grieshoch (embers)." '[62]

The Brownie is found chiefly in the Lowlands and the Northern Isles.

'It seems to have made its way into the Highlands only in recent times,' says J. G. Campbell; yet, 'in the Highlands of Perthshire,' says the same authority, 'previous to the '45, each farm or village had its *bodachan sabhaill*, the little old man of the corn, who helped to thresh the corn, made up the straw into bundles, and saw that everything was kept in order.[63] These brownies had the appearance of old men and were very wise. They always worked at night. In character Brownie was harmless, but he made mischief unless every place was left open at night. He was fed with warm milk by the dairy-maid.' If given a present of new clothes, the brownie donned them and disappeared and was never more heard of.[64]

In Orkney, stacks of corn, called Brownie's stacks, were always safe from molestation. A portion of food used to be set apart in the home for Brownie, and a libation of milk poured into a stone, known as Brownie's stone, to secure his favour and protection.

Traditions of this kind are common on the Continent as well as throughout the British Isles, and seem to indicate a social contact between two very different racial types.

A special kind of brownie, known in the South of Scotland as the Kilmoullach, and in the North-East as the Kiln-carle, is associated with millers and inhabits the killogie. He was of savage disposition.

> Kiln-carle teethless,
> Come oot and make me eesless![65]

Millers were anciently reputed to be 'men of skill', possessing occult powers akin to witchcraft, and the Church looked on them askance. The kilmoullach appears to have been regarded as something akin to the miller's familiar spirit. It was he who held the thread thrown into the kiln on Hallowe'en by the maiden who desired to know the name of her future husband.[66]

In later descriptions, the urisk and the brownie are indistinguishable.

SPIRITS IN ANIMAL FORM

Of supernatural creatures appearing in animal form, the chief is the Kelpie, a water-spirit which was usually seen in the form of a young horse scampering along a river bank. When tired of the sport, he would strike the water three times with his tail, so heavily that each splash sounded like a crash of thunder, and would disappear like a flash of fire into a deep pool.

The kelpie had a magic bridle, and wrought its enchantment by looking through the eyelets of the bridle bit; but the white wizard could undo any spell or enchantment by looking through the eyelets in the opposite direction. If by rare luck a kelpie's bridle comes into your possession, 'look through the holes in the bit of the bridle,' says Highland tradition, 'and you will see myriads of invisible agents, fairies, witches and devils all flying round you, the same as if you had been gifted with the second sight, and all their machinations exposed to your observation.'[67]

The kelpie's bridle is conceivably a relic of the belief in Manannan's steed, the horse of the lord of the ocean.[65]

Only one 'kelpie's bridle' is known to be extant, or to have been so a generation ago. This was the trophy of a daring Macgregor of an earlier age, who had a breathless encounter with a kelpie. Seumas or James Macgregor was one evening tramping the long road home from Inverness to Glenlivet, and sat down to rest at the entrance to Loch Slochd. On rising, still footsore, he thought, 'If only I had my good nag to carry me!' Hardly was the wish formulated when, to his amazement, there stood the familiar beast, bridled and saddled and all. Macgregor mounted him, and they cantered along the lochside in the gathering dusk. Suddenly the horse made to leave the bridle-path in the direction of the loch. In a flash, Macgregor realised that this was not his horse, or any horse at all, but the dreaded kelpie, and calling aloud he invoked the Holy Trinity. At the sound of the sacred name, the kelpie reared violently; horse and rider parted company; and the kelpie plunged into the loch.

When Macgregor came to himself, he was lying between the bridle-path and the loch, with the kelpie's bridle firm in his grasp.

For many generations Macgregor's descendants wrought 'white magic' with the trophy. In the mid-nineteenth century the bridle was in the possession of one Gregor Willox Macgregor, commonly known as Warlock Willie, who lived at Gaulrig, in Strathavon (Banffshire). Willox had also in his possession a healing-stone known as *Clach Ghrigair*, the Macgregor stone, which is said to have ornamented, in earlier times, the battle standard of Clan Gregor. With bridle and stone he made occasional tours of the northern counties, and returned, says Col. Grant Stewart, who knew him personally, 'with the double satisfaction of thinking that while, in the course of his rambles, he had conferred the greatest benefit on suffering humanity, he had at the same time a good deal improved his own pecuniary resources.' Times, however, were changing, and 'Mr Willox is convinced more and more . . . of the truth of the proverb, "A prophet has no honour in his own country." ' Still, he adds, 'It is no rare matter for the inhabitants of both sides of the Avon to fall in with the unfortunate pilgrims inquiring the way to *Taigh Maishter Willox*.[68] His clients included barren women and farmers with ailing cattle, who came from centres as distant as Aberdeen and Inverness.'[69]

Loch nan Dubhrachan, in Skye, is the traditional haunt of a kelpie. Two or three old 'kelpie' tunes have survived on the island and are sung as lullabies. One of these—*Cumha an Eachuisge*—the Lament of the Water-Horse—is based on the legend of a kelpie who assumed human guise and married an island girl, the brown-haired Morag. One day, catching a glimpse of the sand on his breast, she divined the truth, and fled in horror from him and their child. The disconsolate kelpie sings a lullaby to the forsaken babe in the hope of inducing Morag to return.[70]

Loch Treig, in Lochaber, was noted for its water-horses or demon steeds.

A tale of the water-horse once popular in Balquidder is told by Mrs Johnston, a contemporary and friend of Sir Walter Scott.

'A number of little boys had gone to bathe and sport about a dark loch in the wild rugged glen. A beautiful milk-white horse came from the loch, so gentle that it stretched itself out, and pawed, and allured some of the more adventurous to mount its back. Another and another mounted, and the animal still stretched itself to receive its victims, till all were in its power, when it suddenly plunged into the loch, which swallowed up water-spirit and its riders.'

In a foot-note she adds, 'A dark loch on the top of a mountain adjoining Glenogle, that savage and gloomy valley through which a high road between Lochearnhead and Glendochart is carried, was the abode of the kelpie. Some children were certainly drowned there, and Highland superstition allows none of its votaries to perish ingloriously.'[71]

A pool in the North Esk, in Angus, was another haunt of the kelpie. It was possibly this tradition that inspired Violet Jacob's poem, *The Kelpie* (for the poet belongs to an old Angus family), of which two verses run:

> I'm feart o' the road ayont the glen,
>   I'm sweir to pass the place
> Whaur the water's rinnin, for a' fouk ken
> There's a kelpie sits at the fit o' the den,
>   And there's them that's seen his face.
>
> But whiles he watches and whiles he hides,
>   And whiles, gin nae wind manes,
> Ye can hear him splashin' agin the sides
>   O' the rocks and the muckle stanes.[72]

The kelpie is a Caledonian spirit, and is probably of animistic origin. It has been described as 'the personification of the sudden blast of wind or of whirlwind which sweeps over the surface of the lakes and pools . . . . of the Highlands. The latter strikes the water suddenly, leaves behind a ripple like the wake of a living creature swimming beneath the surface, and then, halting for a moment, raises, a few inches above the surface, a dark crest of little waves which bear a remote resemblance to the back and mane of such a creature. But here the Water-horse is the whirlwind charged with the spindrift, which it raises and whirls into its folds as it sweeps over sea-loch and fresh-water lake. When the whirlwind thus charged collapses in its after career over the land, and discharges the water it held in suspense, it leaves behind it no trace of its former existence except, it may be, a pool of water in the place where it vanishes. The collapsed Whirlpool or Waterspout is the dead Water-Horse.'[73]

Some, however, would identify the kelpie with the traditional loch monsters of the Highlands.

Supernatural cattle are also recorded. In Sir Walter Scott's time, belief in the water-bull was still common. One had its lair at Lochawe and another at Loch Rannoch. It was said that they could be killed only with silver shot. Others were associated with the lochs of Llundavra and Achtriachan in Glencoe. St Mary's Loch, in Yarrow, was the haunt of a water-cow of which the Ettrick Shepherd writes:

'A farmer in the neighbourhood got a breed of her that multiplied and throve well until the farmer somehow outraged or offended her; whereupon one fine night the old dam came out of the loch and gave such a roar that the surrounding hills shook again, upon which her progeny, nineteen in number, followed her quietly into the water and were never seen again.'

As late as 1884, rumours were current in Ross-shire that the water-cow had been seen in a loch in the parish of Gairloch.

In Skye there lingers the tradition of the *Gobar Bachach*, the Lame Goat, which wandered over the countryside and invariably lay down in the richest pastures. She was always in milk, and could yield enough to supply a large force of warriors. Her name is given to the last sheaf cut each year in the harvest fields of the island.

THE FAIRY FAITH TO-DAY
It is evident that all the denizens of our Scottish fairy world derive either from the old animism, or from the play of fancy on natural phenomena, or from the belief in ghosts, and that in the course of time 'the fairies' became identified with the primitive folk who inhabited these islands before the coming of the Celtic invaders.

'Bred in a philosophy which strips nature of personality and reduces it to the unknown cause of an orderly series of impressions on our senses,' writes Sir James Frazer, 'we find it hard to put ourselves in the place of the savage, to whom the same impressions appear in the guise of spirits or the handiwork of spirits. For ages the army of spirits, once so near, has been receding farther and farther from us, banished by the magic wand of science from hearth and home, from ruined cell and ivied tower, from haunted glade and lonely mere, from the riven murky cloud that belches forth the lightning, and from those fairer clouds that pillow the silver moon or fret with flakes of burning red the golden eve . . . . Only in poet's dreams or impassioned flights of oratory is it given to catch a glimpse of the last flutter of the standards of the retreating hosts, to hear the beat of their invisible wings, the sound of their mocking laughter, or the swell of angel music dying away in the distance.'[74]

A glimpse of that last flutter of the standards is vouchsafed by one of our contemporary Scottish writers:

'So bred in the bone is a certain kind of belief that the mind, though it reject, can rarely extirpate it. Once, on a stretch of moorland by a rushy pool, I saw a flickering, faint-blue light dancing in the darkness low above the ground. I thought it a will-o'-the-wisp and set out to chase it. But then I heard a little tumbling tune of four or five notes, many times repeated, and the slow-stepping light was dancing in time with them. I had a couple of dogs with me, an Irish setter and a casually bred Irish terrier. They also heard the tune, and stopped, and softly whimpered. The hair on their necks began to bristle, their tails went down, they turned and fled. I was not so much frightened as overcome by a feeling of impropriety, of indecent intrusion, and half a minute later I too retreated. From a hundred yards away I could still hear the tune, very small, but clear as a voice carried over water on a calm evening.

'Do I believe this story? It is perfectly true, and yet I reject the hypothesis that would, in a way, explain it. I am . . . content to be illogical.'[75]

Let us leave it at that.

EIGHT

The Witches

When the grey owl has three times hooed,
  When the grimy cat has three times mewed,
When the tod has yowled three times i' the wud
  At the reid mune cowrin' ahint the clud,
When the stars has cruppen deep i' the drift,
  Lest cantrips pyke them oot o' the lift,
    Up horses a', but mair adowe!
    Ride, ride to Lochar-brig-knowe![1]

Fragment of a reputed witches' rallying song
  from Cromek's *Remains of Nithsdale and Galloway Song*.

Previous to the passing of the statute of 1563 by the Scottish Parliament, there are few references to witchcraft in our records, but from that date on into the eighteenth century, the Mosaic enactment, 'Thou shalt not suffer a witch to live!', was part of the Common Law of Scotland. The last execution was at Dornoch in 1722, and nearly a generation later we find a Scots legal writer treating the subject quite solemnly, even to laying down principles of evidence. After that, the Scots lawyers of the Age of Reason laughed witchcraft out of court. They could not, however, laugh it out of popular belief, as the works of Burns and Hogg testify. It was not until the dawn of the nineteenth century that the fear of witches and warlocks perceptibly lost its hold in the countryside; but it lingered on in the remoter parts of the country, and is, in fact, not yet entirely extinct.[2] (The present writer, as a child in Orkney, was in terror of any strange old woman she encountered lest she should be a witch.)

It is now generally recognised that the hatred and terror the witches inspired derived less from their actual deeds than from the credulity of the commentators of the period, who believed implicitly that the unfortunate creatures who were tortured and hanged or burnt at the stake were endowed by the Devil with supernatural powers which they used for evil purposes. But we live in a scientific age, and the modern anthropologist takes a very different view from that of the medieval theologian. In recent years, a dispassionate investigation of the copious records of the witch-trials all over Europe has revealed the witch-cult as a debased survival of an indigenous European form of nature-worship of great antiquity.

The early monkish historians assume that the British Isles were completely Christianised in the fifth and sixth centuries. It is obvious, however, that the conversion (in any real sense) of a people from their immemorial beliefs to an exotic faith imposed upon them by their rulers is a matter not of years, but of centuries, or even millennia. Thus, long after the pagan world had become nominally Christian, the masses everywhere continued to practise the old rites either openly or surreptitiously, and it was not until the thirteenth century that the Church found itself in a sufficiently strong position to declare open war upon paganism in Europe. In 1484, Pope Innocent VIII issued his famous decree against witches, and during the next two centuries the witch-persecution mania raged throughout Christendom, Catholic and Protestant being united on at least this particular issue. The persecutions began relatively late in Scotland and lingered there relatively long.

It is improbable that witchcraft as practised in Scotland derived directly from Druidism. More likely it was a debased form of that still older Iberian magic which Druidism superseded but did not entirely suppress. The organised witch-cult of the Middle Ages we may assume to have been imported from the Continent. The Earl of Gowrie and Sir Robert Gordon of Gordonstoun were two prominent Scots who were reputed to have studied 'the black art' in Padua and Salamanca, and Michael Scot ('The Wizard') may have also belonged to this school.[3]

Although the medieval witch-cult of Western Europe derived from a primitive, non-selfconscious nature-religion, with sophistication it had become corrupt (as had paganism in ancient Greece) and developed into a pathological cult in which the doctrine and rites of the Christian Church were deliberately parodied, and evil instincts and desires were sanctioned and encouraged. For this development, the attitude of the Church was at least in some measure responsible.

'Theological opinion could not altogether deny the reality behind the beliefs which it reproved, but it did its best to divert the thoughts of the faithful from them. The tragedy of later theology was that by reversing this attitude and by formulating the evil which it wished to extirpate, it became the accomplice of evil and was fascinated by the thing it persecuted.'[4]

It is noteworthy that many of the most enlightened minds in Europe shared the popular view of witchcraft and the general eagerness to stamp it out. Sir George Mackenzie of Rosehaugh, who did his utmost to keep the zeal of the Scottish witch-hunters within bounds, is described by Sir Walter Scott as a man 'who, not doubting the existence of the crime, was of the opinion that on account of its very horror, it required the clearest and most strict probation'. There were many others who shared his solicitude, and saw to it that slanderers were punished by exposure in 'the jougs' or pillory, together with a fine.

Today, most of us who think about witchcraft at all dismiss it as an outworn superstition; but in spite of Miss Margaret Murray's skilful—perhaps too skilful—rationalisation of the phenomena, there are still those who believe that behind the practice of the witches there was some sinister power which science cannot explain. Writing from the Roman Catholic standpoint, Dr Montague Summers maintains that witchcraft, so far from being a primitive belief with pre-agricultural rites, has at its core and kernel commerce between evil spirits and human beings.

Between these two extremes is the view expressed by Dr Evans Wentz: 'Witchcraft in the West, in probably a majority of cases, is a mere fabric of absurd superstitions and practices—as it is shown to be by the evidence brought out in so many of the horrible legal and ecclesiastical processes conducted against helpless and eccentric old people, and other men and women, including the young, often for the sake of private revenge, and generally on no better foundation than hearsay and false accusation.[5] In the remaining instances it undoubtedly arose, as ancient witchcraft (black magic) seems to have arisen, through the infiltration of occult knowledge into uneducated and often criminally inclined minds, so that what had formerly been secretly guarded among the learned, and generally for legitimate ends, degenerated in the hands of the unfit into black magic.'

THE HORNED GOD
The medieval witch-cult was, briefly, a survival of the worship of the Horned God, the god of fertility, the generative principle in nature. One of its main tenets was the belief, common to many ancient religions, that the god, the creator or giver of fertility, was incarnate in a human being or an animal—a belief which involved strange, and, to civilised notions, repulsive rites. Quite naturally the Church, both before and after the Reformation, condemned it as devil-worship; and indeed there is some excuse for the belief that at its celebrations

> There sat Auld Nick in shape o' beast.
> A towsy tyke, black, grim, and lairge.[6]

Auld Nick, otherwise Auld Clootie or (more reminiscent of his origin) Auld Hornie, was merely the rude Doric equivalent of the Egyptian Amen, the Cretan Minotaur, the Celtic Cernunnos and the Greek god Pan.[7]

It is a commonplace of anthropology that whenever a new religion is established, the god or gods of the old religion become the devil or devils of the new. Thus every non-Christian god was regarded as the enemy of the Christian God, or, in other words, as the Devil; and as Miss Murray points out, it was not until the rise of Christianity, with its fundamental doctrine that a non-Christian deity was a devil, that the cult of the Horned God fell into disrepute.[8]

It is not hard to understand why to the uneducated masses (though the worshippers were by no means all uneducated) a god whom they knew and worshipped in person, who lent a flesh-and-blood ear to their prayers and could be relied upon to make a direct and practical response, should be a more satisfying object of worship than the God of the Christians—an incorporeal Being who lived in a Heaven remote from men, and whose followers regarded as sin what was to them sheer joy of living. It is this warm, human element in their relationship that explains the devotion of the witches to their god and their readiness to die for their faith.

SACRIFICE

The most impressive rite in early times was 'the sacrifice of the god', which took place at intervals of seven or nine years. As in other pagan cults, the creature—man or beast—in whom the god was incarnate was sacrificed for the benefit of his people. At the time of the witch-trials, animal sacrifice was the rule.[9] In France, a goat was offered; in Scotland, usually a dog, a cat, or a fowl. In 1608, the Longniddry coven (near Edinburgh) christened a cat at the 'irne zet' (gate) of Seatoun, and 'thairafter cam all bak again to the Deane-fute, quhair (where) first thai convenit, and cuist (cast) ane Kat to the Devill.'[10] Usually, however, the sacrifice was done privately and without ceremony by an individual witch.

The object of the sacrifice was to propitiate the (non-incarnate) god, that he might incline a favourable ear to the petitions of his worshippers.

An allusion to the seven-year cycle and the human sacrifice that prevailed among the primitive population of Scotland is found in the ballad of Thomas the Rhymer (Thornton MS.). The Queen of Elfhame insists that Thomas must return immediately to earth, for

> To-morne of helle the foulle fende
> Amang this folk will feche his fee,
> And thou art mekill man and hende—
> I trow full wele he wolde chose thee.[11]

Again, in the ballad of Tamlane:

And never would I tire, Janet,
   In fairyland to dwell,
But aye at every seven years
   They pay the teind to hell,
And though the Queen maks muckle o' me,
   I fear 'twill be mysel.[12]

ORGANISATION

The organisation of the witch-cult has been aptly described as a sort of congregationalism. There was a 'minister'—the 'devil' or his substitute, the 'officer'—and a body of 'elders'— the coven.

The coven consisted of twelve 'witches' (chiefly women) and the 'devil' or 'officer' who managed the local affairs of the cult. Each coven had its Ring-Leader (leader of the ring dance), its Piper and its Maiden, the last two being peculiar to Scotland.

'We do no great matter without our Maiden,' said Isobel Goudie of the Auldearn coven at her trial in 1662; 'Quhan we are at meat or in any vther place quhateuir, the Maiden of the Coven sits ablow the rest, nixt the divell.'

All the covens in a district were under the authority of a Grand-master or King Deil, the Horned God incarnate. (The witches had come to adopt the phraseology of the Christians.)

The first appearance of the 'devil' in the Scottish records is in 1567, at the trial of Bessie Dunlop of Lyne in Ayrshire. Bessie speaks of her 'devil' simply as 'Thom Reid', and describes him as 'ane honest wele elderlie man, gray bairded', who wore ordinary clothes and carried 'ane quhyte (white) wand' in his hand. Bessie Henderson, of Crook of Devon in Kinross-shire, said the Devil appeared to her in the likeness of 'ane bonnie young lad, with ane blue bonnet'; and Margaret Huggen, of the same coven, describes hers as 'an uncouth man with black cloathes and ane hood on his heid'. His last recorded appearance is at Thurso in 1719, when Margaret Nin-Gilbert[13] met with him in the likeness of a man and confessed that she 'knew him to be the devil or (ere) he parted with her'.

Although ordinarily the 'devil' appears to have been

indistinguishable from an elder of the kirk, he could be imposing and forbidding enough in his ritual attire, which included either an animal's skin, or a mask in the form of an animal's head. Barbara Napier, giving evidence at the trial of the North Berwick witches in 1590, tells how the 'devil' would 'start up in the pulpit, like a mickle black man, with ane black beard sticking out like ane goat's beard, clad in ane black tatie (tattered) gown and ane ewill favoured scull cap on his heid; having ane black buik in his hand'; whilst her fellow-witch, Agnes Sampson, describes him even more dramatically: 'His face was terrible, his nose lyk the bek of an egle, gret bourning eyn; his handis and legis were herry, with clawis upon his handis, and feit lyk the griffon.'[14]

This super-devil turns out to have been none other than Francis, Earl of Bothwell, nephew and heir of Mary Stuart's third husband. We shall hear more of him presently.

ADMISSION RITES

Free consent was necessary for admission to membership of the witch cult. The rites included the formal renunciation of the Christian faith, the baptism, the kiss (*osculum infame*), and the marking. The marking was obviously some form of tattooing, the 'devil' biting or nipping some spot, usually on either the shoulder or the hand, until the blood came, in such a way that when the wound healed, the mark, variously red or blue, became indelible. (The witch hunters invariably searched for the 'devil's mark'.) Then followed the profession of faith and the vow of fidelity.

Isobel Goudie, of the Auldearne (Moray) coven, giving evidence in 1662, deponed:—

'I denied my baptism, and did put the one of my handis to the crowne of my head and the vther to the sole of my fute, and then renuncit all betwixt my two hands to the Divell.'

In Shetland the rite by which a woman might become a witch was even more dramatic:—

'When it is full moon and midnight, the aspirant after unhallowed power goes alone to the seashore and lies down upon the beach *below the flood-tide mark*. She then puts her left hand under the soles of her feet and the right hand on the top of her head and repeats three times, 'The muckel maister Deil tak what's atween dis twa hands!' The devil then appears and clinches the bargain with a shaking of hands. When this is done, there is no retracting. The woman is his slave and he gives her power on land and sea.'[15]

THE COVEN

The ordinary meetings of the coven were held weekly or at short irregular intervals. There was no fixed site. The kirk or kirk-yard was a favourite meeting-place. It is noteworthy that many churches stand on sites where the Celtic monks planted their first 'cells', and which had been still earlier associated with Druidical worship. The old kirkyard of Auldearn, for example, was the site of a Druidical circle before it became a place of Christian burial, and, like the kirkyards at Nairn, Forfar, North Berwick, and elsewhere, housed notable gatherings of witches. Besides the meetings at the parish church, 'in the holfe thairof', the Forfar witches, giving evidence in 1661, mention others on the Insch (island) within the Loch of Forfar; at Petterden, midway between Forfar and Dundee; at 'the Mury-knowes'; and 'near Kerymure (Kirriemuir: Barrie's Thrums). The Aberdeen covens met on St Katherine's Hill; those of Banffshire on the Binhill; those of Deeside between the hill of Craigleuch and Lumphanan; and those of Forres at the Knock of Alves. In the opinion of Mr Brodie Innes, an authority on Scottish witchcraft, it was very probably on the southern slope of this hill, where a little stone circle still stands, that the Forres witches met Macbeth.

There is evidence of a good deal of conviviality at the meetings of the coven. Alison Pierson (Fife, 1588), mentions 'wyne punchounis with tassis (cups) with them' at a gathering in Lothian. Helen Guthrie, at her trial in 1661, related that at a meeting in the kirkyard at Forfar, 'they danced togither, and the ground under them was all fyre flauchter, and Andro Watson . . . . made great merriment by singing his old ballads, and that Isobel Shirrie did sing her song called Tinkletum Tankletum; and that the divell kist every one of the women.' On another occasion Elspet

Bruce, of the same coven, 'gave the divell ane goose in her ane house, and he dated (doted on) her more than them all because she was ane prettie woman'.

The witches commonly carried fir candles at their gatherings. We read how the Strathdon witches went to Pol-nain and there 'went steering themselves to and fro in their riddles, by means of their oars, the brooms, hallooing and skirling worse than the bogles, and each holding in her left hand a torch of fir'.[16]

FAMILIARS

It was customary for the 'devil' to appoint to the witch, on her admission, some species of animal by which she should divine. This was done by observing the direction, pace, and movements of the animal, and the sounds it emitted. Any animal of the species sufficed. The familiar was the link between the witch and the devil, and was often identified with the latter.

Agnes Sampson, 'the Wise Wife of Keith', who was tried in 1590, had a dog called Elva; Alexander Hamilton, in Lothian, had a crow, a cat, and a dog as his divining familiars; a certain Shetland witch had a corbie (the raven was the device on Odin's shield and on the ensign of the Vikings, by whom this bird was held sacred); and as late as 1719 Margaret Nin-Gilbert of Thurso divined by a black horse, a black hen, and a black cloud.[17]

Quite distinct from the divining familiar is the domestic familiar. We have it on the authority of Forbes, a distinguished Scottish lawyer, that 'To some (the Devil) gives certain Spirits or Imps to correspond with, and serve them as their familiars known to them by some off Name, to which they answer when called.[18] These Imps are said to be kept in Pots or other Vessels.' There is, however, no mention of the domestic familiar in the Scottish trials, although it appears frequently in those of the English witches.

THE BROOM

The witch's broom was used by members of the coven as a mode of conveyance to the Sabbaths, and appears in the processional dance. At Aberdeen, for instance, on Rood

Day (Beltane Eve) 1597, the witches foregathered on St Katherine's Hill, 'and there, under the conduct of Satan present with you, playing before you after his form, ye all danced a devilish dance, riding on trees, a long space.'

The original broom, whether for domestic or magical purposes, was a stalk of the broom plant with a tuft of leaves at the end, and this was succeeded by a besom of birch, thorn, twigs, or heather. Besides these, the witches used stalks of ragwort, hemp, bean, or any hollow stalk.

The belief in the power of the witches to fly through the air is ancient and universal, but the number of cases vouched for is disappointingly small and the evidence disappointingly inadequate. In the earlier records, the methods of locomotion described are normal, but in the seventeenth century they become highly coloured. Isobel Goudie (Auldearn) says, 'I had a little horse, and vold say, "Horse and Hattock in the Divellis name!" And then ve vold flie away, quhair (where) ve vold'; and again, 'Quhan (when) ve vold ryd, ve tak windlestrawes, or been-stakes (bean-stalks) and put them betwixt our foot, and say thryse,

> Horse and Hattock, horse and goe,
> Horse and Pellatis, Ho! Ho!

and immediately ve flie away.'

Miss Murray maintains that the riding was ritual, and that far from speeding through the air, the witches merely ambled on the ground. Balzac has another theory:

'The mysteries of the witches' Sabbath, so wonderfully painted in the sixteenth century, are no mysteries for us. The Egyptian ancestors of that mysterious people of Indian origin, the gypsies of the present day, simply used to drug their clients with haschish, a practice that fully accounts for broomstick rides and flights up the chimney . . . and all the fantastic tales of devil-worship.'[19]

TRANSFORMATION INTO ANIMALS
There are numerous references in the trials to the transformation of the witches into cats and hares, and occasionally into dogs, crows and other animals. In the accusation

against Bessie Thom (Aberdeen, 1596–7), for instance, the dittay states that 'there, accompanied with thy devilish companions and faction, transformed in other likeness, some in hares, some in cats, some in other similitudes, ye all danced about the Fish Cross'; and again, Marie Lamont (Inverkip, 1662) tells us that 'the devil turned them into likeness of kats, by shaking his hands above their heads'.

These transformations were, of course, merely ritual.

'They were apparently an attempt,' says Miss Murray, 'to become one with their god or sacred animal by taking on his form.' The nearest approach to an outward change was the wearing of either the skin of an animal or an animal mask. The witches themselves admitted that they were masked, and this is corroborated by the witnesses.

Some of the incantations used to effect the transformations were given by Isobel Goudie at the Auldearn trials:

> I sall gae intil a haire,
> Wi' sorrow and sych and meikle care;
> And I sall gae in the Devillis name,
> Ay quhill I com hom againe.

Reverse

> Haire, haire, God send thee caire,
> I am in ane hairis likeness just now,
> Bot I sall be in a womanis liknes evin now.

Again

> I sall gae intil a catt,
> Wi' sorrow and sych and a blak shat;
> And I sall gae in the Devillis name,
> Ay quhill I com hom againe.

And again

> I sall gae intil a craw,
> Wi' sorrow and sych and a blak thraw, etc.[20]

THE CAULDRON

The Witches' Cauldron, which figures so prominently in

Macbeth, is seldom mentioned in the trials, but the pot with its magical ingredients appears to have been boiled in the presence of the 'devil' and his coven to the accompaniment of incantations, and when ready the contents were distributed to the votaries for use in their cantrips.[21]

Two specimens of the cantrip, rhyme, witch spell, or incantation used at such a ceremony have been preserved in the Galloway tradition. Both are for love potions—one for a man and the other for a woman.

I.

In the pingle or the pan,
Or the haurnpan o' man,
Boil the heart's-bluid o' the tade,
Wi' the tallow o' the gled;
Hawcket kail and hen dirt,
Chow'd cheese and chicken-wort;
Yallow puddocks champit sma',
Spiders ten and gellocks twa;
Sclaters twall, frae foggy dykes,
Bumbees twunty, frae their bykes;
Asks frae skinklin' lochans blue,
Ay, will mak' a better stue:

Bachelors maun hae a charm,
Hearts they hae fu' o' harm:
Ay the aulder, ay the caulder,
Ay the caulder, ay the baulder,
Taps sna' white, and tails green,
Snappin' maidens o' fifteen;
Mingle, mingle, in the pingle,
Join the cantrip wi' the jingle;
Now we see and now we see,
Plots o' paachin' ane, twa, three.[22]

II.

Yirbs for the blinkin quean,
Seeth now whan it's e'en;
Boortree branches, yellow gowans,
Berry rasps and berry rowans;
Deil's milk frae thrissles saft,
Clover blades frae aff the craft;
Binwud leaves and blinmen's baws
Heather bells, and wither'd haws;

> Something sweet and something sour,
> Time about wi' mild and dour;
> Hinnie-suckles, bluidy fingers,
> Napple roots and nettle stingers;
> Bags o' bees and gall in bladders,
> Gowk's spittles, pizion adders;
> May dew and fumart's tears,
> Nool shearings, nowt's neers,
> Mix, mix, six and six,
> And the auld maid's cantrip fix.[23]

Sometimes the cauldron was overturned and the steaming liquid spilled on the ground, the object being to raise fog by sympathetic magic. The cauldron was also used to prepare food for the Sabbaths, everyone present helping himself out of the pot with his horn spoon.

THE WITCH CAKE

Sometimes, instead of the boiling of the cauldron, a witch cake was baked at the meetings of the coven.

> I saw yestreen, I saw yestreen,
> Little wis ye what I saw yestreen:
> The black cat pyked out the grey ane's een
> At the hip o' the hemlock howe yestreen.

> Wi' her tail i' her teeth she whomel'd roun',
> Wi' her tail i' her teeth she whomel'd roun',
> Till a braw star drapt frae the lift abune,
> And she keppit it ere it wan to the grun'.

> She hynt them a' in her mou' and chowed,
> She hynt them a' in her mou' and chowed,
> She drabbled them owre wi' a black tade's blude,
> And baked a bannock—and ca'd it gude.

> She haurned it weel wi' ae blink o' the mune,
> She haurned it weel wi' ae blink o' the mune,
> And withershins thrice she whorled it roun':
> 'There's some sall skirl ere ye be dune!'

> Some lass maun gae wi' a kilted sark,
> Some priest maun preach in a thackless kirk;
> Threid maun be spun for a deid man's sark;
> A' maun be dune ere the sang o' the lark.

Tellna what ye saw yestreen,
Tellna what ye saw yestreen,
There's yin may gaur thee sick and graen
For tellin' what ye saw yestreen.[24]

THE GARTER

The garter, especially a woman's, was long believed to
have magical properties. At weddings, the bride's garters
were unknotted, thrown, and fought for by the guests. The
loosening of the knots (which occurred also at births), was
due, Frazer tells us, to the belief that the witches' knots,
on the principle of homeopathic magic, tied up the bride
and prevented the consummation of the marriage. Similarly they tied up the expectant mother and prevented an easy
birth. Among the witches, the lace or string or garter was
the badge of rank.[25] Although usually worn on the knee,
it was used sometimes as a 'point' or placed in the cap.
In Shetland, the story is told of an eagle in Scalloway
who seized a cock and flew up with it, 'which one of
those enchanters seeing, presently took a string (his garter
as was supposed) and casting some knots thereupon with
the using the ordinary words, the eagle did let fall the cock
into the sea.'

The witches who were in the habit of selling favourable
winds to sailors gave them a knotted string to be used with
the proper incantations. The more knots loosened, the
stronger blew the wind. To raise a tempest, the witch beat
on a wet rag with a piece of timber, saying three times:

> I knot this ragg upon this stane,
> To raise the wind in the Devillis name;
> It sall not lye till I please againe.

Reverse

> We lay the wind in the Devillis name;
> It sall not ryse quhill we lyk to raise it againe.

Sir Walter Scott, on his visit to Orkney and Shetland in
1814, visited a notorious 'witch' at Stromness, who was in
the habit of selling favourable winds to sailors. He describes

her in a note to *The Pirate*:

'He was a venturesome master of a vessel who left the roadstead of Stromness without paying his offering to propitiate Bessie Miller . . . Her fee was extremely moderate, being exactly sixpence, for which, as she explained herself, she boiled her kettle and gave the bark the advantage of her prayers, for she disclaimed all unlawful arts. The wind thus petitioned for was sure, she said, to arrive, though sometimes the mariners had to wait for some time for it . . . She herself was, she told us, nearly one hundred years old, withered and dried up like a mummy. A clay-coloured handkerchief, folded round her head, corresponded in colour to her corpse-like complexion. Two light-blue eyes that gleamed with a lustre like that of insanity, an utterance of astonishing rapidity, a nose and chin that almost met together, and a ghastly expression of cunning, gave her the effect of Hecaté.'

THE SABBATHS

Four times a year the witches held a festival known as a Sabbath. The dates were those of the ancient Quarter Days—the eves of Candlemas, Beltane (known in Germany as Walpurgis night),[26] Lammas, and Hallowmas; the hours, between sunset and cockcrow; the site, some lonely spot on moor or seashore, or beside some hallowed tree or stone, or in an ancient kirkyard.[27]

The main feature of the festival was a religious or magical ceremony in which the leading figure was the 'Devil' or 'King Deil' of the district in the disguise of a horned animal.

The proceedings opened with an act of homage to the 'Devil', or god incarnate, on the part of the worshippers, who renewed their vows of fidelity and obedience, and kissed him on any part of his person he chose to indicate.[28] Sometimes, too, he turned a certain number of times widdershins. Reports of magic accomplished either by individuals or by covens were then made and recorded in a book (by which means a store of well-tried spells and prescriptions were gradually acquired);[29] and with the admissions to the society and the marriages of members the business part of the proceedings ended. There followed the religious service, which in Catholic countries was comparable with Mass, but which in Scotland, as in Sweden, followed the rites of the Reformed Church. The most detailed accounts come from France, and show a devotion equal to that of any Christian Church, the worshippers bowing their heads or lying prostrate, united in prayer to their god.

The religious service was followed by the obscene fertility rites.

'The sexual ritual,' says Miss Murray, 'has been given an overwhelming and quite unwarranted importance in the trials, for it became an obsession with the Christian judges and recorders to investigate the smallest and most minute details of the rite. Though in late times the ceremony had possibly degenerated into a Bacchanalian orgy, there is evidence to prove that, like the same rite in other countries, it was originally a ceremonial magic to ensure fertility.'

In the dittay against Jonet Lucas (Aberdeen, 1597) the last count was, 'the deuill your master, beand in the liknes of ane beast had carnall (deall) with ilk ane of yow'.

The dancing and feasting that ended the proceedings lasted until dawn, the crowing of the cock being the signal for dispersal.

THE DANCES

The dances, which were an important part of the fertility rites, were based on imitative magic. The jumping dance was for the growth of the crops, and the so-called 'obscene' dance for fertility in the domestic animals, when the dancers were disguised as animals, or in human beings when undisguised. The two principal forms are the processional or follow-my-leader dance and the ring dance.[30] The processional dance was most frequently used to bring the dancers to the consecrated ground where the round dance or 'Ring' was to be performed. The Ring usually moved to the left, but where, as in France, the dancers faced outwards, the movement was widdershins, against the sun.

The religious origin of the processional dance is emphasised by the fact that it was often danced in the churchyard. It is recorded that in 1282 the priest of Inverkeithing 'led the ring' in his own churchyard. In 1590 the North Berwick witches 'dancit endlang the kirkyaird,[31] and Gelie (Geillis) Duncan playit on the trump, Jhonne Fian missellit (muffled or masked) led the ring; Agnes Sampson and her dochteris and all the rest following . . . . to the nowmer of sevin scoir of persounes'. At the trial of the covens before the King (James VI), 'Agnes Sampson confessed that upon the night of Allhallow Even last, she was accompanied . . . . with a great many other witches, to the number of two hundred, and that they all went to sea, each one in a riddle or cive (sieve), and went into the same very substantially, with flaggons of wine, making merrie and drinking by the way in the same riddles or cives, to the Kirk of North Barrick in Lowthian, and that after they had landed, tuk handes on the lande, and daunced the reill or short daunse, singing all with one voice,

> Commer, goe ye afore, commer goe ye,
> Gin ye winna goe afore, commer, let me!

'At which time she confessed, that this Geillis Duncan did goe before them, playing the reill or daunse, upon a small trumpe, called a Jewes trumpe, untill they entered into the Kirk of North Barrick.

'These confessions made the King in a wonderful admiration, and sent for the saide Geillis Duncan, who upon the like trumpe did play the saide daunse before the Kingis Majestie, who in respect of the strangeness of these matters, tooke great delight to be present at their examinations.'[32]

The Ring was usually danced around some object such as a standing stone or a cross, or sometimes round the 'devil', either standing or enthroned. At Craigleuch, on Hallowe'en, 1597, the Aberdeen witches 'danced about a great stone a long space, the devil your master playing before you'.

At Auldearn, the Maiden of the coven was nicknamed 'Over the dyke with it', because, said Isobel Goudie, giving evidence in 1662, 'the Devil always takes the Maiden by the hand when we dance Gillatrypes; and as they couped they would cry, "Over the dyke with it!" '

The instrument most favoured by the witches was the

pipe or the trump (jew's harp). Isobel Cockie, of an Aberdeen coven, was accused in 1597 of being at a sabbath on Hallowe'en. 'Thou wast the ring-leader, next Tom Leyis, and because the Devil played not so melodiously and well as thou crewit, thou took the instrument out of his mouth, and took him on the chaps therewith, and played thyself to the whole company.'

The names of some of the witch tunes survive. *Gillatrypes* appears to have been popular in the north-east. In the Elgin Kirk Sessions Records, 2 June 1596, we read that three servant lasses confessed to having been in 'ane dance called *gillitrype* singing ane foull hieland sang'. Then, as we have seen, it appears at Auldearn in 1662. Again we find it at Garmouth in 1731, when Margaret Hoy appeared before the Kirk Session of Speymouth and declared her penitence for her 'indecent postures in unseemly dances (Gillatrypes)'.[33]

At Tranent (Midlothian), in 1659, 'Douglas was the pyper, and the two favourite airs of Auld Clootie were *Kilt Thy Coat, Maggie, And Come Thy Ways With Me*,[34] and *Hulie The Bed Will Fa*'. Again, Barton's wife, of Kirkliston, tried in 1655, stated that 'going to a dancing upon the Pentland-hills, (the Devil) went before us . . . . playing on a pair of pipes. The spring he played was *The Silly Bit Chicken, Gar Cast It a Pickle, And It Will Grow Meikle*'.

THE PRACTICE OF WITCHCRAFT

The use of images of clay or wax figures to injure or kill an enemy is a very early form of sympathetic magic. An image was made to represent the doomed person, was pierced with thorns or pins, and was then dissolved in a running stream or melted before a slow fire. The rite had some chance of success if it came to the victim's ears, but if it failed, the witches were usually prepared to resort to a surer method—either poison or steel. The earliest instance recorded in Great Britain is the attempt on King Duffus of Scotland (962–67).[35]

'The king had fallen ill of a mysterious sickness; and a girl having let fall some suspicious words, some of the guard being sent, found the Lass's Mother with some Hags, such as herself, roasting below a small moderate Fire, the King's Picture made of Wax . . . . The Waxen Image having been found and broken, and these old Hags having been punished with death, the King did in that moment recover.'[36]

The wax image was one of the methods resorted to by the North Berwick witches in their notorious attempt on the life of James VI in 1590. Agnes Sampson, giving evidence, 'affirmed that sche, in company with nyn vther witches, being convenit in the nycht besyd Prestounpannes, the deuell ther maister being present standing the midis of thame; ther a body of wax, schaipen and maid be the said Anny Sampsoun, wrappit within a lynnyng (linen) claith, was first delyuert to the deuell; quilk efter (after which) he had pronuncit his verde (words), delyuerit the said pictour to Anny Sampson, and sche to hir nyxt marrow (companion) and sa euery ane round about, saying, "This is King James the sext, ordonit to be consumed at the instance of a noble man Francis Erle Bodowell (Bothwell)".'

As recently as December, 1883, a *corp creagh*, or clay image, was produced in the Sheriff Court in Inverness, the case being a quarrel between two women. The figure was about four inches long. Around it was wound green worsted thread, and the body was pierced with pins. Sheriff Blair wanted to buy it, but was apparently unsuccessful. Nearly twenty years later there was one in use in South Uist. A clay figure discovered in Glen Urquhart near the home of the intended victim is now in the Pitt Rivers Museum in Oxford.

A few years ago, the present writer came across a witch's cursing-bone, which had come into the possession of a retired teacher living in the village of Fochabers, in Moray. The bone had been the property of an old woman, a reputed witch, who lived near the head of Glen Shira, in Argyll, and who died there at the beginning of the present century. Such was her reputation that even after her death none of the Glen people would touch any of her possessions, and it was the minister of the parish, the Rev. J. Finlay

Dawson, who found the bone upon the window ledge in her cottage. He took it away as a curiosity, and eventually gave it to Miss Helen Warwick, then a member of the staff of Inveraray Grammar School. In 1944 it was presented by Miss Warwick to the Scottish National Museum of Antiquities.

According to tradition, when the 'witch' wanted to 'ill-wish' a neighbour, she took her cursing-bone and made her way to his croft between sunset and cock-crow. She did not go to the dwelling-house, however, but made for the hen-house; and seizing the hen that sat next the rooster (his favourite), she thrawed its neck and poured its blood through the hollow bone, uttering curses the while.

The bone, which appears to be that of a deer, has been stained by age to a deep ivory. It is enclosed in a ring of dark bog oak, roughly oval in shape. This is obviously a phallic symbol, to which the 'witches' were notoriously addicted.

The present writer has also seen and handled the *buin-eagean*, or witch-balls, that were the property of a Highland 'wizard' (now dead) and were said to have been 'worked' by him with dire effect between the two World Wars.[37] Though green in colour, these are probably similar to the witches' 'blew clews' of Lowland tradition.

The witch was the chief enemy of the dairy. A good churning was always coveted, and it was dangerous to give her any milk, as that gave her the power to draw away all the milk or cream of the cow. Helen Gray in Slains was found guilty of taking 'the haill substance of the mylk of my lordis ky and youis (ewes)', and as late as 1826 a woman at Dingwall was accused of charming away the substance of the milk. The witch usually operated by the method known as 'drawing the tether'. While tugging at a hair rope made by taking a hair from the tail of every cow within reach and twisting them together, she muttered an incantation.[38] The Witch of the Carse of Gowrie, it is said, was seen pulling at a hair rope along which streams of milk were flowing, and heard repeating these words:

Mare's milk and deer's milk,
And every beast that bears milk
Atween St Johnston and Dundee,
Come a' to me, come a' to me!

A similar method was 'milking the pot-chain'. When a neighbour's cow was in the act of calving, the witch would place her pot on the chain that hung from the roof-tree near the fire; then, 'by some deevlish cantrip slicht', she contrived to draw all the rich milk from the adjacent byre into her pot. To avert this danger, the moment the calf dropped from the dam, its mouth was opened and a little of the dam's excrement thrust in. By this act the witch's pot filled not with milk, but with water. Another precaution was to milk the first three 'strins' from the dam through a gold wedding-ring or over a silver coin. Salt or urine was sometimes sprinkled over the cow immediately after calving, and it was given 'silvered' water to drink.

Sometimes the witch, in the form of a hare, would sit on the back of a neighbour's cow. At the next milking the neighbour would get no milk, but the witch would have ample.

By similar methods the witches took away the profit from the malt.

They also coveted 'the fruit of the corn'. Isobel Goudie, of the Auldearn coven, relates how 'before Candlemas, we went be-east Kinlosse and ther we yoaked ane plewghe of paddokis. The Devill held the plewgh, and John Yonge in Mebestowne, our officer, did drywe the plewgh. Toads did draw the pleugh, as oxen; qwickens were sowmes, a riglen's horne was a cowter, and ane piece of ane riglen's horne was ane sok.[39] We went seuerall tymes abowt; and all we of the Coven went still (continuously) up and downe with the plewghe, prayeing to the Devill for the fruit of that land, and that thistles and brieries might grow ther.'

The same witness gives the formula used. 'When we take away the fruit of the corn at Lammas, we take wool shears, and cut or clip only three stalks of it and plait other three reeds and say:

> We cut this corn in our lord the devil's name,
> And we shall have the fruit of it hame;

and this thrice over, and so we have the fruit of that field.'

This rite was usually performed at Lammas, before the corn was ripe. In order to sain their crops, farmers used to walk round their fields sunwise with torches or clavies.

The witches sometimes worked woe upon a man's bestial so successfully, it was said, that his 'hail gudis and gear' were bewitched and the man reduced to poverty.

When magical methods failed, the witches did not hesitate to resort to some simpler but surer device, as at Crook of Devon, where, in 1661, Bessie Henderson 'confessed and declared that Janet Paton was with (her) at ane meeting when they trampit down Thos. White's rie in the beginning of harvest, and that (she) had broad soales and trampit down more than any of the rest'. Again, during a great storm the Forfar witches destroyed 'by magic', as they asserted, the old Brig o' Cortaquhie; but one of their number, Helen Guthrie, confessed that they went to the bridge 'with intentione to pull it doune', and that for this end she herself and others of them 'did thrust ther shoulderis against the brig', and that 'the divell wes bussie among them acting his pairt'; and Isobel Smyth, another member of the coven, added, 'wee all rewed that meeting for wee hurt ourselves lifting'.

The witches were believed to have the power to aid or blight fertility. In 1590, Jonet Clark was tried in Edinburgh for the 'gewing and taking of power fra sindrie mennis members', and in the same year and place Bessie Roy was accused of causing mother's milk to dry up. Many midwives practised witchcraft—the better the witch, it was said, the better the midwife—and they were often called in to perform incantations during the events of the farmyard. They also trafficked in the affections, and by means of a love potion could induce a goodly youth come of honest folk to marry 'ane ugly harlot queyne'. Two sweets stuck together with his sweat were believed to give a man power over the woman he desired. Witness the Fausse Sir John in the ballad of *May Colvin*:

> Frae ablow his arm he's pu'd a charm
>   And stuck it in her sleeve,
> And he has made her gang wi' him,
>   Wi'out her parents' leave.

In medical matters the devil often acted as consultant to the witch. Bessie Dunlop (Ayrshire) confessed that 'qhen sundrie persounes cam to hir to seik help for thair beist, thair kow, or thair yow (ewe), or for ane barne (bairn) that was tane away with an evil blast of wind or elf-grippit, sche gaed and sperit (asked) Thom (Tom Reid, her 'devil') quhat micht help thame?' Alison Pierson, the Fife witch, claimed to have learned her craft from her cousin, Mr William Simpson, 'quha (who) sche affermit wes ane grit scoller and doctor of medicin . . . . The saide Mr William tauld hir of ewerie seiknes and quhat herbis scho sould tak to haill thame, and how scho sould vse thame'.

More often than not, the witches seem to have used their powers for good. Marian Grant, who was burnt for witchcraft in Aberdeen in 1597, cured ailing cattle in the name of the Father, the Son, and the Holy Ghost. Bartie Paterson, arraigned before the Lords of the Justiciary in 1607, at the instance of the Presbytery of Dalkeith, cured his patients with a stoup of water from the Dow Loch in Dumfries-shire, making them repeat as they raised it, 'I lift this water in the name of the Father, the Sone, and the Haly Ghaist, to do guid for thair health for quhom it is lifted'. He was condemned. In 1623, Bessie Smith confessed before the Presbytery of Lesmahagow that she had been guilty of 'charming the heart feavers'. She 'appoyntit them the wayburne (plaintain) leaf to be eaten nyne morningis', this charm to be repeated, kneeling:

> For Godes saik,
> For Sanct Spirit,
> For Sanct Arkit,
> For the Nine Maidens that dyed
> Into the Buirtie in the Ladywell bank,
> This charm to be beuk and bell to me,
>   And that sua be.

Bessie was left to the discipline of the kirk session.

The practice of 'unwarrantable healing' was so wide-spread that the Presbyteries were frequently at their wits' end how to cope with it. The herbal remedies and charms had, indeed, as strong a hold on the people as have quack cures in our own time, and it is probable that many of the 'witches' were at least as honest in intention and as success-ful in practice as the average purveyor of these medicines. In 1698, we find the brethren in Sutherland seeking advice on how to cope with the practice of witchcraft among their people, and being recommended to set forth the sin of witchcraft from the pulpit and take action against offenders according to the rules of the Church. Again, in 1737, we find the Synod of Ross protesting 'how greatly God is dishon-oured, the character and persons of innocent people injured and peace disturbed' by certain 'ignorant and superstitious persons' taking it upon themselves to test for witchcraft by such methods as 'scoring abune the breath' (drawing blood above the nostrils), and ordaining that the ministers shall 'in the fullest manner instruct their people against the evil and gross wickedness of such practices', and threatening procedure.

THE WITCHES AND THE FAIRIES

There is plenty of evidence in the records of the witch-trials of comings and goings between the witches and the aborigi-nal mound-dwellers, who seem to have lived a life apart until within three hundred years ago, and to have become identified in the popular mind with the fairies. The attrac-tion of the mound-dwellers was apparently their superior knowledge of the occult and their skill in magic. Traces of this knowledge and skill survive in the remoter—and some not so remote—districts of Scotland. There are women, for instance, who can tell at the first glance under what planet one was born, and others who, if one passes an object be-longing to someone else into their hands, can tell one quite a lot about its owner; whilst 'second sight' is still not so rare a phenomenon in the Highlands and Islands. It seems a pity that science persists in its neglect of this fascinating borderland between the seen and the unseen worlds.⁴⁰

To return to the witches, Bessie Dunlop of Lyne related at her trial in 1567 how her 'devil', Thom Reid, led her one day from her house to the kiln-end, and there she saw 'twelf persounes, aucht wemene and four men. The men were clad in gentilmennis claithing, and the wemene had all plaiddis about thame, and were very semelie lyke to see . . . . They bade hir sit doun, and said, "Welcum, Bessie, will thow go with us?" Bot sche answerit nocht, becos Thom had forbidden hir.' Being asked if she speired at Thom who they were, she answered, 'They were the gude wychties that wynnit (dwelt) in the Court of Elfhame, qha come thair to desyre hir to go with thame.'

In 1588, Alison Pierson of Byrehill, Fife, was 'conuict for hanting and repairing with gude nichbouris (the fairies) and Quene of Elfhame thir diuers zeiris (years) bypast'. She confessed that 'in Grange-mure thair come ane man to hir cled in grene cloathis, quha said to hir, gif (if) scho wald be faithfull he would do her gude. He gaid away thane, and apperit to hir at ane vthir tyme, ane lustie man, with mony mene and wemene with him; and that scho sanit hir (sained herself) and prayit, and past with thame forder nor scho could tell; and saw thame pypeing with merryness and good scheir.'

At Inveraray, in 1677, Donald McIlmichall was tried for 'that horrid cryme of corresponding with the devil', the whole evidence being that he 'entered a fairy hill where he met many men and women, and he playd on trumps to them quhen they danced'.

Lastly, Isobel Goudie of Auldearn, giving evidence in 1662, stated, 'I was in the Downie-hills and got meat there from the Quein of Fearrie, mor than I could eat. The Quein of Fearrie is brawlie clothed in whyt linens, and the King of Fearrie is a braw man, weill favoured . . . Ther wes elf-bullis⁴¹ rowtting and skoylling wp and downe thair and affrighted me . . . As for Elf-arrow-heidis, the Devill shapes them with his awin hand, and syne deliueris thame to the Elf-boyes, who whittis and dightis them with a sharp thing lyk a paking needle⁴² . . . . The Devill wold giw ws the brawest lyk money that ewer was coyned; within fowr and twantie houris it vold be horse-muke.'

HIGHLAND WITCHES
In the Highlands, outside the burghs, there is little or no trace of the witch cult or of 'black' magic.

'The responsible witches of Gaeldom,' writes Kenneth Macleod, 'were highly gifted women who won their place by force of character and by right of service. Each would fight the other, and sometimes all the others, in defence of parochial rights and privileges. Each, too, made full use of all the arts, whether conventional or unconventional, to bring the luck of milk to her own sheilings, or the luck of fish to her own shores.

'But the witches were racial as well as parochial pat-riots. If the kiltless armies sometimes wondered why the mist was so thick and the rock so unexpected in Gaelic territory, there was a woman in a place called Moy who knew. And as likely as not, she was at that very moment handing round silver goblets, with something in them, to the six guests who jested and laughed around the fire, seri-ous business being over. Many a time, too, did those seven big ones, standing on the headland of Knoydart, hurl wind and waves against such sloops of war as carried intentions that might not be good for Gaeldom . . . . Behind Gaeldom stood Gormshuil of Moy and Doideag of Mull and Laorag of Tiree and Maol-odhar of Kintyre and Luideag of the Bens and Corrag, daughter of Iain the Fair, and Cas a' Mhogain Riabhaich from Glencoe . . . . One would cross many a ferry to see the seven old crones dancing hand in hand their circular dance to the rhythm of a madden-ing tune.'[43]

TYPES OF WITCH
In outer appearance, there were probably plenty of witches who corresponded to the unwashed hags with the nutcracker profile of the legend (bathrooms and dentures alike being unknown), but some, at least, were far removed from the popular conception. Of the leading spirits in the notorious North Berwick conspiracy, Agnes Sampson is described as

'a woman not of the base and ignorant sort of witches,[44] but matronlike, grave, and settled in her answers, which were all to some purpose'; John Fian, or Cunynghame, was a schoolmaster; Effie McCalyan was a woman of social position, the daughter of Lord Cliftonhall; and Barbara Napier was also of good family. But the witch who has made the most vivid impression on local folk tradition is Isobel Goudie, of the Auldearn coven, who proved such a mine of information at her trial in 1662. She is described as young and of most attractive appearance, with flaming red hair and strange dark eyes.[45] She was the wife of a farmer, but appears to have been of superior station to her husband, who is described as 'a dull, heavy man'. They lived on a lonely farm on the edge of Lochloy, a mile or two from Nairn, and in the ruins of the neighbouring Castle of Inshoch she met the grey-clad scholar who became her 'devil', and by whom she was baptised as a witch in the kirk of Auldearn, some two miles distant. (The kirkyard is believed to have been originally a site of Druidical worship.) The Castle became their regular meeting-place, and here she was trained in the practice of witchcraft—to make images of clay or wax, to make the moon-paste (the formula is said to be still current in Morocco and Brittany), to use the fairy arrows, and the rest. She also made the acquaintance of Sir Robert Gordon of Gordonstoun, who had been a Privy Councillor of Charles 1, and had become a leading member of the witch cult in Scotland. (The story of his last ride through Elgin to the holy kirk of Birnie, pursued by the Devil, who caught him at last and claimed his soul, is still a tradition in Moray.) Isobel eventually became dissatisfied with her life and gave herself up to justice. In the very church where she had renounced her Christian baptism and been received into the witch cult the Assize met and passed judgment on her; and in the course of her trial, which lasted for four days, she gave the remarkable evidence which has been preserved in Pitcairn's *Criminal Trials*. She was sentenced to be strangled and burned.

Perhaps the most unsavoury character in the history

of witchcraft in Scotland was the notorious Major Weir, of Edinburgh, who was burned in that city in 1670.[46]

In many parts of the country people still point out a 'Witches' Knowe' or a 'Gallows Hill', where the local witches had met their death. The tale is still told of one of the witch-burnings on the Law Knowe (now marked by a circle of trees) on Kilpurney Hill in Perthshire. As she was being conveyed to the spot in a farm cart, the victim saw the country folk hurrying from all directions to get a good position. She nodded and smiled to those who passed her, and turning to her custodians, asked, 'What are they a'fleein' for? There can be naethin' dune till I gang.' When she arrived at the Knowe, the people were still to be seen making their way down the hillside, so the old body placidly seated herself, produced her knitting from a capacious pocket and remarked, 'Ah weel, I'll just thrust a threid till they a' gaither.'[47]

Although the tortures to which the witches were subjected can never be justified, it must be remembered that the witch covens, when the cult was at its height, were hostile to human happiness and even to human life, and were held in terror by the mass of their countrymen.[48]

'By their abandoned and licentious orgies and by their readiness to gratify their employers in any base purpose of revenge, they proved themselves to be a menace to society and a peril to the state,' writes J. M. McPherson; and 'the constituted authorities had to put out a strong hand to deal with this evil power which challenged their supremacy.' The form of the penalties belonged, he points out, to the age, but, on the other hand, profound sympathy must be felt for the innocent victims.

The tragic error of the witch inquisitors was to assume that everyone who adhered to the old nature-religion was intrinsically evil. In point of fact, there were many professing Christians, including high dignitaries of the medieval Church, who had nothing to learn from the witches in the way of evil practices; and had the adherents of the rival faiths been thrown 'throughither' and then sorted out, not in accordance with their profession of faith, but in accordance with their goodness or badness of heart, the result might have given folk to think. However fantastic their beliefs, it is difficult to think without shame and compassion of those victims of our forefathers' misguided zeal, many of whom went to the stake or the gallows with a courage and devotion equal to that of the Christian martyrs.

THE EVIL EYE

Although belief in witchcraft proper is fast dying out in these islands, belief in the Evil Eye or Ill Ee still survives in the remoter rural areas. This belief is age-old and world-wide. It was prevalent in ancient Greece, and the Romans—so Pliny tells us—wore amulets as a protection. In Scotland it has always been associated with the witches, who were believed to owe the faculty to the Devil. Jonet Irving, for instance, was taught by her 'devil' that if she bore illwill to anyone, she should 'look at thame with open eyes and pray evill for thame in his name', and she would get her heart's desire.

Although not confined to either sex, the Evil Eye is chiefly associated with women. Its possessor did not always repel at sight, but there was usually 'something peculiar' in her looks, that made people fear to refuse her if she asked for anything. It was unlucky to meet her on the road, especially if one had set out on a particular errand, and prudent folk either turned back or went round another way.

A deep-set eye was considered particularly baneful.

There are two theories regarding the Evil Eye—one irrational, the other rational. The first is that the possessor cannot help himself, that he may do mischief not only without intending it, but without realising what he is doing.

'When we were in the old place,' said a farmer (in the eighteen-seventies), 'there was a man living up on the hill who would often be helping the farmers round about him when they were thrang. He had the Evil Eye, but he couldn't help it. He would be sorry for it himself. Many a one would be scolding him for hurting their beasts.'

The other theory is that the belief originated in the fear aroused by the hostile look of a neighbour. In the words of an Islay man, 'It is the evil heart going into the eye and causing the Evil Eye.' The Evil Eye is the antithesis of the tender heart or nature apt to sympathy, of all that is symbolised by the Sacred Heart. It expresses either covetousness, as when the possessor seeks to benefit himself at the expense of another and obtain the *toradh* or substance of his cattle—milk, butter and cheese—or the fruits of his labour, or else as envy, when he gets no direct benefit, but has the satisfaction of injuring or diminishing what he envies in the possession of another, such as youth, health and personal beauty. Pretty children and healthy young beasts were in special danger. A child would fall sick; milk would dry up in breast or udder; a colt would fall lame; the hens would lay 'soft' eggs; the butter would refuse to 'come'. Every precaution was taken to avert the danger. If there was time, the child was concealed or sprinkled with 'silvered' water, or one of its garments—usually a stocking— was turned inside out; or the mother would invoke the Trinity, or spit on the child, or throw a small piece of its clothing into the fire. To protect the butter, salt or silver was thrown into the churn. A small gift at parting frequently helped, or a red ember flung after the departing woman.

Sometimes the owner of the Eye would dissimulate by praising what she envied. Such praise was known to be highly dangerous. If the unwelcome visitor remarked, 'He's a bonnie bairn,' the mother would respond, 'God save the bairn!' In the eighteen-nineties, a woman and her little daughter were one day crossing Kessock Ferry to Inverness. On the ferry-boat, the story goes, there was a reputed witch who bent down and said to the little girl, 'What a pretty little mouth you've got!' Almost immediately the child felt her mouth twisting to one side of her face, and thus it remained for a month, till a cure was wrought by a wise woman in Fortrose.

If the person whose child or beast was injured was unsuccessful in counteracting the Evil Eye, his only resource was to consult someone who possessed *eolas*, the secret knowledge that provided an infallible cure. Here and there, through the countryside, such 'canny' or 'skeely' women were to be found. In the Highlands, the effect of the Evil Eye was known as *cronachadh*, harming, ill-wishing, cursing, and the antidote as *beannachadh*, blessing.[49] The possessor of the Evil Eye was feared and avoided; the possessor of *eolas* was held in high repute. The one sought to harm, the other to help; the one to diminish, the other to increase a neighbour's goods; the one to blight, and the other to aid fertility. The one was skilled in dangerous herbs, the other in healing herbs. The one accompanied the rite with a curse, the other with a blessing. Occasionally, however, the power to injure and the power to cure were united in one person. About her there were mixed feelings, and wise folk were at pains to keep on her right side.

Various methods were used to counteract the effects of the Evil Eye.

'My child is *air a cronachadh* with the Evil Eye of that woman,' said the anxious mother; on which the woman possessing *eolas* took a red thread, and when she had spoken 'the words', tied it round the child's neck. The healing-thread is sometimes spoken of as three-ply, and was knotted in a prescribed manner. The knots were used like beads in a rosary, a line of the incantation (without which no charm was effective) being repeated as each knot was passed. One of the many incantations that have been preserved runs as follows:

> An eye covered thee,
> A mouth spoke thee,
> A heart envied thee,
> A mind desired thee.
>
> Four made thy cross:
>   Man and wife,
>   Youth and maid;
> Three will I send to thwart them:
>   Father,
>   Son,
>   Spirit Holy.

I appeal to Mary,
    Aidful Mother of men;
I appeal to Bride,
    Foster-mother of Christ omnipotent;
I appeal to Columba,
    Apostle of shore and sea;
And I appeal to heaven,
    To all saints and angels that be above:

If it be a man that has done thee harm,
    With evil eye,
    With evil wish,
    With evil passion,
Mayst thou cast off each ill,
    Every malignity,
    Every malice,
    Every harassment,
    And mayst thou be well for ever,
    While this thread
    Goes round thee,
In honour of God and of Jesus,
And of the Spirit of balm everlasting.[50]

Both fire and water were effective in counteracting the Evil Eye. The fire rite, known as the Fiery Circle (in Gaelic *Beannachadh na Cuairte*, the Blessing of the Circle) is described elsewhere. The water rite was performed thus:

With a crock of clay or a small wooden clog the healer went to a running stream and stopped at the place where the dead and living cross. She (or he) spoke to no living person from the moment she set out to the moment she returned. On the lower side of the bridge or ford, she went down on her right knee, lifted as much water as she could hold in her cupped hands, and poured it into the crock, repeating the rune:

I am lifting a little drop of water
In the holy name of the Father,
In the holy name of the Son,
In the holy name of the Spirit.[51]

On returning to the house, she sprinkled some of the

water in the ears and along the spine of the person or
animal on whom the Evil Eye had rested, pronouncing
his name and repeating these words:

> Shake from thee thy harm,
> Shake from thee thy jealousy,
> Shake from thee thy illness,
>   In name of Father,
>   In name of Son,
>   In name of Holy Spirit.[52]

The remainder of the water was poured on to a grey stone,
or a 'fixed rock that fails not', or behind the fire-flag.[53]

These incantations are magic formulae to which has been
added the sanction of Christianity. For their deepest instincts told the people that as every poison has its antidote,
so has every evil spell; that as light destroys darkness and
as knowledge destroys ignorance, so good destroys evil.[54]

Notes

CHAPTER ONE. *Introductory*

1. For we have a memory within memory, as layers of skin underlie the epidermis . . . With most of us this anterior remembrance lies dormant, but to some of us are given swift ancestral recollections. Fiona Macleod.

   Freud himself postulates ancestral memory as forming part of the 'unconscious' of the individual.

2. J. W. Flecker, *To a Poet a Thousand Years Hence.*

3. To-day, with our greater understanding, there is humility in the minds of all scientists. The further we penetrate into Nature's secrets, the more clearly we see the ever-receding frontiers of knowledge. Sir Harold Hartley (quoted at the Annual Meeting of the British Association, Edinburgh, August 1951).

4. There are, then, two opposite trends, the ordinary commonsense view of the reality of this world; and the other, towards which mysticism, religion, and physics converge, the view that reality lies outside or beyond us. Prof. Stanley Cook, 'The Relevance of the Science of Religion.'

   Religion has emerged into human experience mixed with the crudest fancies of barbaric imagination. Gradually, slowly, steadily the vision recurs in history in nobler form and with clearer expression . . . The fact of the religious vision, and its history of persistent expansion, is our one ground for optimism. Apart from it, human life is a flash of occasional amusements lighting up a mass of pain and misery, a bagatelle of transient experience. Alfred North Whitehead, *Science and the Modern World.*

   Like music and poetry, religion provides its own justification; like them is witness to its own worth . . . The power of religion to confer happiness, to give peace, has abundant testimony in its favour. W. Macneile Dixon, *The Human Situation.*

   Religion is the sense of trustful relationship with, and dependence upon, an Unseen Power. Prof. H. M. Gwatkin.

   Thou hast made us for Thyself, and our heart is restless till it finds rest in Thee. St Augustine.

5. An old Scottish sentiment or toast runs, The ingle-neuk,

wi' routh (plenty) o' bannocks and bairns!

6. *Ancient Art and Ritual*.
7. De Cupid., div. B.
8. *Ancient Art and Ritual*.

CHAPTER TWO. *Ethnic Origins of the Festivals*

1. Of the two main Celtic languages, Welsh is still very much alive, and in Ireland Gaelic has taken on a new lease of life. In Scotland, the deliberate policy of extirpation has been abandoned, but the decline has not yet been arrested. F.M.M.CN.

2. The name is not derived from the Latin *pictus*, painted, as is commonly supposed. 'It would seem that while the form *Picti* is certainly Latin, it is based on a genuine native form.' W. J. Watson, *Celtic Place-Names of Scotland*.

3. Strictly speaking, there is no such thing as a Celtic race any more than there is an Aryan race. 'There is a group of languages and a certain cultural complex associated with them.' R. A. S. Macallister, *Ancient Ireland*.

4. The traces of the Anglo-Saxon influence, which are so abundant in the southern parts of the island, are rare and slight even in the border counties of Scotland, and scarcely discernible to the north of the Forth. Daniel Wilson, *Prehistoric Annals of Scotland, vol.* II.

    In the eleventh century, after Malcolm II had shattered the Anglian power at Carham (Wark) in Northumbria, Gaelic colonies were planted in the Lothians, and their descendants fused with the earlier settlers. (Such well-known Border names as Scott, Kerr and Douglas are of Celtic origin.) The spread of 'Inglis', the speech of Northumbria, was due mainly to trading connections and to the simplicity of this peasant dialect as compared with the ancient and highly inflected Celtic tongue. F.M.MCN.

5. The resistance of Scotland is especially noteworthy. Eoin McNeill, *Phases of Irish History*.

6. At four terms in the zeir, viz., Alhallowmas, Candilmas, Beltan, and Lambmes. Con. Burghs, I, 60 (1582).

    Candlemas and Lammas have been moved forward in accordance with the New Style of reckoning the year, whereas the Whitsun and Martinmas terms correspond approximately with the Old Beltane and Old Hallowmas. F.M.MCN.

CHAPTER THREE. *The Druids*

1. *Druidh* (Scots Gaelic), *Droaid* (Irish Gaelic), cunning man or magician. The etymology is uncertain; possibly

from the Celtic *dru*, Greek *drus*, an oak—oak-worship being a feature of the cult.

In an Irish version of the Gospels, 'The Wise Men came from the East' is rendered 'The Druids came,' etc.; and in a poem ascribed to St Columba, the line occurs: *Is e mo drai Crist mac De*. Christ the Son of God is my Druid. (Misc. Ir. Archeol. Soc., I, p. 8.)

2. Have not the most authentic religions been solar in origin, germinating from sun-wonder; material and spiritual influences alike finding their fusion in that golden flower of living flame? Sol and soul are in essence one and the same; even as to language similarly derived. The inner light and the outer; are they perhaps simply one? The sun-seed of light which blossoms from the womb of diffused radiant darkness is the same source of being in the universe, in the atom, in ourselves. From that primal impulse we receive our promptings, to act from and with which is life and joy, to deny which is woe and death. Acting awarely with nature's law of cause-and-effect, we should find nature friendly and gracious. Flouting it, we depart from all peace and sanity and happiness, wasting our substance and ourselves in strife. Dion Binghym, in *Little Reviews Anthology*.

Conscience is sun-awareness and our deep instinct not to go against the sun . . . . It is only immoral to be dead-alive, sun-extinct, and busy putting out the sun in other people. D. H. Lawrence.

3. The dates of the invasions are uncertain, but according to the most recent researches (Gordon Childe, etc.) the first was completed in the late Bronze Age, c. 750, and the second about 200 BC.

4. The belief that Britain was the fountain-head of Druidism appears to have been wide-spread, and Procopius, a Byzantine historian of the sixth century, refers to a late form of the belief in the mysterious reputation of the island. (*De Bello Gothico*, Dindorff's Edn. vol. II, p. 559.)

Matthew Arnold speaks of 'the Celtic nearness to nature and her secret'.

5. See Lewis Spence, *The Mysteries of Britain*.

How some of (the) professors of classical mythology would have held their sides and roared at the very notion of a British mythology. Yet all the time it had long been secretly leavening English ideas and ideals, none the less potently because disguised under forms which could not be readily appreciated. Charles Squire, *Celtic Myth and Legend*.

6. Tacitus relates how the Island of Mona (Anglesey)—the great stronghold of Druidism—was attacked, its sacred

groves cut down, its altars laid level, its priests put to the sword.

Evidence of Classical Writers

7. In his *Celtic Religion and Mythology* Mr MacBain points out that the strong priestly caste, divided off from the nobles and the commons, can be paralleled in the Hinduism of India with its rigid caste of Brahmans, who monopolised all religious rites.

8. They even arbitrated in cases of war, and made the opponents stop when they were about to line up for battle. Strabo, *Geographica* IV, c. 197, 4.
    It was then they ceased their slaughtering and maiming on hearing the music of the poets. Quoted by Douglas Hyde, *Literary History of Ireland*.

9. *De Bello Gallico*, Book VI, 13.

10. Diogenes Laertius.
    The universal maxim of the Druids: 'Be brave, that you may survive among the blessed.'
    Hence their warrior's heart hurls them against the steel, hence their ready welcome of death, for who were coward enough to grudge a life sure of its return. Lucan, *Pharsalia*, Book I, 11.
    It is an interesting fact that in the Great War (1914–18) the German military authorities placed the 51st (Highland) Division as the most formidable in the British Army.

11. Don Chrysostom.

12. Diodorus Siculus.

13. Dividiacus was a man of affairs, acknowledged ruler of the Aedui, and a politician and diplomatist of established reputation through the whole of Gaul; it was, in fact, an important diplomatic mission that took him to Rome on the occasion when he was the guest of Quintus Cicero and discussed divination with Tully. T. D. Kendrick, *The Druids*.

14. There is a tradition (though some scholars dispute it) that Pythagoras was schooled in philosophy by the Druids of Galatia. Plato based his philosophy mainly on Pythagoreanism, the western school of thought, incorporating many of its fundamental tenets and assumptions, although he was also influenced by the eastern school of Asia Minor. Indeed, it is not until we come to Plato that we find a merging of these two streams in a philosophy that is at once derivative and profoundly original.

15. (Of Birth and Death) On either hand we behold a birth of which, as of the moon, we see but half. We are outside the one, waiting for a life from the unknown; we are inside the

other, watching the departure of a spirit from the womb of the world into the unknown. To the region whither he goes, the man enters newly-born. We forget that it is a birth, and call it death. The body he leaves behind is but the *placenta* by which he drew his nourishment from his mother Earth. And as the child-bed is watched on earth with expectancy, so the couch of the dying, as we call them, may be surrounded by the birth watchers of the other world, waiting like anxious servants to open the door to which this world is but the wind-blown porch. George Macdonald, *Robert Falconer*, p. 350.

16. Henri Hubert, *The Greatness and Decline of the Celts*.

17. We have . . . the most weighty and explicit testimony—Strabo's, Caesar's, Lucan's—that this (Celtic) race once possessed a special, profound, spiritual discipline, that they were, to use Mr Nash's words, 'wiser than their neighbours'. Matthew Arnold, *Study of Celtic Literature*, II.

18. Lewis Spence, *The Mysteries of Britain*.

19. *The Silver Bough*.

Sacrifice

20. Traces of totemism can . . . . be discerned in the tribal or clan names of the Picts . . . . The name of the Orkney Islands, Orcades, is undoubtedly Keltic. In Irish literature the islands are called *Inse Orc*, Isles of the Orcs, i.e. Boars, whilst *Inse Cat*, Isles of the Cats—Shetland or Caithness—are also mentioned. Watson accordingly concludes that the Orcs were just the totemic boar clan, presumably of the Picts. Gordon Childe, *Prehistory of Scotland*.

21. Sacrifice ceased to be a spiritual bond in proportion as it came to be regarded as the making of offerings for the purpose of obtaining favours in return. F. B. Jevons, *Comparative Religion*.

22. The study of the history of the development of a hypothesis from savage idolatry to a highly cultivated metaphysic (the Bible) is as interesting, instructive and reassuring as any study can be to an open mind and an honest intellect.

. . . . (Micah) raises the conception of God to the highest point it has ever attained by his fiercely contemptuous denunciation of the blood sacrifices, and his inspired and inspiring demand, 'What doth the Lord require of thee but to do justly, and to love mercy, and to walk humbly with thy God.' Before this victory of the human spirit over crude superstition Noah's God and Job's God go down like skittles.

. . . Later on comes Jesus, who dares a further flight. He suggests that godhead is something which incorporates itself in man: in himself, for instance.

. . . This is an advance on the theology of Micah; for

man walking humbly before an external God is an ineffective creature compared to man exploring as the instrument and embodiment of God with no other guide than the spark of divinity within him. It is certainly the greatest break in the Bible between the Old and New Testament. Yet . . . we find Paul holding up Christ to the Ephesians as 'an offering and a sacrifice to God for a sweet-smelling savour', thereby dragging Christianity back and down to the level of Noah. None of the apostles rose above that level, and the result was that the great advances made by Micah and Jesus were cancelled; and historical Christianity was built up on the sacrificial altars of Jehovah, with Jesus as the sacrifice. George Bernard Shaw, *The Adventures of the Black Girl in Search of God*.

23. He, the Emperor Claudius, very thoroughly suppressed the barbarous and inhuman religion of the Druids in Gaul, which in the time of Augustus had merely been forbidden to the Roman citizens. Pomponius Mala, *De Situ Orbis* III, 2, 18 and 19.

24. If (Augustus) forbade Roman citizens to take part in Druidical worship, his purpose was political: to withdraw Gauls who had received the citizenship from a strongly nationalist influence. *Cambridge Ancient History*, vol. X, 492.

Organisation

25. John Knox, who had no use for a 'pented bred' (painted board), or ikon, was evidently a chip of the old Druidic block. F.M.MCN.

26. The practice of holding the Quarterly Communion service out on the hillside—a very solemn and impressive ceremony it is—has not yet entirely died out in the Highlands.

27. The first community founded by St Bride was Kildare, 'the cell of the oak'.

28. Moses struck the rock with a magic rod. Kings have sceptres. Neptune has a trident, popes and bishops croziers, high civil officials have a mace of office, in the Roman Church wand-like objects are used to perform benedictions, and all over the world there are the wands of magicians and the medicine-men. Evans Wentz, *The Fairy Faith in Celtic Countries*.

The Highlanders retain a tradition of the *slatan drui'achd*, which they say was a white wand. James Logan, *The Scottish Gael*.

It was traditionally made from the wood of the yew tree.

29. Specimens of this crescent, in gold, called *cornan* by the Irish, have been found in Ireland.

The Druids in Scotland

30. In a passage of *Táin bó Cúalange* (Windisch's ed., p. 672 f), King Conchobar remains silent until the Druid Cathbadh has replied to the bringer of important tidings. 'For such was the rule of Ulster. The men of Ulster must not speak before the King, and the King must not speak before his druids.' *Ancient Laws of Ireland,* I. 22.

31. See Adamnan's *Life of St Columba.*

32. Eratesthenes, the Greek chronologer and scholar, speaking of the arrow with which Apollo slew the Cyclops, writes that 'he (Apollo) hid the arrow among the Hypeneans where he had his winged temple.' (Apollo had rays for arrows.)

33. The Druidic rites on Iona are imaginatively reconstructed by Fiona Macleod:

It was while the dew was yet wet on the grass that Bride came out of her father's house and went up the steep slope of Dun-I . . . . When at last, a brief while before sunrise, she reached the summit of the Scuir, she found three young Druids there, ready to tend the sacred fire the moment the sun-rays should kindle it. Each was clad in a white robe, with fillets of oak leaves; and each had a golden armlet. One stepped forward . . . . 'Hast thou come to pray?'

But at that moment a low cry came from one of his companions. He turned, and re-joined his fellows. Then all three sank upon their knees, and with outstretched arms hailed the rising of God.

As the sun rose, a solemn chant swelled from their lips, ascending as incense through the silent air. The glory of the new day came soundlessly. Peace was in the blue heaven, on the blue-green sea, on the green land.

. . . . In what strange, mysterious way Bride did not see; but as the three Druids held their hands before the sacred fire there was a faint crackling, then three thin spirals of blue smoke rose, and soon dusky red and wan yellow tongues of flame moved to and fro. The sacrifice of God was made. Out of the immeasurable heaven He had come, in His golden chariot. Now, in the wonder and mystery of His love, He was re-born upon the world, re-born a little fugitive flame upon a low hill in a remote island. Great must be His love that He could die thus daily in a thousand places: so great His love that He could give up His own body to daily death, and suffer the holy flame that was in the embers He illumined to be lighted and revered and then scattered to the four quarters of the world.

Bride could bear no longer the mystery of this great love. It moved her to an ecstasy . . . . Bowing her head, so that the glad tears fell warm as thunder-rain upon her hands, she rose and moved away. *The Sin-Eater.*

34. *The Clans, Septs and Regiments of the Scottish Highlands*, by Frank Adam, revised by Sir Thomas Innes of Learney, Lord Lyon King of Arms.

35. *Scots Heraldry.*

36. The Celtic missionaries allowed the pagan stock to stand, grafting their Christian cult thereon. Hence the blending of the pagan and Christian in these poems, which to many will constitute their chief charm. A. Carmichael, Introduction to *Carmina Gadelica.*

   A popular form of the proverb was the triad. The Ossianic formula for efficiency runs: Strength in our hands,/Truth on our lips,/Purity in our hearts.
   Survivals of Druidical beliefs and practices

37. *The Mysteries of Britain.*

38. Along with a number of leading ministers, there were appointed Sir Archibald Johnstone of Warriston, Clerk Register; Mr Thomas Nicholson, His Majesty's Advocate; and several prominent lawyers and physicians. See the Church records of the period.

   The manner in which these measures were received by their congregations is described in John Buchan's *Witchwood.* Much of this so-called Druidism was merely archaic magic. F.M.MCN.

39. See p. 58.

40. Both in *Carmina Gadelica.*

   Sùil Dhé mhóir,
   Sùil Dhé na glòir,
   Sùil Righ nan slògh,
   Sùil Righ nam bèo,
      Dòrtadh oirnne
         Gach òil agus ial,
      Dòrtadh oirnne
         Gu fòill agus gu fial.
   Glòir dhuit fhéin,
      A ghréin an àigh.
   Glòir dhuit fhéin, a ghréin,
      A ghnùis Dhé nan dùl.

   Ri faicinn domh na gealaich ùir,
      Is dùth domh mo shùil a thogail.
   Is dùth domh ma ghlùn a leagail,
      Is dùth domh mo cheann a bhogadh,
   Toir cliù dhuit féin, a ré nan iùl,
      Gum faca mi thù a rithist,

Gum faca mi a' ghealach ùr,
  Ailleagan iùil na slighe.
Is iomadh neach a chaidh a null
  Eadar ùine an dà ghealaich,
Ged tha mise a' mealtainn fuinn,
  A ré nan ré's nam beannachd!

CHAPTER FOUR. *The Gods*

1. *The Greek View of Life.*
    The Celtic Gods
2. *Religion of the Ancient Celts.*
3. Prof. O'Rathaille.
4. Angus Og, the God of Youth, in whom the characters of Dionysos, of Apollo, of Baldur the Beautiful all mingle and meet. Patrick Geddes, *The Masque of Learning.*
5. The legend of the Holy Grail is one of the most striking instances of the fusion of Druidical and Christian beliefs, for it derives in part from the Magic Cauldron of Celtic paganism and in part from the Sacred Chalice of Christianity—the vessel in which Christ at the Last Supper instituted the Blessed Sacrament, and which contained His Blood. The legend of the Grail has been treated by a succession of poets, who developed its ethical and mystical import, so that the Grail became the symbol of man's loftiest aspirations.
6. When the Forth and Clyde Canal was being cut, several Roman altars were unearthed and are now in Glasgow University Museum.
7. The Anglo-Saxon invasion of Southern Britain led to a confederation of the Celtic peoples from Cornwall northwards, and an attempt was made to place the joint armies under a supreme commander-in-chief. The most notable of the successive holders of this office was Arthur, who fell in battle—most probably at Camelon, near Falkirk—in 537.

    Against the extravagant Welsh claims that the Arthurian cycle had its origin in the Principality must be set the researches of Skene, Stuart Glennie, and others who show that the place-names of the cycle are more plentiful in Scotland than in England or Wales, and maintain that Arthur's main exploits took place in Scotland, all the twelve battles being fought on the territory between the two Roman walls. Arthur's soldiers are referred to as 'Men of the North', and Sir Edward Anwyl is obliged to admit that Arthur himself 'came from the zone of the North', although he maintains the southern origin of the cycle. Duncan H. MacNeill, in a letter to the author.

Pre-Historic Temple on the Clyde

8.   Headed by the late Ludovic Mann.

9.   It was universally believed in ancient times that an evil spirit or dragon emerged at regular intervals and attempted to devour the sun or the moon and thereby destroy the cosmos. The celestial fight appears in the Egyptian myth of Horus and Set (Set being the eclipse-causing demon), and also in Celtic and Teutonic legend. Allegorically, it is the fight between good and evil. The priests sought to avert the danger by rites and ceremonies, and there was great rejoicing when the victory of Light over Darkness, of Good over Evil was won. In many countries sanctuaries were erected to commemorate the passing of the eclipse and the commencement of a new astronomical era.

The Gods Commemorated in Place-names

10. Much of the earliest Welsh poetry treats of the Britons of Strathclyde and their doings, and genealogies of the leading families of the fifth and sixth centuries are extant. These are to be found in Skene's *Picts and Scots* and elsewhere.

11. 'There was a lad was born in Kyle,' writes Burns, alluding to himself; and in the poem, *The Twa Dogs*, he refers to the local tradition: 'Twas in that place o' Scotland's isle/That bears the name o' Auld King Coil.' At Coilsfield, in the parish of Tarbolton, there is a circular mound in which sepulchral remains have been discovered. It is known locally as 'Coel Hen's Tomb'.

12. Annan is in fact the Gaelic genitive case of a British Anau, as Manann is the genitive of a British Manau. Professor W. J. Watson, *Celtic Place-Names of Scotland*.

13. Ibid.

CHAPTER VE. *The New Faith*
The Death of Pan

1.   In ancient Greece, despite the dominance of the Olympian hierarchy, these dark, primitive and often orgiastic fertility-cults, which long pre-dated the rise of the anthropomorphic gods, persisted underground, as they continued to do centuries later under Christianity. F. M. MCN.

2.   Primitive man regarded the sowing of the seed of plants as a process of impregnating the mother earth by means of a male fertilising agent which resulted in renewed birth. Moreover, both the seed that was sown and the seminal fluid of the male were regarded as analogous, functionally, to the rain which causes the crops to grow. Once the significance of this view-point is grasped, the understanding of all the

seeming complexity of the primitive religions of agricultural peoples becomes relatively a simple matter. J. W. Bews, *Human Ecology.*

3. *St Francis of Assisi.*

   The New Faith

4. Most of the historical founders of religions and a majority of religious philosophers . . . have divided human beings into a minority of individuals capable of making the effort required to 'attain enlightenment', and a great majority incapable of making such efforts . . . Jesus of Nazareth taught that 'many are called, but few are chosen', and that there were certain people who constituted 'the salt of the earth', and who were therefore able to preserve the world, to prevent it from decaying. The Gnostic sects believed in the existence of esoteric and exoteric teaching, the latter reserved for the many, the former for the few who were capable of profiting by it. The Catholic Church exterminated the Gnostics, but proceeded to organise itself as though the Gnostic belief in esoteric and exoteric teachings were true. For the vulgar it provided ceremonial, magically compulsive formulas, the worship of images, a calendar of holy days. To the few it taught, through the mouth of the mystics, that such external 'aids to devotion' were (as Buddha had pointed out many centuries before) strong fetters holding men back from enlightenment or, in Christian phraseology, from communion with God . . . . Here are two distinct religions for two distinct kinds of human beings. Aldous Huxley, *Ends and Means.*

5. 'But,' said Adam, 'I've seen pretty clear, ever since I was a young un, as religion's something else besides notions. It isn't notions sets people doing the right thing—it's feelings . . . . And I found it better for my soul to be humble before the mysteries o' God's dealings, and not to be making a clatter about what I never could understand.' George Eliot, *Adam Bede.*

6. Q.4. What is God? A. God is a Spirit, infinite, eternal, and unchangeable, in His being, wisdom, power, holiness, justice, goodness, and truth. *The Shorter Catechism.*

7. The whole matter of the union with God consists of purging the will of the affections and desires, so that the vile and human will may become Divine Will, being made one with the Will of God. St John of the Cross.

   The supreme height of individual self-expression and union with the universe are one. John Holms. Quoted by Edwin Muir in *The Story and the Fable.*

8. Christ's estimate of human personality, its divine origin,

its spiritual nature, its supreme value, its boundless pos-
sibilities, has been rightly called his most original contribution to human thought . . . All irreverent treatment of
human personality in individual relationships or social institutions—that is essentially anti-Christ. . . . Racial prejudice,
social pride, industrial cruelty, war, personal selfishness and
lust—these are the real sins against the real God, and they
have one common quality: they treat human personality
with contempt. Dr H. E. Fosdick, *Adventurous Religion*.

In every individual organism an individual nature, an
individual consciousness is spontaneously created at the
moment of conception . . . . There is in the nature of
the infant something entirely new, underived, underivable,
something which is, and will forever remain, *causeless*. And
this something is the unanalysable, indefinable reality of in-
dividuality.

This causeless created nature of the individual being is
the same as the old mystery of the divine nature of the soul.
Religion was right and science is wrong. Every individual
creature has a soul, a specific individual nature the origin
of which cannot be found in any cause-and-effect process
whatever. . . . . It means that science abandons its intellectual position and embraces the old religious faculty. But it
does not become thereby less scientific; it only becomes at
last complete in knowledge. D. H. Lawrence, *Psychoanalysis
and the Unconscious*.

The fact is there have never been many Christians.
There have been many believers in the semi-pagan accretions which ecclesiastical Christianity has held in common
with other faiths, but Christians who shared the reverence
of Jesus for human personality have been few and far between. That is the real challenge to us. What have sectarian
differences to do with reverence for human personality:
What have theological wrangles in common with the cause
that Jesus of Nazareth had at heart? E. J. Strover, Art.
'Reverence for Human Personality' in *The Modern Churchman*, Sept., 1945.

9. He abideth patiently,
    He listeneth readily,
    He understandeth mightily,
    And he pardoneth utterly.
                    Old MS.

10. So, too, in our own times.

I cannot pretend that Seth and Dinah were anything
else but Methodists . . . of a very old-fashioned kind. They
believed in present miracles, in instantaneous conversions,

in revelations by dreams and visions; they drew lots, and sought for divine guidance by opening the Bible at hazard; having a literal way of interpreting the scriptures which is not at all sanctioned by approved commentators. . . . Still—if I have read religious history aright—faith, hope and charity have not always been found in direct ratio with a sensibility to the three concords; and it is possible, thank Heaven, to have very erroneous theories and very sublime feelings. George Eliot, *Adam Bede.*

11. The first to tolerate Christianity was Constantine, whose mother is believed to have been a British princess, 'Elen' or Helen, who is associated by tradition with the family to which Coyl the Old (Old King Cole) belonged—one of the ruling families of Strathclyde. Whether the legend be true or false, it is certain that Constantine's father settled in York, which was then the capital of Roman Britain; that he took part in the wars against the Caledonians; and that he died in Britain. See Collingwood and Myers, *Roman Britain,* 282.

12. The Church has remained up to our own day, as it were, a remnant of the Empire. Throughout all the Middle Ages the Church is no other than the old Rome, regaining its authority over the barbarians who conquered it, imposing upon them its decretals, as it formerly imposed its laws, governing them by its cardinals, as it once governed them by its imperial legates and its pro-consuls. Renan, *Influence of the Institutions, etc. of Rome.*

13. Up to 287 AD, adherence to Christianity invited persecution by the Roman officials.

The Pictish Church

14. B. Aquitaine, 310 AD, a Gaulish Celt.

15. B. Hungary, c. 336, among a Celtic remnant.

16. Whether the statement ascribed to Bede that Ninian was instructed at Rome is a fact, a surmise, or a medieval gloss is disputed by scholars.

We may suspect the monk of Jarrow of recording not a fact, but rather an inference of his own time, which witnessed the establishment in a far more intense form, of the religious influence of Rome over the British Church, after the long seclusion following the fall of the Empire and the Teutonic invasion, but the journey of Ninian is quite in keeping with the spirit of his age. James Mackinnon, *Culture in Early Scotland.*

17 Candida Casa . . . is simply a translation of 'Logo-Tigiac' or 'Leukoteiac', the name of the bothy on St Hilary's farm near Ligugé where St Martin organised his 'family' or community. A. B. Scott, *The Pictish Nation and Church.*

18.   This name, lifted from the Greek nurseries, was in St
       Martin's time a current title among the Greek Christians
       for a Christian minister. Ibid.
           The name survives in Papa Stour (Shetland), Papa
       Westray (Orkney), Pabbay (Outer Hebrides), and else-
       where.

19.   This relationship has been compared to that of the chaplain
       to the battalion commander in a modern British regiment.

20.   Place names such as Kilbride, Kilbrennan, Kilmartin, Kil-
       marnock and Kilmalcolm denote the sites of these primitive
       churches.

21.   Bede tells us in his *Ecclesiastical History* that the south-
       ern Picts received the true faith from St Ninian, whereas
       St Columba was the first to teach the Picts 'beyond the
       mountains to the north', and most historians have assumed
       from this statement that the Grampian mountains constitute
       the northernmost limit of St Ninian's missionary labours.
       Many recent writers, however, take the view that Bede,
       who was untravelled, took his geographical details from
       the library at Jarrow and thus fell a victim to Ptolemy's
       notorious error with regard to Scotland, which he places in
       the North Sea at right angles to England, so that the west
       coast faces north and the east coast faces south. If Bede did
       indeed follow Ptolemy, the mountain range he refers to is
       not the Grampians, but Drum-Alban, the Dorsal Range or
       'backbone' of Scotland—the ridge which divides the Scot-
       tish Highlands lengthwise in two, and which runs roughly
       northwards from the head of Loch Lomond to Ben Hee in
       Sutherland.
           . . . The fact that many commemorations of St Ninian
       are found on the eastern side of Scotland, both north and
       south of the Grampians, and that the disposition of the well-
       known symbol-marked stones extends from the Forth to the
       Shetlands would appear to corroborate this view; but it is
       by no means unanimously accepted, and the argument con-
       tinues. F. M. McN.
                     The Columban Church

22.   Fiace's hymn to Patrick, composed about 800, begins with
       the statement, 'Patrick was born at Nemthur', and a gloss
       adds that this is the name of a city in North Britain,
       namely Al Cluada, that is Dumbarton (Dun Breatann,
       fortress of the Britons), 'once the acropolis of the Britons
       of Strathclyde'. See W. J. Watson, *Celtic Place-Names of
       Scotland*.

23.   Columba was trained first by St Finian of Moville, who was
       himself trained at Candida Casa, and later by St Finian of

Clonald, whose own teachers had been educated there. Thus Columba can be claimed as a direct spiritual descendant of St Ninian. F.M.McN.

24. The dominions of the Pictish King, Brude, are believed to have extended from the Forth to the Shetlands, and the Scots of Argyll were tributary to him. F.M.McN.

25. Their names linger in many parts of Scotland. Loch Columcille in Skye and Inchcolm (Colum's Isle) in the Firth of Forth commemorate two of the many monasteries founded by St Columba himself .... The name of the martyr Donnan survives in Kildonan, of Blane of Bute in Dunblane, of Mun in Kilmun, of Finnan in Glenfinnan, of Maelrubha in Loch Maree. Up and down the western seaboard and through the Isles are scattered the remains of little Celtic chapels and monastic cells built by these holy men. F. M. McNeill, *Iona: A History of the Island*.

26. Writing of the Galatians, Dean Farrar says that as Celts they had brought their old Druidism with them into Asia, and he attributes their acceptance of St Paul's teaching and their 'impulsive affection' as perhaps due, in some measure, to the affinities presented by the new religion to the loftiest and noblest of their own beliefs. *See* his *Life of St Paul*, Chap. XXIV.

(Ye) received me as an angel of God .... I bear you record that, if it had been possible, ye would have plucked out your own eyes, and have given them to me. St Paul, *Epistle to the Galatians*, IV, 14, 15.

27. The only recorded martyrdom in the history of the Celtic Church in Scotland is that of St Donnan, who was slain on the island of Eigg at the instigation of a Pictish Queen—not, it is said, because she was hostile to his religion, but because he was distracting her shepherds from their duties. F.M.McN.

Romanisation

28. Not to be confused with the great Augustine (of Hippo).

29. What is clear from all the story of his (Columba's) life is the complete independence of all his actions: there is no opposition to the Pope; there is simply no reference to the Pope at all. J. A. Duke, *The Columban Church*.

30. In the fifteenth century, when the islands were pledged to Scotland as part of the dowry of Princess Margaret of Denmark on her marriage to James III, they were transferred from the ecclesiastical jurisdiction of Trondhjem to the Archbishopric of St Andrews. F.M.McN.

31. As late as the thirteenth century, the *Cele De* (Culdees) maintained the worship of the Celtic Church in places as

far apart as St Andrews, Dunkeld, Iona and Dornoch. They were finally absorbed in the Roman Scotic Church. See A. B. Scott, *The Pictish Nation and Church*, 516.

32. To Queen Margaret's biographer, a devout priest, any rite not sanctioned by Rome was 'barbarous'.

33. Unity and conformity are not the same thing. Were this more clearly understood, a Commonwealth of Churches might achieve the unity which, in the modern world, an Imperial Church bent on uniformity cannot hope to achieve. F.M.McN.

34. Although they acknowledged the sovereignty of the Pope in spiritual matters, in temporal affairs the Scots retained their independence of judgment—witness the Declaration of Arbroath, that remarkable letter sent in 1320 (six years after Bannockburn) by 'the Earls, Barons, Freeholders, and the entire Community of Scotland' to Pope John XXII, with whom Edward II of England had been intriguing. After recounting the wrongs and cruelties they had suffered under Edward I, their liberation by Robert the Bruce, and the renewed threat from Edward II, they continue:

'Wherefore, we most earnestly beseech your Holiness, as the Viceregent of Him who giveth equal measure to all, and with whom there is no distinction, either of persons or nations, to admonish Edward to content himself with his own dominions, esteemed in former times enough for seven kings, and allow us Scotsmen, who dwell in a poor and remote country and seek nought but our own, to remain in peace . . . . Should your Holiness, however, give too credulous ear to the reports of our enemies and persist in favouring the English to our confusion, in spite of what we tell you, then the slaughter of our bodies, the perdition of our souls, and all that train of evils that shall follow . . . . will the Most High, we believe, impute to you.

'And to Him as the Supreme King and Judge we commit our Cause.'

Reformation

35. Superstition increased as piety attached itself more and more to formal observances. James Mackinnon, *Culture in Early Scotland*.

In all churches one encounters the type described by Dr Fosdick as 'a baptized pagan, with a correct theology, whose human relationships are untouched by the spirit of the Master'. F.M.McN.

36. The established Churches of Scotland and England might be described as the left and right wings of the Reformation. It is noteworthy that whilst Scotland reverted to type

and adopted a democratic system of church government, England, with its feudal tradition, retained its ecclesiastical hierarchy. F. M. MCN.

37. The Scottish Church does not produce mystics in the accepted sense of the word, for its greatest spirits have always felt that, as George Macleod expresses it, 'Despite the mystical insistence, yet the feeding-ground of mystical experience is constant practical concern.' And he quotes Dostoevsky's words: 'Love in practice is a harsh and terrible thing compared with love in dreams.'   F. M. MCN.

In the second of the present series of Gifford lectures in Natural Theology (delivered in Edinburgh), the Rev. C. E. Raven, D.D., . . . examined the two types of mysticism, negative and positive, and showed how the first led to world-rejection and the second to world-acceptance; but he argued that the two were not to be sharply distinguished and that in the effort to bring daily life in its multiple details into conformity with the pattern of the eternal, there was room for both elements. *The Scotsman.*

38. And he (the minister) told of the rising of Christ, a pin-point of the cosmic light far off in Palestine, the light that crept and wavered and did not die, the light that would yet shine on all the world, nor least the dark howes and hills of Scotland. Lewis Grassic Gibbon, *Sunset Song.*

39. Dr George Macleod.
'The Christian Myth'

40. The theologian believes in one God in whom the entire universe exists, and he cannot agree to a doctrine in which human goodness is in conflict with an irredeemably evil part of creation. It disrupts the universe, he says. And his dogma goes beyond this to propound a plan with a sacrifice and a son of God, by whom the evil in the world is to be redeemed. This is the Christ of orthodox belief. Through him charity is said to have come into the world.

Now there are many men to-day who embrace the Christian charity but cannot accept this theology. Not only is its anthropomorphic character unconvincing, with its other-world so impossibly like our own, but the Christ so conceived, with his sacrificial death and his resurrection in the spring, is obviously no other than the vegetation spirit of a dozen pagan religions, concerned with nothing more spiritual than a tribal food supply. The priests claim that their doctrine of redemption is the essence of Christianity. To me it is irrelevant; it is something taken over from pagan ritual, grafted on to the Christian legend. Some spokesmen of the Church (I remember particularly the Dean of St Paul's) have declared that without this mystical theology, as they call it, and the salvation they dispense, Christianity becomes mere 'vague uplift'. To me the ethics of charity with its irrationally inspired opposition to all that natural evil are far more worthy of the name of mysticism. W. B. Honey, in a broadcast talk on 'Christian Values in a World of Conflict'; from *The Listener*, 29 April, 1948.

And now abideth faith, hope, charity, these three; but the greatest of these is charity. St Paul 1 Corinthians, XIII, 13.

41.   The myth reveals the unconscious history of the race just as the dream reveals the unconscious history of the individual. Both show the same kind of expression in concrete image and dramatic form. William Halse Rivers, 'Dreams and Primitive Culture', Intern. Univ. Reading Course, Section VII.

42.   The fact is that most of us need bridges to take us across from the seen to the unseen, from appearance to reality, from time to eternity, express it how we will. A good bridge is one that takes us across, and this is the function of dogma, myth, and cultus. Or we may picture religious teachers as opticians, whose task it is to provide, for eyes of every degree of capacity, spectacles to help them to see the invisible. There can be no standardised orthodoxy. We must be very wary of such words as heretic and obscurantist. Dr W. R. Inge, 'Retrospect and Prospect' in *The Modern Churchman*, Sept. 1945.

The Christianising of the Festivals

43.   Some of the mythical saints of the early Celtic Church are resolvable into pagan gods—e.g. St Bride, who derives from a Celtic goddess of the same name. F.M.MCN.

44.   Hospinian, De Fest. Christ., cap. IV.

45.   Hildebrand, *De Diebus Sanctis*.

CHAPTER SIX. *Magic*

1.   *Keekit*, peeped; *ferlie*, marvel; *gey*, very; *unco gear*, strange things; *camstairie*, an obstinate, unmanageable person.

2.   *Natural History*, XXX, 13.

3.   Whilst the priest offers up prayers, the magician utters spells. F.M.MCN.

4.   *The Fairy Faith in Celtic Countries*.

5.   *Totem and Taboo*.

The Airts

1.   He's tied his steed to the kirk-style,
     Syne wrang-gaites roun' the kirk gaed he. Old Ballad.

2. In 1928 the present writer witnessed a funeral in the Hebrides where the approach to the graveyard was made *deiseil*, though this meant taking a longer and more circuitous route than the direct approach. F.M.McN.

3. Dùin an uineag a tuath,
    Dùin gu grad an uineag a deas,
    Agus dùin an uineag an iar,
    Cha d' thàinig fuath riamh o'n ear.
    J. G. Campbell, *Witchcraft and Second Sight*.

The Quarter Days

1. Rev. J. G. Campbell, *Superstitions of the Highlands and Western Islands of Scotland*.

2. Rev. W. Gregor, *Notes on the Folklore of the North-East of Scotland*.

3. As the majority of the young men on the island used to bear one of half-a-dozen patronymics—Macleod, Mackenzie, Matheson, Morrison, Nicolson and Macaulay—there was a fair chance that the name of the future husband was correctly divined. F.M.McN.

The Frith

1. *Carmina Gadelica*, vol. II.

2. It is not improbable that the surname Freer or Frere is a derivative from *frithir*. Progenitors of persons bearing this name were astrologers to the kings of Scotland. A. Carmichael in *Carmina Gadelica*, vol. II.

3. A. Goodrich-Freer, *The Outer Isles*.

The Quarter Cakes

1. *Carmina Gadelica*, vol. II.

Moon Magic

1. De Is. et Os., p. 367.

2. De Aug. Scient. III, 4.

3. In his *Archeological Evidence on the Early Christianity of Scotland*, Dr G. A. Frank Knight points out that Apurcrossan was beyond the Dalriadic kingdom and the jurisdiction of Iona, and alludes to Maol Rubha as a 'revered father of the Pictish Church'. From his *muinntir* or community missionaries were sent through all the glens of Ross-shire, the farthest east church being Fordyce, near Portsoy.

4. Amulree, for example, in Perthshire, is *Ath Maol Ruibhe*, Maol Rubha's Ford, and ancient fairs at Dingwall and Tain were known as *Féill Ma Ruibhe*, St Mourie's Fair.

5. St Maol Rubha's Chapel stood formerly on Isle Maree, one of the many fairy-like islands on this lovely sheet of water. F.M.McN.

Earth Magic

1. If we could become possessed of a different sort of vision, so

that the earth was no longer opaque and so that microscopic beings appeared of normal size, we should immediately realise that the unseen (earth) world is as teeming with life, movement, and complex activities as the visible air world above. Nina M. Hosali, M.Sc., in *The Unseen World*, Jan., 1948.

The natural foundation of man's life, said Mr Muir, was the earth and the store of solar energy which animated it. Up to the rarest achievements of philosophy and art this was the source from which all human productions emanated. It was of importance that this source should remain perpetually accessible to man and not be obstructed by the mass of secondary things which he draws from it.

The modern world of finished products was designated by Mr Muir as a secondary world: complete and self-contained, it isolated man from the primary source of life. This secondary world was void of origins, containing only ends: it had no principle of growth, but merely a technique of exchanging things. In Mr Muir's opinion this state of affairs was unsatisfactory and unnatural. Among other remedial measures designed to establish a natural harmony in things he suggested that the absolute division between town and country should be broken down by bringing the town into the country and the country into the town. This policy, indeed, was essential to intelligent town planning. Report of a lecture by Edwin Muir at Czecho-Slovak House, Edinburgh, from *The Scotsman*, 14 September, 1942.

Our past was in the earth and our roots are in the past. We live for a little on the surface, drawing from our roots and sending new shoots to the Sun. The earth beneath, the sun above, and we the children of their union. That is all we know, and perhaps all we need to know to find the power that has serenity at its heart. Neil Gunn, *Sun Circle*.

2. *See* A. Goodrich Freer, *The Outer Isles*.

3. See *The Clans, Septs and Tartans of the Scottish Highlands*, by Frank Adam, revised by Sir Thomas Innes of Learney, Appendix VII.

4. A church was built on the Moot Hill in the early seventeenth century, and it was here, in 1651, that the last Scottish coronation—that of Charles II—took place.

5. Hume, in his History of the Douglases, writes: 'When Robert Bruce was crowned, 27th March, 1306, Sir James, the eighth Lord Douglas, assisted and cast into a heap, as did the other barons, a quantity of earth off his lands of Douglas, which making a little hill is called *Omnis Terra*. This was the custom of those times.'

6. 'All Cromarty people,' says Professor Watson, who is a native of that district, 'are familiar with the belief that the final judgment is destined to take place on the Moor of Navity.'

7. *Weirdless*, luckless; *pine*, grief, pain.

The Gudeman's Croft

1. G. Henderson, *Popular Rhymes*.
    Saft, soft; *craft*, croft; *taft*, toft, homestead.

Fire Magic

1. O. E. *niedfyr*, from the same root as the German *nieten*, to churn; hence churned fire, fire produced by friction.

    The people look upon fire as a miracle of divine power provided for their good—to warm their bodies when they are cold, to cook their food when they are hungry, and to remind them that they, too, like the fire, need constant renewal mentally and physically. Alexander Carmichael, *Carmina Gadelica*.

2. The ready page, with hurried hand,
    Awaked the need-fire's slumbering brand.
    Scott, *Lay of the Last Minstrel*.

    The need-fire (*teine-eiginn*), which is used in Scotland on special occasions, is unknown in Ireland. Its place is taken by the Blessed Turf. Eleanor Hull, *Folk Lore of the British Isles*.

3. *The Golden Bough*.

4. The nine time nine—a sacred number.

5. Dr D. J. Macleod, Introduction to Martin's *Description of the Western Isles* (1934 edn.).

6. Ibid.

7. *In the Hebrides*.

8. J. Spence, 'On Folklore Days and Seasons' in *Trans. Buchan Field Club*, 1888–90.

Water Magic

1. *British Calendar Customs*, Scotland, vol. I.

    A few of our Scottish springs have ascertained medicinal properties, notably those at Strathpeffer and Bridge of Allan, but the majority have none. F.M.MCN.

2. In the Holy Wells of the Isles there lived, through countless generations, a trout which, in the thoughts of the folk, was accounted pious as a monk and worldly-wise as a Druid. To such a trout went the maid of the song for tidings of her absent lover. Kenneth Macleod, Introduction to 'The Troutling of the Sacred Well', in the *Songs of the Hebrides*, vol. II.

3. Dr D. J. Macleod, Introduction to Martin's *Description of the Western Isles*

4.   St Adamnan (679–704), *Life of St Columba*.
5.   Martin's *Description of the Western Isles*.
6.   The name *Holy Fair* was later used to denote a sacramental occasion. See Burns's poem of that name.
7.   *Description of the Western Isles*.
8.   In Egypt, ... a nail-tree may be seen in a sacred grove of long-thorned acacias at the village of Nezlet Batrân, in the Gizeh area, south of Cairo, and not far from the great pyramids. D. A. Mackenzie, *Scottish Folk-lore and Folk-life*.

Queen Victoria visited the well in September, 1877, and fixed her offering to the tree. (See Dixon's *Gairloch*.) The poet Whittier wrote, to commemorate his visit:
And whoso bathes therein his brow
   With care or madness burning,
Feels once again his healthful thought
   And sense of peace returning.

9.   . . . . St Fillan's Blessed Well,
Whose springs can frenzied dreams dispel,
And the crazed brain restore.
Sir Walter Scott.

10. A Roman Catholic ceremony of pre-Reformation times was revived at Orton, Speyside, yesterday, when over 500 priests and pilgrims from all parts of the North of Scotland marched in procession through the fields of St Mary's Well, whose waters have been reputed for centuries to possess miraculous healing properties.

. . . Many of the pilgrims drank the water from the well, and a number carried away supplies for the use of the sick and infirm. *The Scotsman*, 31 July, 1935.

11. Old Ronald certainly believed in those mysteries that remained from the old natural religion of the countryside. . . . It was certainly a religion of life: its greatest concern being the constant renewal of life by fertility and the need to protect it from mischance. It must have been a religion of true, not induced, humility, based on an appreciation of man's place among the forces of nature. Man had no thought that he might control those forces: he must live under, and, if possible, by them, for if he ran counter to them they might destroy him. Therefore he must try to run with them. Most of the primitive beliefs seem to have been inspired by the need to keep in step with nature. There is something like an empirical, a scientific attitude. The forces of nature are neither friendly nor hostile: impersonal forces—not a pantheon of temporal gods; but they have the laws of their being and unless men take heed of those laws,

disaster will come. John R. Allan, *The North-East Lowlands of Scotland*.

12. One of the Nine Maidens, St Fyndoca, erected a sanctuary on the lovely, peaceful island of Inishail, on Loch Awe, in the shadow of Ben Cruachan, and hither, for centuries, the clans of the adjoining territories—Campbells, MacArthurs, MacCalmans, MacCorkindales and others—brought their dead for burial. F.M.MCN.

13. J. M. MacKinlay, *Folklore of Scottish Wells and Springs*.

14. *Book of Days*.

15. Aberdeen Kirk Session *Records*, 23 November, 1630.

16. Guthrie, *Old Scottish Customs*.

17. Hanway in his *Travels* says that the practice of hanging rags at wells was common in Persia, and Mungo Park found it among some African tribes.

18. *Daily Record* (Glasgow), 7 May, 1934.
    The usual procedure is to 'silver' the water by dropping in a silver coin before drinking and wishing. F.M.MCN.

19. Ebenezer Henderson, as quoted in *Country Folklore*, vol. VII, p. 14.

20. At Crianlarich, a woman of the district told Dr Maclagan, that within the last thirty years (from 1902), she had known people come considerable distances to take water from a well between the old Priory and the Kirkton burying-ground, over which 'the living and the dead' were wont to pass. It was used for curing cattle injured by the Evil Eye. A silver coin was generally put into the vessel in which the water was carried.

21. Mr D. A. Mackenzie relates in his *Scottish Myth and Legend* how this 'silver water' was given him as a child to cure an illness believed to have been caused by the Evil Eye.

Magical Objects

1. Examples are to be seen in the Scottish National Museum of Antiquities. F.M.MCN.

2. The witches of Mongolia carry on their incantations by means of the scarlet silken thread. C. F. Gordon-Cumming, *In the Hebrides*.

3. Ibid.

4. A friend of the present writer's, a Roman Catholic, who lives in the Hebrides, has in her possession a Virgin's Nut on which a small silver cross has been mounted, and which has been blessed by a former bishop of the diocese. Late one evening, in 1936, a young man arrived breathless at her door and begged her to lend him the nut. His wife was expecting her first child and was already in labour; a friend of his had lost his wife in similar circumstances and he was resolved to

take no risks. The nut was safely returned with the news that all had gone well.

5. A. Polson, *Our Highland Folklore Heritage*.
6. The present writer recollects this charm being used in her own home in the Orkneys in the first decade of the present century. Jane had been doing her weekly churning, but the butter wouldn't come. It was bewitched, she said. Owld Jess, who was known to have the Evil Eye, had passed by her window that morning. For three successive weeks there was no butter. Jane went off to consult a wise woman of her acquaintance. She refused to tell us what advice she had received, but invited us all to stand around at the next churning. The butter came in no time, and from the churn Jane triumphantly produced a silver coin!

Magical Animals

1. See vol. II. *Candlemas*.
2. See vol. III. *Hallowmas*.

Magical Plants

1. J. B. Hannay, *Sex Symbolism in Religion*.

    The oak-tree is pre-eminently the holy tree of Europe. Not only Celts, but Slavs, worshipped amid its groves. To the Germans it was their chief god. The ancient Italians honoured it above all other trees; the original image of Jupiter on the Capitol at Rome seems to have been a natural oak-tree. So at Dodona, Zeus was worshipped as immanent in a sacred oak. Evans Wentz, *The Fairy Faith*.

2. Quoted by Frazer in *The Golden Bough*.
3. Violet Jacob, *The Rowan*.

    Flegged, frightened; *whaup*, curlew.

    If the rowan succeeded in keeping the witches away, it was impotent against a worse enemy, the factor, the agent of the de-scotticised laird to whom money had come to mean more than men, and social ambition than the laws of kinship and human kindness; and in many a deserted glen from Skye to Angus, the rowan stands pathetically beside the roofless cottage and reddens each autumn—for shame, it might be said, at one of the darkest blots in Scottish history. F.M.MCN.

4. *Folklore or Superstitious Beliefs in the West of Scotland within this Century* (1879).
5. Because life is one at the Spring Festival, the young man carries a blossoming branch bound with the wool of the young sheep. Jane Harrison, *Ancient Art and Ritual*.
6.   Badan de'n chaorrunn
          Thig o' aodann Ealasaid,
        Cuir snaithn' dearg 'us sreang as,

Cuir sid an ceann a chrathadair,
　'S ged thigeadh buidseach Endor
　　Gun ceannsaicheadh Alein Dall.
J. G. Campbell: *Witchcraft and Second Sight in the Scottish Highlands.*

7.　　　　Làir dhubh bhreabach,
　　　　　Feadh nan creagan,
　　　　Làir dhubh bhreabach,
　　　　　'S i'na ruith.

　　　　'Làn an dùirn de chaora dearga
　　　　　Chum a teanachd
　　　　　'S i'na ruith.
Ibid.

8.　Mrs Nan Dall, 'Scots Herbal Lore' in *Proceedings of the Scottish Anthropological and Folklore Society*, vol. III, No. I (1938).

9.　Brand, *Antiquities.*

10.　Fortingall, a village at the mouth of Glen Lyon, is rich in memorials of past ages, and claims to be the birthplace of Pontius Pilate, who is said to have been born during his father's embassy to the King of the Caledonians, who dwelt in the Round Tower of Donegal near by. The yew tree is believed to have been in existence at that period. Even yet it puts forth branches, and an offshoot flourishes beside it. The tree is now protected by a wall, which has gratings to allow ventilation. See A. M. Stewart, *A Highland Parish: the History of Fortingall.*

11.　　　　Buainidh mis' an t'iubhar àigh
　　　　Roimh chòig aisnean croma Chriosd
　　　　An ainm an Athair, a Mhic, 's an Spioraid Naoimh,
　　　　Air bhàthadh, air ghàbhadh, 's air ghriobhadh.
J. G. Campbell: *Witchcraft and Second Sight in the Highlands of Scotland.*

12.　　　　Buainidh mis' a chaithair làir
　　　　Mar bhuain Muire le dà làimh,
　　　　Buainidh mi le m'neart i,
　　　　'S buainidh mi le m' ghlaic i.
Ibid.

13.　　　　Buainidh mise a mòthan,
　　　　　An luibh a dh'òrduich Criosd,
　　　　　Cha n'eil eagal Iosga teine dhuit
　　　　　No cogadh nam ban sidh.
Ibid.

14.　　　　Buainidh mise am mòthan
　　　　　Fo ghréin guil an Dòmhnaich

> Fo laimh na h'òighe,
> An ainm na Teòra
>   A dheònaich a fhàs.
> Fhad 's ghleidhe's mi am mòthan
>   Gun lochd mo shùil,
>   Gun lot mo bheul,
>   Gun sprochd mo chridhe,
>   Gun chlibe mo bhàs.

Carmina Gadelica IV, 135.

15. Ibid.
16.
> Achlusan Challum Chille,
> Gun sireadh gun iarraidh,
> Cha d'thoir iad as do chadal thu,
> Is cha ghabh thu fiabhrus.
> Buainidh mis' an donn duilleach,
> Luibh a fhuaireadh an taobh bearraidh.
> Cha tugainn e do dhuine
> Gun tuilleadh air mo bheannachd.

J. G. Campbell, *Witchcraft and Second Sight*.

17. Greek ορχις (orchis), a plant with roots in the shape of testicles. Mirabilis est orchis herba, sive serapias, gemina radice testiculis simili. Pliny.
18. J. G. Campbell, *Witchcraft and Second Sight*.
19. John Cameron, *The Gaelic Names of Plants*.
20. MacCulloch: *The Misty Isle of Skye*.
21. Pratt's *Buchan*.
22. Thomas Wilkie, 'Old Rites, etc. in the South of Scotland' in the *Proceedings* of the Berwickshire Naturalists' Club.
23.
> Tagh seileach nan allt,
>   Tagh calltainn nan creag,
> Tagh fearna nan lón,
>   Tagh beithe nan eas.
> Tagh uinnseann na dubhair,
> Tagh iubhar na leuma,
> Tagh leamhan a bruthaich,
>   Tagh duire na gréine.

Carmina Gadelica, IV.

Magical Stones

1. In the Sma' Glen, on the haugh between the road and the river Almond, about eight miles from Crieff, lies a boulder eight feet high which is known as *Clach Osein*, or Ossian's Stone. It was removed by the builders of Wade's road from its original site, where, according to an ancient tradition, it marked the grave of the blind bard of the Fingalian tales.
F.M.MCN.

> In this still place, remote from men,

Sleeps Ossian, in the narrow glen.
Wordsworth.

2. John Smith, the Glasgow vaccinator, in 1771, was the first of the exponents of the famous theory that the plan of Stonehenge is in deliberate relation with the movements of the heavenly bodies. T. D. Kendrick, *The Druids*.

3. What Emerson wrote many years ago about Stonehenge applied equally to Callanish: 'We are not too late to learn much more than is known of this structure. Some diligent Fellowes or Layard will arrive, stone by stone, at the whole history, by that exhaustive British sense and perseverance, so whimsical in its choice of objects, which leaves its own Stonehenge or Choir Gaur to the rabbits, while it opens pyramids and uncovers Nineveh.' *English Traits*, XVI.

4. See Magnus Spence, *Standing Stones and Maeshowe of Stennis* (pamphlet).

5. See D. A. Mackenzie, *Scotland, the Ancient Kingdom*.

6. See Anna J. Mill, *Medieval Plays in Scotland*.

7. See Canon J. A. MacCulloch, *Religion of the Ancient Celts*.

8. In Ireland, the stone, Lia Faill, was known locally as Bod Fhearguis, penis Fergusii, whoever Fergus may be. It is the organ and symbol of reproductive power. R. A. S. Macalister, *Ancient Ireland*.

9. The present writer heard it many a time in her childhood.

10. *Scottish Calendar Customs*, I.

11. The legend is referred to in an article, 'The Stone of Destiny', by D. M. Heyde, in *The Scots Magazine*, May 1954.

In *Highways and Byeways in Central Scotland*, Seton Gordon says that he was informed by the Earl of Mansfield, whose seat is Scone Palace, that about a hundred and fifty years ago two employees on the Dunsinane estate discovered on the east side of Dunsinane Hill an opening which led to an underground chamber, and here they found, resting on pillars, a slab of stone with traces of hieroglyphics. On a subsequent visit, however, they found the entrance blocked by a landslide.

According to Alexander Hutcheson, the Dundee archaeologist, and author of *Old Stories in Stone*, the site of Macbeth's fort on the summit of Dunsinane Hill was excavated in 1818, at the instigation of Mr Nairn, the then laird of Dunsinane, and the underground chamber re-discovered. Beside the Stone, says Mr Heyde, there were two plaques bearing an inscription which has been translated (or mistranslated): 'The shadow of a kingdom till sylphs in air carry me to Bethel.' The stone, which was very heavy and thought possibly to be of meteoric origin, was carted away.

'I have ascertained locally beyond reasonable doubt,' says Mr Heyde, 'that the stone is known to have been taken in the first instance to Bandirran, near Balbeggie, but its subsequent disposal remains a mystery.'

12. Since the above was written, the lifting of the Stone by young Scottish patriots in 1950 has focussed on it the eyes of the world.

13. Frank Adam: *The Clan, Septs and Regiments of the Scottish Highlands* (Appendix x), revised by Sir Thomas Innes of Learney.

14. The Roman god Terminus was a sacred boundary stone.

15. See J. M. MacKinlay, *Folklore of Scottish Wells and Springs*.

16. Cf. Jeremiah VII, 18: The children gather wood, and the fathers kindle the fire, and the women knead their dough, to make cakes for the queen of heaven.

17. D. A. Mackenzie, *Scottish Folklore and Life*.

Mr Mackenzie relates the curious experience of a young doctor who was acting locum to a Dingwall doctor in or about 1915, and attended a patient not far from the holed rock.

On his second visit, he found that the illness had taken a serious turn, and he spoke to the patient's mother, who puzzled him greatly by remarking 'He is sure to recover, doctor; the cakes were taken last night.' The southerner was puzzled and asked what she meant. 'Oh, it's just a saying we will have,' came the evasive answer. The doctor consulted the writer, who suspected that the reference was to a folk custom, and he ultimately discovered that the cake-divination custom was often practised by women, assisted by children, who gathered dry sticks for the fire but were sent away before the cakes were baked and deposited. The local clergymen, doctors, and school-teachers, and even some of the husbands of the women guilty of perpetuating the pagan custom were quite unaware of it.

18. The Auld Hoose o' Gask was the birthplace of Baroness Nairne, who immortalised it in her song, 'The Auld Hoose'.

19. There is another kind of egg held in high renown by the people of the Gallic provinces . . . . In the summer, numberless snakes entwine themselves in a ball, held together by a secretion in their bodies and by a spittle. This is called *anguinum*. The Druids say that hissing serpents throw this up in the air, and that it must be caught in a cloak, and not allowed to touch the ground; and that one must instantly take to flight on horseback, as the serpents will pursue until some stream cuts them off. They pretend that these eggs can

only be taken on a certain day of the moon . . . . I myself
have seen one of these eggs; it was round, and about as
large as a smallish apple; the shell was cartilaginous, and
pocked like the arms of a polypus. The Druids esteem it
highly. Pliny: Nat. Hist. XXIX, 52.

20. C. Rogers, *Scotland Social and Domestic*.

21. A picture of the stone is published in the *Proceedings of
the Society of Antiquaries of Scotland*, vol. IV (1860–2).

22.   Bogam thu sa bhùrn
             A leug bhuidhe, bhòidheach, bhuadhar,
             Ann am bùrn an thior-uisg,
             Nach d'leig Bride a thruailleadh
             'An ainm nan Abstol naomh,
             'S Muire Oigh nam béusan
             'N ainm na Trianaid àrd,
             'S nan aingeal deabrach uile:
             Beannachd air an leug:
             'S beannachd air an uisge,
             Leigheas tinneas cléibh do gach
                   creatur ciùirte.
Proc. Soc. Anti. Scot., vol. XXVII.

23. At a meeting of the Synod of Glasgow on 25 October, 1638,
Gavin Hamilton of Raploch preferred a complaint against
Sir Thomas Lockhart of Lee 'anent the superstitious using
of ane stone set in silver for the curing of diseased cattle';
but the Synod decided that the water in which the stone
was dipped was given 'without using onie wordes, such as
charmers use in their unlawful practices, and considering
that in nature there be monie things seen to work strange
effect, qrof (whereof) no humane witt can give a reason,
it having pleasit God to give unto stones and herbes a special
virtue for the healing of monie infirmities in man and beast',
the matter be dismissed with an admonition to the Laird of
Lee to use the stone 'wt the least scandall that possibly may
be'. See the *Records* of the Synod of Glasgow.

24. To quote only one or two: Passing over Drummossie
Moor, near Inverness, he foretold that before many generations had passed the ground would be stained with the
best blood of the Highlands.
     Fulfilled in 1746, when the Battle of Culloden was
fought on this site.
     Of Tom-na-hurich, the 'fairy hill' of Inverness, he fore-
told (a) that ships would one day sail round the back of
it, and (b) that it would one day be under lock and key,
and the fairies secured within.
     (a) Fulfilled in 1847, when the Caledonian Canal,

begun by Telford in 1803, was completed; (b) fulfilled in 1860, when the hill was made into a cemetery.

One that puzzled the folk greatly: 'The day will come when fire and water shall run in streams through all the streets and lanes of Inverness.'

Fulfilled in 1826–9 with the introduction of gas and water through pipes into every corner of the town.

Some of the prophecies have not been fulfilled. F.M.MCN.

25. A large stone slab, now covered under the sand, lying a few yards west from the road leading from Fortrose to Fort-George Ferry, and about 250 yards north-west of the lighthouse, is still pointed out as marking the spot where this inhuman tragedy was consummated. Alexander Mackenzie: *The Prophecies of the Brahan Seer*, with an introduction by Andrew Lang.

26. With regard to the four Highland lairds, who were to be buck-toothed, hare-lipped, half-witted, and a stammerer—Mackenzie, Baronet of Gairloch; Chisholm of Chisholm; Grant, Baronet of Grant; and Macleod of Raasay—I am uncertain which was which. Suffice it to say that the four lairds were marked by the above-mentioned distinguishing peculiarities, and all four were contemporaries of the last of the Seaforths. Sir Bernard Burke, *Vicissitudes of Families*.

We believe Sir Hector Mackenzie of Gairloch was the buck-toothed laird, the Chisholm, the hair-lipped; Grant, the half-witted; and Raasay the stammerer. Alexander Mackenzie: *The Prophecies of the Brahan Seer*.

27. See *The Dictionary of National Biography*.

The Horseman's Word

1. John R. Allan: *The North-East Lowlands of Scotland*.

Magic in the Modern World

1. *Magic: Substance and Shadow (in Thurm Lecture)*, Proc. Scot. Anthrop. and Folk-lore Society, 1938.

2. Though the Greeks, with all their wisdom, failed to realise that in life beauty could not be achieved by adherence to the straight line, they did discover and apply this principle in architecture. In their supremely beautiful building, the Parthenon, there is actually not a single straight line. Situated as the temple is, on the height of the Acropolis, the lines, had they been straight, would have appeared crooked, whereas, being crooked in the right way, they appear straight; the building would have appeared 'dead', whereas it is 'alive', its pillars 'breathing' like the stems of flowers.

What is the secret? It is (according to the archaeologist

whose lectures the present writer attended on the spot) that beneath the apparent irregularity lies a hidden symmetry, all the vertical lines converging to an invisible point in space. Thus, by substituting what is called dynamic symmetry for geometric symmetry, a beauty unparalleled in architecture has been achieved.

It may be that the same principle holds good in human affairs. The nation, the group, the individual who persists in building upwards in a straight line, concentrating on its (or his) immediate and selfish interests, is bound, sooner or later, to 'gang aglee'. The secret of good building is to keep constantly in mind that 'invisible point in space' which may be identified with the Divine Will, towards which all human effort should be directed. This demands the sacrifice of all selfish interests, but offers instead the fulfilment of one's true interests, which are never at variance with those of others. F.M.MCN.

CHAPTER SEVEN. *The Fairies*

1. *Harles*, drags; *weird*, fate, destiny; *braw*, brave, fine; *hinny*, honey; *Glamourie*, magic, enchantment; *intil't*, in it; *siller*, silver; *abune*, above; *dowf*, dull, heavy, spiritless; *whinny*, covered with gorse; *haar*, sea-mist; *syne*, then; *strength*, stronghold; *ha'*, hall; *fludes*, floods; *sough*, breathe, sigh.

2. Beyond the Polar Circle, in the heart of forlorn Finnish Lapland, lives a small tribe, the Scolt Lapps . . . . Unlike so many primitive races, they have firmly rejected all efforts to bring them the comforts of our civilisation. They will not have even radio sets in their huts. The noise that comes from a box, they say, spoils the voice of the trees and the never-ending melody of the virgin forest. No wonder if Nature, in return for their faithfulness, has preserved in them the old powers we generally call 'second sight'. Telepathy among them is a commonplace; it even enables them to make appointments with one another when they are miles apart. They dream of a place and time, and meet as easily as if they had arranged it by telephone.

A Scolt Lapp will look at you with his clear transparent eyes . . . . and he will see your real face, your 'second face' behind the mask . . . . At times it makes him sad, looking into other people's eyes, to find something like a drooping flower in them, slowly fading from lack of care and proper watering.

. . . . We need to know that on the confines of Europe are some people who preserve those precious powers we have had to lose in our constant endeavour to master Nature. Robert Crottet, 'Children of the Wild', in *Time and Tide*, 15 Nov., 1947.

3. An Elgin correspondent of *The Scotsman*, 8 January, 1925, tells how he accompanied a man to a small farm in the parish of Dallas, in Moray, to buy a cow. A few days after he brought it home, the cow died as a result of a mishap. The buyer returned to the same farm and bought a second cow, to the surprise of the farmer, who thought he was taking a great risk. On receiving the price, the farmer put into the purchaser's hand a flint arrowhead, saying 'Tak ye that wi' her. Ye'll be nane the waur o't onywey.'

4. See Margaret Murray: *The Witch Cult in Western Europe*.

5. His researches in fairy lore won the author, who is an American, the degree of Docteur-des-lettres of the University of Rennes and the Research Degree of B.Sc. of Oxford.
     Fairyland

6. *Celtic Place-Names of Scotland*.

7. Macbain: *Celtic Mythology and Religion*.

8.   How beautiful they are,
        The lordly ones
        Who dwell in the hills,
        In the hollow hills.
        They have faces like flowers,
        And their breath is a wind
        That blows over grass
        Filled with dewy clover.
Fiona Macleod: *The Immortal Hour*.

9. A comparison between the Silver Branch of the Celts and the Golden Bough of the Ancients is drawn by Dr Evans Wentz in his *Fairy Faith*, and may be thus summarised:—

     The Golden Bough was in the gift of the queen of that underworld called Hades as the Silver Branch was in the gift of the Celtic fairy queen. Each seems to have been the symbolic bond between that world and this, offered as a tribute by all initiates who made the journey in full human consciousness; 'and, as we suspect, there may be even in the ancient Celtic legends of mortals who make that strange voyage to the Western Otherworld and return to this world again, an echo of initiatory rites—perhaps druidic—similar to those of Prosperine as shown in the journey of Aeneas, which, as Vergil records it, is undoubtedly a poetical rendering of an actual psychic experience of a great initiate.'

10. *The Voyage of Bran.* Translated from the Irish Gaelic by Dr Kuno Meyer.

11. And even as he spoke, a light began to glow and to pervade the cave and there was everywhere a wandering ecstasy of sound: light and sound were one; light had a voice, and the music hung glittering in the air . . . 'I am Aengus; men call me the Young. I am the sunlight in the heart, the moonlight in the mind; I am the light at the end of every dream, the voice for ever calling to come away; I am desire beyond joy or tears. Come with me, come with me: I will make you immortal; for my palace opens into the gardens of the Sun, and there are the fire-fountains which quench the heart's desire in rapture.' A.E.
   The Secret Commonwealth

12. First published (owing to Sir Walter Scott's interest) in 1815; republished in 1893 (edited by Andrew Lang); and published again in 1933 by Eneas Mackay of Stirling, with an introduction by R. B. Cunninghame-Graham and a drawing of the Fairy Hill of Aberfoyle by D. Y. Cameron. The Rev. Robert Kirk was a student of theology at St Andrews: his Master's degree, however, he took at Edinburgh. He was (and this is notable) the youngest and seventh son of Mr James Kirk, minister of Aberfoyle, the place familiar to all readers of *Rob Roy*. . . . He was employed on an '*Irish*' translation of the Bible, and he published a psalter in Gaelic (1684). Little is known of his life. He married, first, Isobel, daughter of Sir Colin Campbell of Mochester . . . and secondly the daughter of Campbell of Forday . . . He died (if he did die) in 1692, aged about fifty-one. Andrew Lang: Introductory Comment on *The Secret Commonwealth*.

13. The ancient scientists called life a Circle. In the upper half of this Circle, or here on the visible plane, we know that in the physiological history of man and of all living things there is first the embryonic or pre-natal state, then birth; and as life, like a sun, rises in its new-born power towards the zenith, there is childhood, youth, and maturity; and then, as it passes the zenith on its way to the horizon, there is decline, old age, and, finally, death; and as a scientific possibility we have in the lower half of the Circle, in Hades or the Otherworld of the Celts and of all peoples, corresponding processes between death and a hypothetical but logically necessary re-birth. Evans Wentz: *The Fairy Faith*.

14. Isobel Goudie, a member of the Auldearn (Moray) coven, tried in 1662, confessed to stealing milk from a cow by magic: 'We plait the rope the wrong way, in the Devil's

name, and we draw the tether between the cow's hind feet, and out betwixt our forward feet, in the Devil's name, and thereby take with us the cow's milk.'

15.   It was alleged against Isobel Sinclair, an Orkney witch tried in 1633, that during seven years, 'sex times at the reathes (quarter days) of the year, shoe hath been controlled with the Phairie; and that be thame, shoe hath the *second sight*: quhairby (whereby) shoe will know giff (if) thair be ony fey bodie (anyone destined to die shortly) in the hous.'

Second Sight is much too well authenticated to be rejected. The present writer has heard the Medical Officer of Health for a Highland county, among others, express his conviction of the reality of the phenomenon. F.M.MCN.

A friend of the present writer who was much interested in 'psychic' matters, when in India met a Scottish doctor who had specialised in neurology and had an intimate knowledge of native life and thought, and was surprised to learn that he considered there were far more remarkable phenomena in the Scottish Highlands, such as the phantom funerals foreshadowing a death.

The faculty of second sight he attributed to the high development of the sympathetic nervous system as compared to the cerebro-spinal system in a simple people living in close and harmonious contact with nature—one might call it 'in tune with the elements'—but the faculty, he held, tends to decline where this contact is slackened or lost or where the cerebro-spinal system is the more fully developed. It seems to be almost a matter of blood versus brain. F.M.MCN.

The faculty (of second sight) is so apt to the spiritual law that one wonders why it is set so apart in doubt . . . . I believe, not only because there is nothing too strange for the soul, whose vision surely I will not deny, while I accept what is lesser, the mind's prescience, and what is least, the testimony of the eyes.'   Fiona Macleod: *Iona*.

Experiments claimed to prove the age-old belief that human beings can, at times, obtain fleeting glimpses of future events have been carried out by Mr S. G. Seal, of the Mathematics Department of Queen Mary College, London University. To the scientific the faculty is known as precognitive telepathy.

The experiments were conducted from a purely scientific point of view. Reported in *The Scotsman*, 4 December, 1944.

16.   *The Mysteries of Britain*. The early Celtic peoples undoubtedly drew many of their fairy traditions from a memory of Druidic rites of divination. Evans Wentz: *The Fairy Faith*.

Popular Beliefs about Fairies

17. Malory relates that when Queen Guinevere advised her knights of the Round Table that on the morrow (May Day) she would go a-maying, she warned them all to be well-horsed and dressed in green, for green is the fairy colour, and symbolises eternal youth and resurrection or re-birth, as the earth in spring-time is re-clad in green.

During the ceremonies of initiation into the ancient Mysteries, it is supposed that the neophyte left the physical body in a trance state, and in full consciousness . . . . entered the subjective world and beheld all its wonders and inhabitants; and that coming out of that world he was clothed in a robe of sacred green to symbolise his own spiritual resurrection and re-birth into real life—for he had penetrated the Mystery of Death and was now an initiate. Evans Wentz: *The Fairy Faith*.

In modern masonry, which preserves many of the ancient mystical rites, and to some extent those of initiation, as anciently performed, green is the symbol of life's immutable nature, of truth and victory. Robert Macoy: *General History of Freemasonry*.

18. On Greek vases the human soul is depicted as a pygmy issuing from the body through the mouth: and this conception existed among Romans and Teutons. Like their predecessors, the Egyptians, the Greeks also often represented the soul as a pygmy with butterfly wings. . . . According to Caedmon, who was educated by Celtic teachers, angels are small and beautiful, quite like good fairies. Evan Wentz: *The Fairy Faith*.

19. Quoted by Thomas Keightly in *The Fairy Mythology* (1850 edn.).

20. *Carmina Gadelica*.

21. *Mell*, mix; *Weirdless wicht*, ill-fated creature.

The Fairy Hills

22. In the Middle Ages the Crusader Knights of the Order of St John of Jerusalem established a church here, on the route of the Pilgrim's Way to the shrine of St Ninian at Whithorn.

23. See *Songs of the Hebrides*, vol. I, Introduction to 'A Fairy Plaint'.

Fairy Gifts

24. *Songs of the Hebrides*, vol. I, 'Dunvegan Cradle Croon'.

25. Her masterpiece, 'Kismul's Galley', unknown beyond the islands until it slipped into Mrs Kennedy-Fraser's net, has been sung by Chaliapin in the great European capitals.

The 'Taking' of Mortals

26. Thomas Learmonth of Ercildoune (1226–97). (The
     Russian poet Lermontov is believed to be a descend-
     ant.) Mr Lewis Spence conjectures that 'True' Thomas
     is a corruption of 'Druid' Thomas. A fragment of the
     Rhymer's Tower stands above the Leader at the south
     end of Earlston (originally Ercildoune) in Berwickshire.
     A cairn marks the spot where the Eildon tree once stood.
     F. M. MCN.

     Huntly Bank and the adjoining ravine, called, from im-
     memorial tradition, 'The Rhymer's Glen', were ultimately
     included in the domain of Abbotsford. The scenery of this
     glen forms the background of Edwin Landseer's portrait of
     Sir Walter Scott, painted in 1833. J. G. Lockhart, Note to
     Sir Walter Scott's *Poems*.

27. Many of the prophecies attributed to Thomas the Rhymer
     have been preserved. Among them are these:

          The Burn o' Breid
          Sall rin fu' reid,

     fulfilled in the Battle of Bannockburn.

          When the heron leaves the tree,
          The Laird o' Gight sall landless be.

     The castle and lands of Gight, in the parish of Fyvie,
     Aberdeenshire, came, in or about 1479, into the possession
     of William Gordon, third son of the second Earl of Huntly.
     He was killed at Flodden in 1513. On 12 May, 1785,
     Catherine Gordon, heiress of Gight, married the Hon. John
     Byron. Tradition says that about the time of their marriage
     the herons which had nested for years in a fine tree near the
     castle left and took up their abode in the woods of Haddo
     House. The Gight estate was sold soon after the marriage.
     Catherine Gordon became the mother of Lord Byron.

          As lang's this stane stands on this craft,
          The name o' Keith sall be alaft;
          But when this stane begins to fa',
          The name o' Keith sall wear awa.

     The stone referred to stood near the Castle of Inverugie,
     the seat of the Keiths, Earls Marischal, one of whom was
     Field-Marshal to Frederick the Great. The Stone was re-
     moved in 1763 and built into the church of St Fergus,
     then being erected. A year later the estates were bought
     by Lord Pitfour.

     One of the most celebrated prophecies is that of the
     accession of a Scottish king to the throne of England:

          Howe'er it happen for to fa'
          The Lyon sall be lord o' a';
          The French Quene sall beare the sonne

> Sall rule all Britains to the sea,
> Quhilk o' the Bruce's blood sall come
> As neare as to the nint degree.

In his poem, 'Ane New Yere Gift To The Quene Quhen Scho Come First Hame', written in 1561 to celebrate the return of Mary Stuart to the land of her birth, Alexander Scott alludes to his prophecy:

> If saws be sooth to show thy celsitude,
> What bairn should brook all Britain by the sea?
> The prophecy expressly doth conclude,
> The French wife of the Bruce's blood should be:
> Thou art by line from him the ninth degree,
> And was King Francis' party maik and peer;
> So, by descent, the same should spring of thee,
> By grace of God, against this good new year.

Five years later, Mary gave birth to the son who was to unite the crowns of Scotland and England.

But perhaps the most widely known of all the Rhymer's prophecies concerns the family of Haig:

> Tide, tide, whate'er betide,
> There's aye be Haigs o' Bemersyde.

For more than seven hundred years there have been Haigs at Bemersyde, an estate in the Border country. They were a race of 'bonnie fechters': Haigs fought with Wallace and Bruce, and on the fields of Otterburn and Flodden, and a Haig led the British armies to victory in the first World War. In 1921, Bemersyde House was presented by national subscription to Field-Marshal Earl Haig, and on his death passed to his son. F.M.McN.

28. *Ferlie*, wonder; *ilk*, each; *tett*, strand; *harp and carp*, play and recite (as minstrel); *weird*, doom; *daunton*, intimidate.

29. Introductory Comment to *The Secret Commonwealth*.

30. *Yorlin*, yellow-hammer; *hindberrye*, raspberry; *minny*, mother; *or*, ere; *walk*, grassy path, glade; *wene*, dwelling; *maike*, mate; *his lane*, alone; *happ'd*, covered.
    The Changeling

31. Allan Cunningham, *Traditional Tales*. Kain-bairns, children paid in tribute by the witches to their Devil.
    The Trolls

32. Delattre, *English Fairy Poetry*.

33. *Demonology and Witchcraft*.

34. In the writer's childhood, a mound called Dingishowe, at the narrow isthmus dividing the parishes of St Andrews and Deerness, was the reputed gathering-place, on Midsummer Eve, of the trows of the East Mainland of Orkney.

Tutelary Beings

35. Fiona Macleod.

36. In 1921, the present writer was told by the late Gillespie McNeill, the bard of Colonsay and a contributor to the *Songs of the Hebrides*, that his grandmother, who belonged to the adjacent island of Jura, used to carry a cogie of milk to the hill after the milking and spill it on one of the 'fairy circles' as an offering to the *sithe*, or fairies. This custom was once widely prevalent. F.M.MCN.

37. In Wales, one of the names of the fairies is *Y Mamau*, The Mothers. It may be that the fairies represent the ancient group of 'Earth Mothers' who caused the grass to grow, the corn seeds to sprout in the earth, the trees to bud, blossom, and bear fruit. D. A. Mackenzie, *Scottish Folklore and Folk-Life*.

38. A unique map, embroidered in wools by the members of the Kinloch S.W.R.I., which depicts pictorially the history and landmarks of the surrounding districts, includes the Green Lady of Ardblair. F.M.MCN.

39. The reputed home of the 'Green Lady' in the heart of Stonehaven's Old Town has just been demolished . . . . For a long time, the house where she was supposed to appear was empty. First intruders in the 'Green Lady's' abode were the war-time Home Guard, who passed an unofficial requisitioning order and used the property for battle practice. Privates were sceptical, tough N.C.O.'s openly scornful about the ghost story. But the name stuck. Parade orders were often 'House-to-house fighting at the Green Lady'.

    . . . There is no real evidence as to who the lady was supposed to have been in her earthly existence. What is certain is that aged fisher folk will still speak of the High Street-Shorehead corner as 'The Green Lady' long after the history-steeped walls and tiled roofs of the Old Town have been replaced by modern dwellings. *The Weekly Scotsman*, 25 March, 1948.

40. Rev. W. Gregor, 'Notes on Beltane Cakes', *Folklore*, vol. VI.

41. Otherwise there might have been no George Macdonald and no Ramsay Macdonald, whose forebears were refugees from Glencoe.

42. Tha caoineachag bheag a bhròin,
    A dòrtadh deòir a sùla,
    A'gul 's a' caoidh cor Clann Dòmhuill,
    Fàth mo leòin! nach d' éisd an cumha.
    Carmina Gadelica.

43. Fiona Macleod.

44. In Britanny, the night washerwomen were a troop of ghosts

. . . . They washed, they dried, and they sewed the shrouds of the dead men who yet walk and talk (those doomed to die before the following November), singing:—

> Till there come Christian's saviour,
> We must bleach our shrouds
> Under the snow and the wind.

Foyer Breton, vol. I, p. 144.

45. Fiona Macleod.
46. Rev. A. M. Macfarlane, in *Trans. Gael. Soc. Inverness*, vol. XXXIV.

The Sluagh

47. *Carmina Gadelica.*
48. The late Rev. David Duncan, Musselburgh.
49. Frazer, in *The Golden Bough*, tells us that Breton, German, Slavonian and Esthonian rustics throw knives, sickles, or forks, sticks, or stones into a passing whirlwind; whilst among the Bedouins of East Africa, 'no whirlwind sweeps across the path without being pursued by a dozen savages with drawn creeses, who stab into the centre of the dusty column in order to drive away the evil spirit that is believed to be riding on the blast'.

Traces of Animism

50. Compare Shelley:
> The moveless pillar of a mountain's weight,
> Its active, living spirit.

51. Mrs Johnston, *Clan Albyn.*
52. *Celtic Place-Names of Scotland.*

The Merfolk

53. *Scenes and Legends.*
54. Peter Buchan, *Annals of Peterhead.*
55. A. Polson, *Our Highland Folklore Heritage.*
56. Hugh MacDiarmid, 'A Daughter of the Sea' (*Shetland Lyrics*).

Spirits of the Forest

57. Gael. *ar*, on, and *usige*, water.
58. *Celtic Place-Names of Scotland.*
59. Sir Walter Scott 'heard it told that the celebrated free-booter, Rob Roy, once gained a victory by disguising a part of his men with skins so as to resemble the ourisks', or shaggy men.
60. *Folklore in Lowland Scotland.*
61. *Scottish Folk-lore and Folk-life.*

The Brownies

62. William Grant Stewart, *Popular Superstitions of the Highlands.*
63. Cf. *The Mannikin of the Cattlefold (From the Hebrides).*

In the Black Forest, a new boat drove away a nix, one of the little water-people with green teeth who came and worked with the country folk. See Thomas Keightley, *Fairy Mythology*.

64. *Scottish Folk-lore and Folk-life*.

65. *Eesless*, useless.

66. W. Gunnyson, *Illustrations of Scottish History, Life and Superstition*.

Spirits in Animal Form

67. Dr George Henderson, *Survivals of Belief among the Celts*.

68. *Popular Superstitions of the Highlands*.

69. An aunt of the present writer's recollects that when staying with her brother-in-law, the Rev. Donald Robertson, at Ballindalloch (Banffshire) in the summer of 1891 or 1892, they entertained a footsore woman who had tramped from Inverness and was on her way 'to consult someone who had a kelpie's bridle'.

Sir Robert Bruce Lockhart, whose mother was a Macgregor, and who spent most of his school holidays in the Glenlivet country, recalls the story of Warlock Willie in his book, *My Scottish Childhood*.

70. Collected by Miss Frances Tolmie. See *The Journal of the Folk-Song Society*, vol. XVI.

71. *Clan Albyn*.

72. *Sweir*, reluctant; *fouk*, folk; *whiles*, occasionally; *gin*, if; *manes*, moans.

73. Rev. A. M. Macfarlane, 'Myths Associated with the Mountains, Springs and Lochs of the Highlands' in *Trans. Gael. Soc. Inverness*.

The Fairy Faith Today

74. *The Scape-Goat*.

75. Eric Linklater, *The Man on My Back*.

CHAPTER EIGHT. *The Witches*

1. *Tod*, fox; *wud*, wood; *ahint*, behind; *clud*, cloud; *cruppen*, crept; *cantrips*, witches' spells; *pyke*, pick, steal; *lift*, sky; *but mair adowe*, without more ado.

2. In October, 1947, a will was disputed in the Scottish Land Court at Stornoway, on the ground that the testator had believed in witchcraft and had accused a neighbour of walking three times round his croft, against the sun, to take the milk from his cow, and of putting a spell on his sheep, as a result of which some of them had gone lame.

Lord Gibson, giving judgment, said, 'Even supposing it had been proved that he was superstitious, there is not a tittle of evidence that any belief he held had affected his ability to make a will.' The case is reported in *The Scotsman* of 18 October, 1947.

3. John Ruthven, Earl of Gowrie (c. 1578–1600) proceeded from Edinburgh University to Padua, where he studied the natural sciences, including chemistry. He was concerned in the Gowrie conspiracy, and 'it is characteristic of James I that he should have directed a special inquiry into the reputed dealings of Gowrie in the Black Art'. (See D.N.B.)

Sir Robert Gordon of Gordonstoun, in Moray, popularly known as Sir Robert the Warlock, was a reputed man of science who had travelled much on the Continent for his improvement. He was 'somewhat of a favourite with James II, who made him a gentleman of his household and took an interest in his scientific inventions'. Two letters addressed to him by Samuel Pepys are (or were) preserved at Gordonstoun. (See D.N.B.).

Michael Scot (c. 1175–1234), mathematician, astrologer, alchemist, physician and scholar, became attached to the court of the Emperor Frederick II in Sicily and appears to have been celebrated all over Europe as a magician. He is mentioned by Dante in the *Inferno* (c. 20), by Boccaccio as 'a great master of necromancy', and by Sir Walter Scott in *The Lay of the Last Minstrel*. (See D.N.B.).

4. F. M. Powicke, in *The Spectator*, 18 April, 1941.

5. A notorious instance was that of the unfortunate Lady Glamis (née Douglas), widow of the sixth Lord Glamis. A relative of her husband, whose advances she had rejected, persuaded the King, James V, that she and her son were plotting to destroy his (the King's) life by witchcraft. They were tried and sentenced to death, and on a fine summer day in 1537 Lady Glamis was burnt as a witch upon the Castlehill in Edinburgh, 'with great commiseration of the people in regard to her noble blood, being in the prime of her years, of a singular beauty, and suffering all, though a woman, with man-like courage.'

Fortunately the death sentence on her son was deferred, and he was ultimately set free: otherwise King George VI would have had to go elsewhere than Glamis for his bride. The King was, of course, a direct descendant of James V, and, as Sir Robert Bruce Lockhart has pointed out, 'the quarter-centenary of her (Lady Glamis's) death coincided almost to the day with the coronation of her direct descendant, the former Lady Elizabeth Bowes-Lyon, as Queen of Britain.' F.M.MCN.

The Horned God

6. Burns, *Address to the Deil*.

Burns' 'Deil' is a curious compound of the Devil of the Bible and the 'devil' of the witches:

> O thou! whatever title suit thee,
> Auld Hornie, Satan, Nick, or Clootie,
> Wha in yon cavern grim and sootie,
>   Clos'd under hatches,
> Spairges about the brunstane cootie
>   To scaud poor wretches!
>
> Let warlocks grim and wither'd hags
> Tell how wi' you on ragweed nags
> They skim the muirs, an' dizzy crags
>   Wi' wicked speed;
> And in kirk-yards renew their leagues,
>   Owre howkit deid.

Spairges, splashes; *brunstane*, brimstone; *cootie*, bucket; *scaud*, scald; *howkit*, dug-up.

7.   Here is a characteristic deil-rhyme:—

> The deil sat suppin' the auld wife's kail,
>   With a hey sing ho, and a tow, row, row!
> But she raxed a het coal to the neuk o' his tail,
>   And loudly screiched he at the scutherin' lowe!
> He girned, he growled, he gabbered and grat,
>   With a hey sing ho, and a tow row row!
> And doun on the ingle he shivered the pat,
>   As he flew up the lum wi' his tail in a lowe!

Quoted by James Grant in *Harry Ogilvie*.

Kail, broth; *raxed*, reached; *screiched*, screeched; *scutherin'*, scorching; *lowe*, flame; *girned*, complained; *gabbered*, gabbled; *grat*, wept; *pat*, pot; *lum*, chimney; *lowe*, flame.

8.   See *The Witch-Cult in Western Europe*.

9.   It was the sacrifice of the Horned God himself.
     Margaret Murray, *The Witch-Cult in Western Europe*
                    Sacrifice

10.   Pitcairn, *Criminal Trials*.

11.   *Fende*, fiend; *mekill*, big; *hende*, handsome.

12.   *Teind*, tithe.
                    Organisation

13.   Nin, from Gael; *nighean*, daughter (of).

14.   James VI's spirited manual on witchcraft—*Demonologie* (Edinburgh 1597)—was inspired not by mere childish credulity, but by personal experience, for the witches had given him a bad fright. At the trial (in his presence) of the North Berwick witches, in which three covens were implicated, the charge was high treason; they had plotted the

death of the King and Queen by witchcraft. First of all, it transpired, they had performed incantations to raise a storm in order to wreck the ship on which the King was returning with his bride from Denmark—and the storm that actually arose nearly effected their purpose; then they tried the method of melting a wax image, and it is evident that they were prepared to use poison as a last resort.

The significance of the witches' attempt, as well as the identity of the 'devil' by whom it was instigated, transpired in the evidence, during which Barbara Napier admitted the motive to have been 'that another might rule in his Majesty's place and the government have gone to the Devil'; for Bothwell, whose father was an illegitimate but subsequently legitimised son of James v, had a strong claim to be regarded as heir male to the throne should James die without issue. Owing to the loyalty of the witches he contrived to elude punishment, but his power was broken by the execution of the leading spirits of his band, and he was obliged to flee the country. See Margaret Murray, *The Witch-Cult in Western Europe*.

A woodcut of the 'Devil' preaching to the North Berwick witches appears in the pamphlet, *News from Scotland, declaring the Damnable Life and Death of Dr Fian*, London, N.D. (1591).

Admission Rites

15. J. M. E. Saxby, 'Folklore from Unst', in the Rev. Biot Edmonston's *Home of a Naturalist*.

Compare the Rev. Robert Kirk's account of the initiation into second sight, p. 111.

The Coven

16. W. Grant Stewart, *Highland Superstitions and Amusements*.

Familiars

17. Divination by animals, called by the Romans augury, was common in classical times. F.M.MCN.

18. Jock (of Jock's Lodge, now a well-known Edinburgh landmark) tells how his mother, who was 'brankit and burnt' as a witch, had cast an evil spell on a local laird.

'What had the laird done to provoke such vengeance?'

'He shot her urchin—a hedgehog that folk ca'd her familiar. It slept in a cozy neuk o' her bed at nicht, but I thocht it weel awa, for it was a sair rival to me, and aye got a share o' my sowans and kail.' James Grant, *Harry Ogilvie*.

The Broom

19. *Cousin Pons.*

Transformation into Animals

20. *Sych*, sighing; *quhill*, while; *shat*, a sudden sharp pain; *thraw*, twist or wrench; throe.

21. The said Elspet did cast a cantrip on hir kow, that she colde not eate nor give milk. *Records of the Presbytery of Cupar*, 1649.

22. From MacTaggart's *Gallovidian Encyclopedia*.

Pingle, a small tin goblet with a long handle, used for preparing a child's food; *haurnpan*, skull; *tade*, toad; *gled*, old horse; also kite; *hawcket*, chopped; *chicken-wort*, chickweed; *gellocks*, earwigs; *foggy*, mossy; *bumbee*, bumble bee; *bykes*, hives; *ask*, eft, newt, kind of lizard; *skinklin*, sparkling.

23. *Yirbs*, herbs; *quean*, maiden; *bourtree*, elder; *gowans*, daisies; *thrissles*, thistles; *binwud*, bindweed; *blinmen's baws* (blind men's balls), the common puff-ball; *bluidy fingers*, foxgloves; *napple roots*, a sweet wild root, apparently heath-peas; *gowk's spittles*, frothy matter frequently seen on the leaves of plants; *pizion*, poison; *fumart*, pole-cat; *nool*, small horn; *nool's shearings*, probably hartshorn shavings; *nowt's neers*, ox kidneys.

cf. Shakespeare, *Macbeth*, Act IV, Sc. I.

The Witch Cake

20. Cromek, *Remains of Nithsdale and Galloway Song*.

Pyke, pick; *hip*, shoulder of hill; *howe*, hollow, valley; *whomel*, turn quickly round; *lift*, sky; *keppit*, caught; *wan to*, reached; *hynt*, gathered up; *haurn*, toast, fire; *whorl*, whirl; *thackless*, roofless; *sark*, shirt; *gaur graen*, make groan.

The Garter

25. Was the lady who dropped the garter when dancing with Edward III and was overcome by confusion a witch? Margaret Murray, *The Witch Cult in Western Europe*.

The Sabbaths

26. On Walpurgis-Nacht, the witches held an 'International' on the Brocken, in the Harz Mountains. They rode on magpies' tails, and after the sabbath danced until they had danced away the winter's snows.

27. In Macbeth's time, two of the most famous witches in Scotland lived one on each side of Macbeth, the one at Collace, the other not far from Dunsinnan House, at a place called the Cape . . . . By their counsel, Macbeth built a lofty castle upon the top of an adjoining hill, since called Dunsinnan. The moor where the witches met, which is in the parish of St Martin's, is still pointed out by the country people, and there is a stone still preserved, which is called the Witches' Stone. Quoted by W. C. Hazlitt in *Faith and Folklore*.

28. Boguet (1589) says, 'Ils le baisent aux parties honteuses de derrière.'

29. A woman attainted for sorcery by the Presbytery of Perth stated that she had a book containing magical knowledge which was 'her Goodsire's, her Grandsire's, and was a thousand years old'. Her son, Adam Bell, read it to her. See the *Records* of the Presbytery of Perth.

   A manuscript book of magical recipes known as the *Red Book of Appin* is known to have been extant at the beginning of the nineteenth century. When last heard of, it seems to have been in the possession of the now extinct family of Stewart of Invernayle. Another, known as the *Book of the Black Art*, was still spoken of with bated breath during the present writer's childhood in Orkney. This book, or a copy of it, was in the possession of a man in the West Mainland who, having repented of his misdeeds and having tried in vain to get rid of it, took it to the minister of the parish, who buried it deep in the Manse garden; and there, presumably, it remains. (See a letter from Mr P. Leith, Stennis, in *Orkney Folklore*.) The minister was the Rev. William Clouston, Minister of Sandwick and Stromness, 1794–1832.

   The present writer recollects hearing from an old servant that the only way to get rid of a copy of the Book of the Black Art was to burn it leaf by leaf with a leaf of the Bible. F. M. McN.

   Michael Scot the Wizard's book is said to have been interred with him in Melrose Abbey.

   The Dances

30. Reginald Scott, quoting Bodin, says, 'These night-walking, or rather night-dancing witches brought out of Italie into France that dance which is called La Volta.' This is said to be the origin of the waltz.

   Survivals of the processional dance are the Furry dance of Cornwall and the Farandole of France.

31. Of the original church, only a porch remains to mark the site of the churchyard where three covens of witches met to compass the death of the King. It stands not far from the modern harbour. F. M. McN.

32. Pitcairn, *Criminal Trials*.

33. This was evidently a lascivious dance with obscene postures, and may very well have descended from the witches' assemblies then broken up. J. M. McPherson, *Primitive Beliefs in the North-East of Scotland*.

34. This song is included in the Skene Manuscript (early seventeenth century), a collection of lute airs and dance

music, and the air is published in Daunay's *Ancient Melodies of Scotland* (1838). The words, which are described as 'not quite ladylike', are preserved in Skene.

The Practice of Witchcraft

35. Hector Boece (1465–1536), *The Chronicles of Scotland*.
36. Duff (Dubh) or Duffus was the son of Malcolm I. 'So notable was his character for uprightness and gentleness that he was included among the martyrs of the Church and reckoned among the saints.' He was buried in Iona.

 Forres had a bad name for witches, and a *Witches' Stone* in the hedgerow at the base of the Cluny Hill marks the spot where three witches were executed for plotting the death of Macbeth's ancestor, King Duffus. *A. A. Road Book of Scotland*, see *Forres*.

37. We should deceive ourselves if we imagined that the belief in witchcraft is even now dead in the mass of the people. On the contrary, there is ample evidence to show that it only hibernates under the chilling influence of rationalism, and that it would stir into active life if that influence were ever seriously relaxed. Frazer, *The Golden Bough*.
38. One of these hair ropes is in the possession of an old man in Stirlingshire.
39. 'Toads did draw the plough as oxen, couch-grass was harness, a gelded animal's horn was the coulter and a piece of a gelded animal's horn the sock.' All the parts of the plough connoted barrenness for the owner of the soil.

The Witches and the Fairies

40. The belief in occult science is far more widely spread than scholars, lawyers, doctors, magistrates and philosophers imagine. The instincts of the people are ineradicable . . . . The occult sciences, like many natural phenomena, are passed over by the freethinker or the materialist philosopher, *id est*, by those who believe in nothing but visible and tangible facts, in the results given by the chemist's retort and the scales of modern physical science . . . . They make no progress, for the greatest intellects of two centuries have abandoned the field . . . . It is strange that someone has not restored the teaching of the occult philosophies, once the glory of the University of Paris, under the title of anthropology. Balzac, *Cousin Pons*.
41. Dogs of the Chow type were kept by the Neolithic people as watchdogs. Margaret Murray, *The Witch Cult in Western Europe*.
42. A witch-rhyme used in shooting elf-arrows at strayed travellers was given by Isabel Goudie at her trial in 1662:—

 I shoot yon man in the Devillis name,

He sall not win heil hame;
And this sall be also trew,
Thair sall not be ane bit of him blew.
  Highland Witches

43. *Songs of the Hebrides*, vol. III.
  Types of Witch

44. The near descendants of 'the base and ignorant sort of
witches' are described by Scott in *The Bride of Lammer-
moor*:

The lame woman and the octogenarian sibyl . . . had hob-
bled into the garden to gather rosemary, southernwood, rue,
and other plants proper to be strewed upon the body, and
burned by way of fumigation in the chimney of the cottage.
The paralytic wretch . . . was left guard upon the corpse,
lest witches or fiends might play their sport with it.

The following low croaking dialogue was necessarily
overheard by the Master of Ravenswood:

'That's a fresh and full-grown hemlock, Annie Winnie—
mony a cummer langsyne wad hae sought nae better horse
to flee ower hill and how, through mist and moonlight, and
light doun in the King of France's cellar.'

'Aye, cummer! but the very deil has turned as hard-
hearted now as the Lord Keeper, and the grit folk that hae
breasts like whinstane. They prick us and they pine us, and
they pit us on penny-winkles for witches; and, if I say my
prayers backwards ten times over, Satan will never gie me
amends o' them. . . . . But ne'er mind, cummer! we hae
this dollar of the Master's, and we'll send doun for bread
and for yill, and tobacco, and a drap brandy to burn, and
a wee pickle saft sugar—and be there deil or nae deil, lass,
we'll hae a merry night o't.'

Here her leathern chops uttered a sort of cackling
ghastly laugh, resembling to a certain degree, the cry
of the screech-owl.

'He's a frank man, and a free-handed man, the Master,'
said Annie Winnie, 'and a comely personage . . . . He wad
make a bonny corpse—I wad like to hae the streaking and
winding o' him.'

. . . . 'Mak haste, sirs,' cried the paralytic hag from
the cottage, 'and let us do what is needfu', and say what is
fitting; for, if the dead corpse be na straughted, it will girn
and thraw, and that will fear the best o' us.'

Pine, to cause pain; *penny-winkles*, an instrument of
torture; *yill*, ale; *straughted*, straitened; *girn*, grin;
thraw, twist.

45. See Isabel Cameron, *A Highland Chapbook*.

46. The Great Montrose walked to his execution escorted by the Town Guard of Edinburgh under the command of Major Weir, later to become notorious as a warlock. F. M. MC N.

47. See *The Book of Meigle (Scottish Women's Rural Institutes)*.

48. Trystes, where the whole warlocks and witches of a county were assembled, are yet remembered among the peasantry with terror; they are wont to date their age from them, thus—'I was christened o' the Sunday efter Tibble Fleucher's Hallowmas rade.' Cromek, *Remains of Nithsdale and Galloway Song.*

The Evil Eye

49. Projects undreamed of by past generations will absorb our immediate descendants; forces, terrific and devastating, will be in their hands . . . . With the hopes and powers will come dangers out of all proportion to the growth of man's intellect, to the strength of his character, or the efficiency of his institutions. Once more the choice is offered between Blessing and Cursing. Winston Churchill, *Thoughts and Adventures.*

50. *Cronachdain Suil.*

> Chuìrnich suil thu,
> Thurmaich bial thu,
> Rùnaich cridh thu,
> Smuainich miann thu.

Index

Ab 35F, 39
Abaris 18
Abbotsford 204
Abbeys:
   Dryburgh 41
   Holyrood 41
   Jedburgh 41
   Melrose 41
   Pluscarden 41
Aberdeen 70, 86, 131, 145, 157
   Bishop of (1349) 86
   Kirk-Session Records 21, 59, 191
   University of 41
Aberdeenshire 60, 66, 83, 92, 121
Aberfeldy 127
Aberfoyle 107, 112, 116, 201
Abernethy 67
Abertarff 127
Achtriachan 133
Acorns 79
Acropolis 198
'Adam and Eve' 83
Adam, Frank 176, 188, 196
Adder Stone 92
Address to the Deil 209
A.E. 201
Aegar 26
Aengus *see* Angus
Aerial Hosts 81, 123-4
Aides 26
Airts, the 49-50
Alchemy 47
Alder 84
Alein Dall (Blind Allan) 77
Alexander III 89
All Saints' Day 45
All Souls' Day 10
Allan, John R. 66, 100, 191, 198
Alves, Knock of 142

Amber (Charm) 73, 78
Amen 138
Amulets 72FF
Amulree 187
Ana, Anan or Anu 26, 30
Ancestral Memory 169
Angles, the 8, 38
Anglesey 171
Angus, Aengus or Oengus 27, 30,
   105, 177, 201
   County of 63, 67, 127
Animals, Magical 74FF
Animism 124F
Annan 30, 178
Annwn 27, 110
Antioch, Bishop of 45
Anu *see* Ana
Anwyl, Sir Edward 177
Aphrodite 27
Apollo 27, 175
Apple as Magical Plant 79, 105F
Apples, Dooking for 23, 72
Applecross 55
Apurchrosan 55, 187
Ara 55
Arbroath, Declaration of 184
Arch-Druid 18, 93
Ardblair 121
Ardnacallich 121
Ardvorlich, Stewarts of 93
Ares 27
Argyll 8, 37, 126
Arles, Council of 35
Arnold, Matthew 171, 173
Arran 94, 105
Arrows, Apollo's 175
   Elf or Fairy 93, 161
Arthur 27F, 104, 177
Aryan Languages 7

SELECT BIBLIOGRAPHY

Adamnan, St: *Life of St Columba*.
Allan, John R.: The North-East Lowlands of Scotland.
Arnold, Matthew: *Study of Celtic Literature*.
Banks, Mrs Mary Macleod: *British Calendar Customs
    (Scotland), Scottish Lore of the Earth, its Fruits,
    and the Plough*.
Barbour, John Gordon: *Unique Traditions, Chiefly of the West
    and South of Scotland*.
Cameron, Isabel: *A Highland Chapbook*.
Campbell, John Gregorson: *Witchcraft and Second Sight in the
    Scottish Highlands; Superstitions of the Highlands and Western
    Islands of Scotland*.
Carmichael, Alexander: *Carmina Gadelica*.
Chambers, Robert: *The Book of Days*.
Childe, Gordon: *Pre-History of Scotland*.
Collingwood and Myers: *Roman Britain*.
Cromek, R. H.: *Remains of Nithsdale and Galloway Song*.
Dalyell, J. G.: *The Darker Superstitions of Scotland*.
Dickenson, G. Lowes: *The Greek View of Life*.
Duke, J. A.: *The Columban Church*.
Fosdick, H.E.: *Adventurous Religion*.
Fox, W. Sherwood: *Greek and Roman Mythology*.
Frazer, Sir James: *The Golden Bough*.
Freud, Sigismund: *Totem and Taboo*.
Goodrich-Freer, Ada M.: *The Outer Isles; More Folk-lore from
    the Hebrides*.
Gordon-Cumming, Constance F.: *In the Hebrides*.
Grant, Mrs Katherine: *Myth, Tradition and Story from Western
    Argyll*.
Gregor, Rev. Walter: *Notes on the Folk-lore of the North-East
    of Scotland*.
Harrison, Jane: *Ancient Art and Ritual*.
Henderson, Dr George: *Survivals in Belief Among the Celts*.
Hubert, Henri: *The Greatness and Decline of the
    Celts*.
Hull, Eleanor: *Folklore of the British Isles*.
Innes, Sir Thomas, of Learney: *Scots Heraldry;*

Introduction to *The Clans, Septs and Regiments of the Scottish Highlands* (Frank Adam).

Kendrick, T.D.: *The Druids.*

Kirk, Rev. Robert: *The Secret Commonwealth of Elves, Fauns and Fairies.*

MacBain, Alexander: *Celtic Mythology and Religion.*

MacCulloch, Canon J. A.: *Eddic Mythology; The Religion of the Ancient Celts.*

Mackenzie, Alexander: *Prophecies of the Brahan Seer.*

Mackenzie, Donald A.: *Scottish Myth and Legend; Scotland the Ancient Kingdom; Scottish Folk-lore and Folk-life.*

MacKinlay, J. M.: *Folklore of the Scottish Wells and Springs.*

Mackinnon, Rev. James: *Culture in Early Scotland.*

Maclagan, Dr R. C.: *The Evil Eye in the Western Islands; Occasional Papers.*

Macleod, Rev. Dr George: *We Shall Re-build.*

Macleod, Rev. Dr Kenneth: Notes to *The Songs of the Hebrides* (Marjorie Kennedy-Fraser and Kenneth Macleod).

McNeill, F. Marian: *Iona: a History of the Island.*

McPherson, Rev. J. M.: *Primitive Beliefs in the North-East of Scotland.*

Malinowski, Bronislaw: *Magic: Substance and Shadow* (Im Thurm Lecture).

Martin Martin: *Description of the Western Islands of Scotland* (c. 1695).

Meyer, Kuno (Trans.): *The Voyage of Bran.*

Miller, Hugh: *Scenes and Legends of the North of Scotland.*

Milne, James: *Myths and Superstitions of Buchan.*

Murray, Dr Margaret: *The Witch-Cult in Western Europe.*

Napier, Dr James: *Folklore or Superstitious Beliefs in the West of Scotland.*

Pennant, Thomas: *A Tour in Scotland, 1769; A Tour in Scotland and Voyage to the Hebrides, 1772.*

Pitcairn, Robert: *Criminal Trials.*

Polson, Alexander: *Our Highland Folklore Heritage.*

Ramsay, John, of Ochtertyre: *Scotland and Scotsmen in the Eighteenth Century.*

Robertson, Joseph: *The Book of Bon Accord.*

Rogers, Charles: *Scotland, Social and Domestic.*

Saxby, Mrs Jessie M. E.: *Shetland Traditional Lore.*

Scott, Rev. Dr A. B.: *The Pictish Nation and Church.*

Scott, Sir Walter: *Letters on Demonology and Witchcraft; Minstrelsy of the Scottish Border.*

Simpson, Eve Blantyre: *Folklore in Lowland Scotland.*

Skene, W.F.: *Chronicles of the Picts, Chronicles of the Scots.*

Smith, William Robertson: *Religion of the Semites.*

Spence, Lewis: *The Mysteries of Britain.*
Squire, Charles: *Celtic Myth and Legend.*
Stewart, Col. W. Grant: *Popular Superstitions and Festive Amusements of the Highlands of Scotland.*
Watson, Dr W. J.: *Celtic Place-Names of Scotland.*
Wentz, W. Y. Evans: *The Fairy Faith in Celtic Countries.*
Wilson, Daniel: *Prehistoric Annals of Scotland.*
Gaelic Society of Inverness: *Transactions. Orkney Folklore.*
Scottish Anthropological and Folklore Society: *Proceedings.*
Society of Antiquaries of Scotland: *Proceedings.*